CAMRA'S
Good
Cider
Guide

CAMRA supports REAL CIDER AND PERRY

CAMPAIGN CAMRA for REAL ALE

CAMPAIGN FOR REAL ALE

CAMRA'S

Good Cider Guide

Published by the Campaign for Real Ale
230 Hatfield Road
St Albans
Hertfordshire AL1 4LW

www.camra.org.uk/books

ISBN 1-85249-195-7

A CIP catalogue record for this book is
available from the British Library

Printed and bound in the United Kingdom
by William Clowes, Beccles, Suffolk

Head of Publications: Joanna Copestick
Project Editor: Emma Lloyd
Editorial Assistance: Judy Mallinson
Designer: Paul Welti
Design Production Services: Keith Holmes, Redbus
Cover Photography: Gus Filgate
Maps: Perrott Cartographics

Acknowledgements:
Many thanks to the Apple Committee for all
their help with this book, all CAMRA branches,
Ted Bruning, Vicky Gorman and Rupert Watts

CAMRA would like to thank the following cider producers
for permission to reproduce photographs and labels:

Lambourn Valley Cider Company; Green Valley Cyder Ltd;
Lyme Bay Winery; Wiscombe Cider; Little Thatch Cider;
Crooked End Farm Organics; Mr Whiteheads Cider
Company Ltd; Cider Museum & King Offa Distillery; Gregg's
Pit Cider & Perry; Ledbury Cider & Perry Company; Oliver's
Cider & Perry; Crippledick Cider Co; K.S. Jordan; Crone's;
Upton Cider Company; Ermie & Gertie's; Perry's Cider; Rich's
Farmhouse Cider; Thatchers Cider Company Limited;
Suffolk Apple Juice & Cider Place; Barkers Real Cider &
Perry; Norbury's Cider; Troggi; Ralph's Cider & Perry; Toloja.

Additional photography: Pages 1, 4, 94, 103-105, 107-108,
122-123 Dave Matthews; pages 7-8 Gillian Williams; all
other photographs (unless stated) from the CAMRA archive.

Contents

Introduction

CAMRA's Relationship with Real Cider and Perry

In 2006 CAMRA will be 35 years old, and since 1977 has supported and campaigned for real cider and perry. As a consumer organisation CAMRA recognises the fact that the key to having more real cider and perry in pubs across the country is availability and distribution. Real cider and perry should not just be something you pick up on your holidays, or the drink of secret groups of enthusiasts. It should be an essential part of every pub-goer's experience. A glass of still, live cider or perry (i.e. not carbonated or pasteurised) is a glass of liquid sunshine and a tonic against our bland multi-national keg ciders. The French, I understand, refer to our keg ciders as 'cidre industriel'. I would urge you to seek

AN ORCHARD ADDS TO THE BEAUTY AND BIODIVERSITY OF THE LANDSCAPE
THROUGHOUT THE YEAR, SHOWN HERE IN FULL BLOOM.

THE WINDOWS OF AWARD-WINNING KEVIN MINCHEW'S PRESSING SHED CONTAIN BEAUTIFULLY COLOURED STAINED GLASS IMAGES SHOWING THE RIPENED FRUIT OF A CIDER APPLE TREE READY FOR HARVESTING.

out real cider and perry and consciously choose to support these products which are inexorably linked to the earth.

Over 30-odd years our approach to real cider and perry has understandably developed. Fifteen years ago most CAMRA beer festivals had one or two polycasks (a plastic container which holds approximately 40 pints) of real cider or perry dotted around the stillage among the beers. Now most Festivals include cider in their title e.g. Stockport Beer and Cider Festival and have a dedicated bar. Year on year cider and perry sales are increasing as more people like you decide to awaken their taste buds.

In 2005 the National Cider and Perry Championships, hosted by Reading Beer and Cider Festival, saw 100 different ciders and perries judged for Gold, Silver and Bronze Awards for both drinks. This competition has grown by approximately 10% year on year for the past five years and represents the cream of real cider and perry which is available each year. Most Festivals however have a good selection of ciders and perries for you to try.

In 2003 real cider and perry came of age when CAMRA declared October to be National Cider & Perry Month. Two years on, October is firmly fixed on each Branch and Region's planner with trails, tastings, visits, pressings, and

KEVIN MINCHEW PROUDLY
HOLDS HIS AWARD, ANOTHER IN
RECOGNITION OF MANY YEARS
SUCCESS IN PRODUCING HIGH
QUALITY CIDERS AND PERRIES.

presentations being arranged. A Cider and Perry Pub of the Year competition was launched in 2004 and new competitions are being planned for future years. The first National Cider Pub of the Year (2005) is the Miners Arms in Whitecroft, Gloucestershire. Each year October promises to be bigger and better than before and we are forging links with significant external cider and perry groups to develop October further still.

Another real cider and perry-related award is the prestigious Pomona Award. The Award is named after the Roman Goddess of Fruit and is made to the person or organisation that has done the most for cider or perry in the previous 12 months. Nominations are made by CAMRA Members via the monthly members' newspaper, *What's Brewing*. The Pomona Award has been won by Kevin Minchew for his protection of rare trees (and his delicious cider, which is featured on the cover of this book); by Gerry Alton at Brogdale (home of the National Soft Fruit Collection) for his work with cider apples and perry pears; Johnson's Cider on the Isle of Sheppey for planting an orchard of standard trees; and Cymdeithas Seidr Cymru, the Welsh Cider Society, for the energy and enthusiasm of its members, which has made cider and perry a familiar sight in Wales (for more information see www.welshcider.co.uk). The 2005 Pomona award was won by Dunkertons for their tireless work establishing cider and perry as a premium product since their founding in 1979, for being the first producer in Herefordshire to be awarded Soil Association certification in 1988 and for their extensive orcharding work.

Check out CAMRA's website www.camra. org.uk, see what's happening and join in with us!

Gillian Williams
CAMRA'S DIRECTOR OF CIDER & PERRY CAMPAIGNING

CAMRA's National Champion Cider and Perries from 2000-2005

2000

Cider
Gold: Westons – Old Rosie
Silver: Gwatkin – Yarlington Mill
Bronze: Luscombe – Dry

Perry
Gold: Dunkertons – Perry
Silver: Westons
Bronze: Gwatkin – Oldfield

2001

Cider
Gold: Westons – Old Rosie
Silver: Dunkertons – Organic
Bronze: Gwatkin – Foxwhelp

Perry
Gold: Hecks
Silver: Franklin
Bronze: Gwatkin – Oldfield

2002

Cider
Gold: Gwatkin – Yarlington Mill
Silver: Cornish Orchards
Bronze: Burrow Hill – Sweet

Perry
Gold: Minchews – Blakeney Red
Silver: Hindlip – Sweet
Bronze: Hecks – Hendry Huffcap

2003

Cider
Gold: Summers – Medium
Silver: Gwynt Y Ddraig – Medium
Bronze: Hecks – Hangdown

Perry
Gold: Hartlands – Sweet
Silver: Double Vision – Medium
Bronze: Barkers – Dry

2004

Cider
Gold: Gwynt Y Ddraig – Medium
Silver: Upton – Sweet
Bronze: Dunkertons – Medium

Perry
Gold: Gwatkin – Blakeney Red
Silver: Summers
Bronze: Butford Farm – Dry

2005

Cider
Gold: Ralph's – 3B's

Silver: Upton – Sweet
Bronze: Newton Court – Medium

Perry
Gold: Gwynt Y Ddraig – Red &
Green Longdon
Silver: Minchews
Bronze: Hecks – Farmhouse

COMMON GROUND
The orchard champions

THE apple, it is believed, originated in the mountains between China and Kazakhstan. When and how it came to these shores we can't know; but when it did, it found a warm welcome. Here we have worked with nature on and off for two millennia or more to produce over 2,000 eating and culinary varieties and many hundreds more cider varieties. Many of them are particular to place, each carrying their own stories. Pears, plums, damsons, cherries, medlars, hazel nuts and walnuts have equally interesting biographies, but the symbolism surrounding the apple gives it power. It links Eve with Isaac Newton, Laurie Lee and Sophie Grigson.

Apples are grown in the UK from north of Inverness to Cornwall. Most have a history that relates to their place of origin. Some areas such as Devon, Somerset, Herefordshire, Essex and Kent have developed particular landscapes of apple orchards and their attendant birds, bees, and butterflies, rich habitats and knowledgeable people. Common Ground found to its chagrin in the late 1980s that no-one was championing these old orchards and the traditions and skills that lived alongside them, and the losses were already grave. We began a campaign both to conserve old orchards and to promote new community orchards, city orchards, school orchards, new mixed uses for tall tree orchards, and to spread enthusiasm for eating and drinking the apple and all of the other fruits and nuts we can grow here. They are good for us and excellent for wildlife, they add lustre to the landscape, and they have rich cultural associations.

In 1990 we invented Apple Day, inviting CAMRA's cider group among many others to join us in Covent Garden on 21 October. This has become an annual moment to celebrate, right across the country, everything that the fruit and the trees represent and give to us. And through hundreds of people working to give thousands a good day out, interest in the fruit and the orchards has grown. Common Ground works to give courage to others to do things for themselves. Out of the confidence nurtured by putting on Apple Day in Bath grew the new generation of Farmers Markets. Groups have grown across the counties including the Marcher Apple Network on the Welsh border, Orchard Link in the South Hams of Devon, Hertfordshire Orchards Initiative, East of England Apples & Orchards Project, Cheshire Orchards Project, the Ayrshire Apple Network and many more.

IDDESLEIGH ORCHARD, DEVON BY JAMES RAVILIOUS FOR COMMON GROUND

The momentum for orchard conservation is growing, but every year reasons for the removal of orchards multiply. The worst thing is that loss is stealthy. Many cider apple producers and commercial fruit producers live on the edge of viability. The smallest ripples on the world market or in legislation may push them to the edge. Many small growers keep their orchards out of affection, as a memory bank or to keep nature near at hand. Fruit growers receive no national support save countryside stewardship grants for environmentally friendly practice or terminal grubbing grants which prompt commercial apple growers to have bonfires every few years because of overproduction of eating/cooking apples in mainland Europe.

But a tectonic shift is happening in 2005 as the European Union changes over to single farm payments in the name of more care for the environment. Grants will now be based upon acreage rather than animal headage or crop tonnage payments. Confusion about the eligibility of orchards has led to some grubbing up, even though traditional orchards with grazing are likely to attract grant aid. Small owners with just a few acres of long-established tall tree

PHOTOGRAPH BY JAMES RAVILIOUS FOR COMMON GROUND

orchard rich in wildlife may feel that pulling the trees out is a sensible precaution, in order to safeguard their pension, or their children's inheritance. Defra has been bombarded with good arguments for thinking this through.

Common Ground would like to see real, sympathetic support for culture and nature at the local level. Why? Here is an answer specific to one county, we look

forward to a day when we can transpose it to all the rest. There are some places which still hold a direct link with the land through threads of culture, there are some aspects of life which hold fragile keys to doors behind us and doors ahead of us. Somerset is one of these places, cider is one of those things. Next time you are drinking in the landscape, remember: When we lose an orchard, we sacrifice not simply a few old trees – bad enough, some would say – but we risk losing forever varieties particular to the locality, the wildlife, the songs, the recipes, the cider, the hard but social work, the festive gatherings, the look of the landscape, the history under our noses, the wisdom gathered over generations about pruning and grafting, aspect and slope, soil and season, variety and use. We sever our links with the land.

Looked at from a different angle, if we lose the real cider we lose the need for cider barrels, flagons, wassail bowls, mugs, tools, troughs, presses... people. We lose interest in the artefacts and the buildings often particular to their place. They are devalued, left to rot, mislaid, broken up; and with them fades the knowledge, the self-esteem and soon the orchards, the varieties, the wildlife... the community of interest overlaying the community of place which makes local distinctiveness reverberate with authenticity.

Everything is dependent upon everything else: culture and nature, when so finely tuned as in a landscape with apples, is not a still-life but an intimately woven working world. A world that people are proud to live and labour in, a world that outsiders want to look into.

Let us not throw it away.

COMMON GROUND, now based in Shaftesbury, Dorset, plays a unique role in linking nature and culture, working to inspire, inform and involve all people in learning about, enjoying and taking more responsibility for their own locality. We champion popular involvement and inspire celebration as one starting point for local action to improve the quality of ordinary places and everyday lives. We have initiated many projects and publications, including the *Common Ground Book of Orchards* (2001) and *England in Particular* a book about local distinctiveness (Hodder & Stoughton). For information on Apple Day and Orchards across the country please see: www.commonground.org.uk and www.england-in-particular.info

The *Common Ground Book of Orchards* (2001) is available at £25 inc p&p (Cheques to Common Ground please) from: Common Ground, Gold Hill House, 21 High Street, Shaftesbury, Dorset SP7 8JE.

Producers

Key to Map

 Location of Cider Producer

 Location of Cider Outlet

Cider Producers
England

Berkshire

Lambourn Valley Cider Company
The Malt House
Great Shefford
Hungerford RG17 7ED
☎ (01488) 648441
sales@lambournvalleycider.co.uk
www.lambournvalleycider.co.uk

The Lambourn Valley Cider Company was founded in December 1995 by Roy Bailey to produce real Berkshire cider from local apples. Fruit of all types is used – cookers, eaters, crab apples and even some genuine cider apples such as Dabinett, which are grown in gardens and on farmland in the countryside around Newbury.

Cider/Perry
Royal County Cider, 7% ABV
(bottled/draught)
King's Ransom Cider, 6.8% ABV
(bottled/draught)
Spartan Cider, 7.5% ABV
(bottled/draught)
Old Berkshire Perry, 6% ABV
(bottled/draught)
King John's Perry, 7.4% ABV
(bottled/draught)

Annual Production
600-700 gallons

LAMBOURN VALLEY'S ROY BAILEY ENJOYS THE FRUIT OF HIS LABOUR.

A SPECIAL MAKING OF CIDER AT LAMBOURN TO CELEBRATE THE QUEEN'S 50TH ANNIVERSARY.

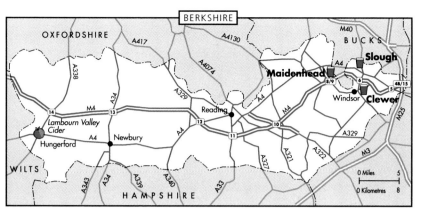

Sales
No direct sales available

Outlets
Outlets include:
Swan Inn, Hungerford (01488 668326)
Royal Oak, Newbury Street, Wantage
(01235 763129)
Glue Pot, 5 Emlyn Square, Swindon
(01793 523935)
Inn with the Well, Ogbourne St George,
Marlborough (01672 841445)
Oakdale Arms, 283 Hermitage Road,
London (020 8800 2013)

Wholesaler
Jon Hallam (01291 627242)

Cambridgeshire

Cassels Cider
37 Riverside
Cambridge CB5 8HL
☎ (01223) 501455
books@jlcassels.freeserve.co.uk

Jim and Lucy Cassels founded Cassels
Cider in 1995. Jim is originally from
'Devon farming stock' and has planted a
small orchard of West Country cider
apples, which he blends with local
Cambridgeshire apples to produce his
prize winning dry cider.

Cider
Cassels Dry, 7% ABV (sterile
bottled/draught)
Cassels Medium, 7% ABV (draught)
Dabinett, 6.5% ABV (sterile
bottled/draught)
Yarlington Mill, 6.5% ABV (sterile
bottled/draught)

Annual Production
1,500 gallons

Sales
Visitors welcome by appointment only,
farm gate sales available

Directions
Close to Shelford Station on
Cambridge-London Liverpool Street line.
Phone for directions

Outlets
Cambridge Blue, Gwydir Street,
Cambridge (summer only) (01223 361382)
Live & Let Live, Mawson Road,
Cambridge (01223 460261)
Waggon & Horses, Milton, Cambridge
(01223 860313)
Longbow, Stapleford, Cambridge
(01223 566855)
Queen's Head, Newton,
Cambridge
(01223 870436)

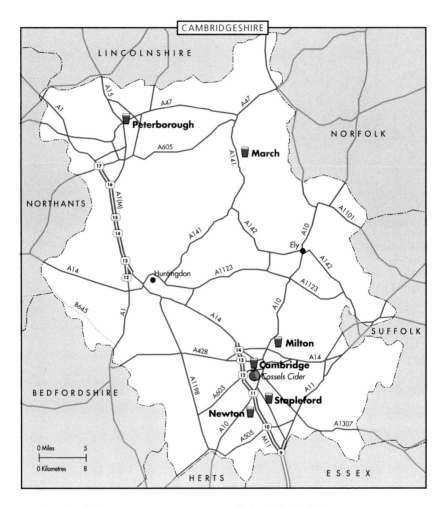

Bacchanalia Off Licence,
Mill Road,
Cambridge
(01223 315034)

Cheshire

Cheshire Cider
Eddisbury Fruit Farm
Kelsall CW6 0TE

☎ (01829) 751255
m.dykes@eddisbury.co.uk
www.eddisbury.co.uk

Cheshire cider began producing
commercially in 1996. It is made
from varieties of dessert and
culinary apples.

Cider
Cheshire Cider (Sweet/Medium/Dry),
6.4% ABV (bottled;
pasteurised/draught)

Annual Production
7,000 litres

Sales
Visitors welcome. Farm shop open
10am-4pm every day

Directions
From Chester take the A556 towards
Manchester. After the roundabout
near Tarvin take the left fork then
turn right at the traffic lights into
Kelsall village. From the centre of the
village turn right up Yeld Lane and
Eddisbury Fruit Farm is 1 mile on, on
the right hand side

Outlets
Many local stockists, please phone for
information

Cornwall

Cornish Cyder Farm
Penhallow
Truro
TR4 9LW
☎ (01872) 573356
karen@thecornishcyderfarm.co.uk
www.thecornishcyderfarm.co.uk

The largest cider maker in
Cornwall, established 20 years ago.
They make farm scrumpy, sparkling
cider, apple brandy, fruit wine, jams
and chutneys. The farm is a visitor
friendly environment with tours, a
museum, tractor rides and
comprehensive shop. They also
have a fully licensed on site
restaurant.

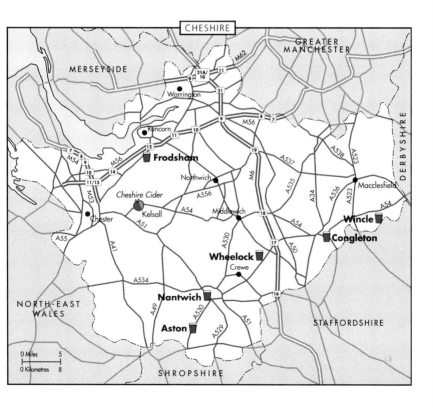

Cider

Cornish Scrumpy Medium Sweet/Medium Dry, 7.4% ABV (bottled; pasteurised)
Vintage Cyder, 7.4% ABV (bottled; pasteurised)
Table Cyder, 4.5% ABV (bottled; pasteurised)

Annual Production
60,000 gallons

Sales
Visitors welcome. Shop is open 9am-6pm all year round, 9am-8pm in the summer (July-August)

Directions
On the A3075, 8 miles from Newquay at Penhallow

Outlets
Available in Threshers and Victoria Wines in the South West region
Sainsbury's, Tescos & Morrisons throughout Cornwall

Cornish Orchards
Westnorth Manor Farm
Duloe
Liskeard
PL14 4PW
☎ (01503) 269007
apples@cornishorchards.co.uk
www.cornishorchards.co.uk

In 1999 Westnorth Manor farm changed from dairy farming to apple juice and cider production. A passion for good food and the older traditional apple varieties has provided a pastime and business. Cornish Orchards are now producing draught and bottled ciders, specialising in bottle-fermented and oak matured cider suitable for serving with a meal. They also produce Veryan Cyder using fruit harvested at Veryan and produced to the recipe and methods used by the original owner.

Cider

Draught Cider, 6.7% ABV (draught)
St Cubys, 5% ABV (bottle conditioned)
Westnorth Manor, 7.5% ABV (bottled)
Black & Gold (dry), 6.2% ABV (bottled; pasteurised)
Black & Gold (sparkling), 5.8% ABV (bottled; pasteurised)
Farmhouse, 5.5% ABV (bottled; pasteurised)

Annual Production
80,000 litres

Sales
Visitors welcome. Shop on site open Monday-Friday 10am-5pm, Saturday 9.30am-12.30pm

Directions
From the A38 Bodmin/Liskeard road, turn off to Looe on the B3254. 3.5 miles to the village of Duloe, then 0.5 miles further on towards Looe

Haye Farm Cider
Haye Farm
St Veep
Lostwithiel
PL22 0PB
☎ (01208) 872250

Cider has been made at Haye farm since the 13th-century and they continue to make it the same way, using apples from their own old orchards. The cider is 100% juice, barrel fermented naturally from the living wild yeast already in the apple skins.

Cider
Haye Farm Cider, 7% ABV (bottled/draught)

Sales
Visitors are welcome. Farm gate sales are available seven days a week from 8am till late

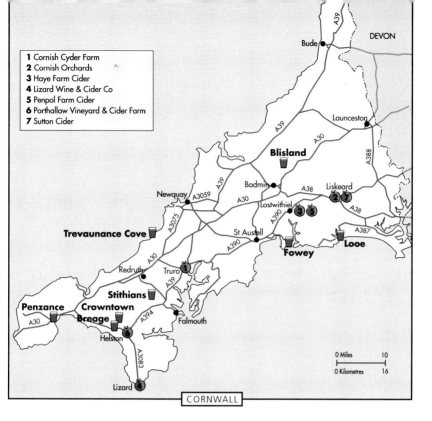

1 Cornish Cyder Farm
2 Cornish Orchards
3 Haye Farm Cider
4 Lizard Wine & Cider Co
5 Penpol Farm Cider
6 Porthallow Vineyard & Cider Farm
7 Sutton Cider

Directions
Follow signs to Lerryn then to St Veep

Outlets
Numerous local farms, shops and public houses

Lizard Wine & Cider Co Ltd
Lizard Cider Barn
Hirvan Lane
Predannack, Lizard TR12 7AU
☎ (01326) 241481

Founded in 1999, Lizard Wine & Cider Company blend ciders, country wines, meads and liqueurs. The Lizard Cider Barn was rebuilt from one of the old wartime buildings of the RAF at Predannack Airfield and has a production capacity of 5,000 gallons of cider a year. The barn was equipped to continue cider making for the many orchards on farms where traditional skills were being lost. Cider apples from up to 16 local growers have been processed and this is helping to stimulate cider apple growing again. All ciders can be tasted in the Cider Barn shop.

Cider
Dry/Medium/Sweet, 6.8% ABV (bottled; sterile filtered)

Sales
Visitors welcome. Shop open 10am-6pm 7 days a week March-November. Also sells a wide range of wines, liqueurs, fudge etc

Directions
Take the A3083 from Helston and carry on approx 4-5 miles

Penpol Farm Cider
Middle Penpol Farm
St Veep
Lostwithiel
PL22 0NG
☎ (01208) 872017

The Langford family have been making traditional cider at Middle Penpol Farm for nearly 60 years. Farming is first and foremost and producing cider is a side line, mainly for family and friends. The cider is naturally fermented, no additives are used and all the apples used are local.

Cider
Traditional Farm Cider (Medium) (draught)

Annual Production
1,000 gallons

Sales
Visitors Welcome. Farm gate sales available all reasonable hours (not Sunday afternoon)

Porthallow Vineyard and Cider Farm
St Keverne
Helston
TR12 6QH
☎ (01326) 280050

Porthallow Vineyard started cider making in 1985. They also produce wines and liqueurs.

Cider
Cornish Blacksmith Cider, 7% ABV (bottled)

Annual Production
1,000 gallons

Sales
Visitors welcome. Shop on site open 11am-5am daily except Saturdays

Sutton Cider
Sutton House
Upton Cross
Liskeard PL14 5BA
☎ (01579) 363258

Sutton Cider was founded in 2001. Sutton House Farm produced its own cider until 1955 for workers on the estate. It has 20 acres of apple trees and the current owners have put back 120 cider apple trees over recent years. The cider is made using a Cornish beam press and fermented in oak barrels.

Cider
Sutton Cider (Medium Dry), 7% ABV (draught)

Annual Production
250 gallons

Sales
Visitors welcome. Farm gate sales available

Directions
Ask at Upton Cross Post Office

Outlets
Cornish beer festivals
Blisland Inn, The Green, Blisland (01208 850739)

Derbyshire

Stagge Cider
11 Huntingdon Avenue
Bolsover
Chesterfield S44 6EE
☎ (01246) 825121

Stagge Cider is a home based, small scale producer founded in 2001. At present James Lee is looking to make his cider available locally and is experimenting with a range of fruit ciders.

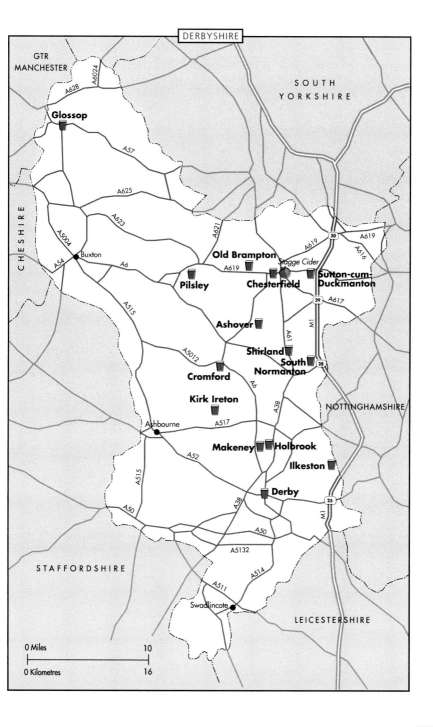

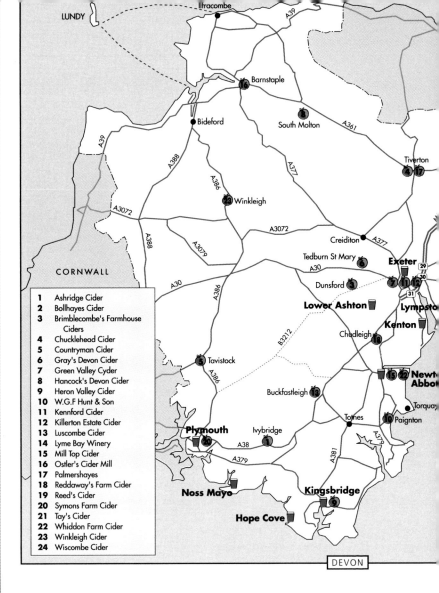

Key to map

1. Ashridge Cider
2. Bollhayes Cider
3. Brimblecombe's Farmhouse Ciders
4. Chucklehead Cider
5. Countryman Cider
6. Gray's Devon Cider
7. Green Valley Cyder
8. Hancock's Devon Cider
9. Heron Valley Cider
10. W.G.F Hunt & Son
11. Kennford Cider
12. Killerton Estate Cider
13. Luscombe Cider
14. Lyme Bay Winery
15. Mill Top Cider
16. Ostler's Cider Mill
17. Palmershayes
18. Reddaway's Farm Cider
19. Reed's Cider
20. Symons Farm Cider
21. Tay's Cider
22. Whiddon Farm Cider
23. Winkleigh Cider
24. Wiscombe Cider

Cider
Stagge Cider (Dry), 6% ABV (bottled; sterile filtered)

Annual Production
50-100 gallons

Sales
No direct sales available

Devon

Ashridge Cider
Ashridge Farm
Modbury, Ivybridge PL21 0TG
☎ (01548) 831131
orders@ashridgecider.com
www.ashridgecider.com

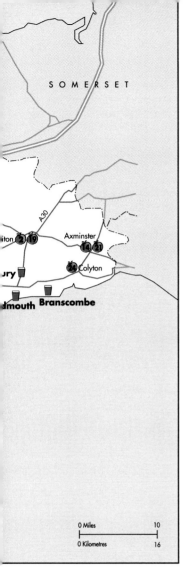

orchards. Although small, Ashridge has received considerable acclaim.

Cider/Perry
Ashridge 'Brut', 8% ABV (bottle fermented)
Ashridge 'Devon Blush', 8.5% ABV (bottle fermented)
Perry (occasional)

Annual Production
1,500 gallons

Sales
Through website only

Awards
Devon County Show 2003: 1st prize & Reserve Champion
Royal Bath & West Show 2003: 1st & 2nd prize
Taste of the West Product Awards: Silver 2003 & 2004
Devon County Show 2004: 2nd & 3rd prize
Devon County Show 2005: 1st & 2nd prize & Reserve Champion
Hereford International Cider & Perry Competition 2005: 1st prize

Outlets
Riverford Farm Shops, Totnes, Devon
Green Valley Cyder, Clyst St George, Exeter, Devon

Bollhayes Cider
Vigo Ltd
Dunkeswell
Honiton EX14 4LF
☎ (01404) 890262
sales@vigoltd.com

Ashridge Cider specialises in the production of high quality sparkling cider using the traditional method (or methode champenoise). Devon's appley answer to champagne! Established in 1997, production is limited to 9000 bottles per annum. All apples are handpicked from organic certified

Bollhayes Cider is produced at Bollhayes Park Farm, Clayhidon from apples grown in traditional orchards in and around the Blackdown Hills. Production started in 1988. Bollhayes Cider is a member of the Guild of Southwest Cider Makers, which promotes the production of high quality, traditional ciders made from pure, fresh local juice. Bollhayes sister company, Vigo Ltd, sells equipment to cider juice and wine makers on a hobby and commercial scale.

Cider/Perry
Bollhayes Bottle Fermented Devon Cider (Dry), 8% ABV (bottled)
Total Eclipse Bottle Fermented Cider (Medium Dry), 8% ABV (bottled)
Bollhayes Draught Cider, 8% ABV (draught)
Bollhayes Perry, 8% ABV (bottled)

Annual Production
1,500 gallons

Sales
Visitors Welcome. Sold from Vigo Ltd 9am-5pm Mon-Fri excluding bank holidays

Awards
Devon County Show 2005: 1st prize
Bath & West Show 2005: 1st prize

Outlets
Wallaces of Hemyock (farm shop), Hill Farm, EX15 3UZ (01823 680017)
Culm Valley Inn, Culmstock, EX15 3JJ (01884 840354)
Merry Harriers, Forches Corner, Clayhidon, EX15 3TR (01823 421270)
Half Moon Inn, Clayhidon, Devon, EX15 3TJ (01823 680291)

Wholesaler
Merrylegs (01626 770845)
Jon Hallam (01291 627242)

Brimblecombe's Farmhouse Ciders
Farrants Farm
Dunsford EX6 7BA
☎ (01647) 252783
brimblecombes@aol.co.uk

Cider was first made at Farrants Farm over 450 years ago. You can still see some of the old implements including the mill. Cider is made in the original cob barn in the traditional way by making a cheese from straw and pressing the apples in a twin screw press. Anyone who visits Farrants cannot fail to go away with a sense of folklore and history as the atmosphere and setting takes you back through the ages.

Cider
Farmhouse Dry/Sweet, 7% ABV (draught)
Vintage Dry/Sweet, 7% ABV (draught)

Annual Production
1,000-1,500 gallons

Sales
Visitors welcome. Shop on site open 11am-6pm from Easter until end of October

Directions
On the B3212 between Longdown and Dunsford. Just past the intersection with the B3193

Chucklehead Cider
South Hayne Farm
Shillingford EX16 9BL
☎ (01398) 361376

Chucklehead Cider was founded in 1993. Michael and John Dinnage use a blend of locally sourced cider apples.

Cider
Chucklehead Cider, 7% ABV

Annual Production
6,000 gallons

Sales
Visitors welcome but by appointment only

Countryman Cider
Felldownhead
Milton Abbot, Tavistock PL19 0QR
☎ (01822) 870226

In 1858 the Lancaster family purchased equipment to make cider on their farm. This tradition continued for five generations until 1972 when a new hydraulic mill and press were installed. The old press and equipment is on display in the North Cornwall Museum at Camelford. The new equipment, located in 15th-century stone barns, enabled production on a commercial scale, which reached an annual peak of 23,000 gallons. In 1989 an orchard was planted, which now enhances the tourist walkabout.

Cider
Medium Sweet/Dry, 6.5% ABV (bottled/draught)
Gold Label, 7% ABV (bottled/draught)

Annual Production
10,000 gallons

Sales
Visitors are welcome to wander in the orchard and to see the press, mill and displays. Tasters are given. The shop is open 9.30am-6.30pm Monday-Saturday. As well as cider, apple brandy apertif, perry, apple juice, wines and pottery is sold

Directions
On the B3362 (Tavistock to Launceston road) just north of Milton Abbot – follow brown signs

Awards
Devon County Show 2004: 1st prize

Outlets
Numerous around Cornwall and Devon, please ring for details

Gray's Devon Cider
Halstow, Tedburn, St Mary EX6 6AN
☎ (01647) 61236
ben@graysdevoncider.co.uk

Devon's longest established cider maker,

making traditional farm cider from apples grown by themselves and from local farmers orchards.

Cider
Sweet/Medium/Dry, 6.5% ABV (bottled/draught)

Annual Production
9,000 gallons

Sales
Visitors are welcome. Farm gate sales available Monday-Saturday 9am-5pm

Directions
OS grid reference SX823923

Outlets
Darts FarmClyst St George, Devon
English Cider Centre, Firle, East Sussex
Old Inn, Widecombe, Devon

Green Valley Cyder Ltd
Darts Farm, Clyst St George
Exeter EX3 0QH
☎ (01392) 876658

Founded in 1989 by ex Whiteway employees wishing to continue the best traditions of cider making locally. The business is now beneficially integrated into the Darts Farm complex and has a thriving retail trade.

Cider
Devon Farm Cider, 6.8% ABV (bottled/bottled; sterile filtered/draught)
Rum Tiddlytum (seasonal), 7% ABV (bottled/draught)
Stillwood Village, 8.3% ABV (bottled; sterile filtered)

Clyst Orchard, 8.3% ABV (bottled; sterile filtered)
Dragon Tears (dry), 4.7% ABV (bottled; carbonated)
St George's Temptation (sweet), 4.7% ABV (bottled; carbonated)

Hancock's Devon Cider
Clapworthy Mill
South Molton
EX36 4HX
☎ (01769) 572678

Many generations of the Hancock family have been making their natural, traditional cider as well as apple juice and wine. Most of the apples are grown at Clapworthy Mill, with others sourced locally.

Cider
Sweet/Medium/Dry, 6-8% ABV

Annual Production
10,000 gallons

Sales
Visitors are welcome. The shop is open seven days a week, all year. Monday-Saturday 9am-5pm, Sunday 10am-4.30pm

Directions
From junction 30 (M5) take A376 towards Exmouth. After 2 miles follow brown tourist signs for Darts Farm at Clyst St George

Outlets
Fountain Head, Branscombe, Devon
Beer Engine, Newton St Cyres, Devon
Old Church House Inn, Torbryan, Devon
Turf Hotel, Exminster, Devon
Bridge, Topsham, Devon

Wholesalers
RCH Brewery, West Hewish, Somerset (01934 834447)
John Reek, Merrylegs (07776 013787)
Jon Hallam (01291 627242)

Annual Production
5,000 gallons

Sales
No direct sales available – the business is now wholesale only

Outlets
Off licences and pubs throughout Devon

Heron Valley Cider Ltd
Crannacombe Farm
Hazelwood
Loddiswell
Kingsbridge TQ7 4DX
☎ (01548) 550256
steve@heronvalley.co.uk

This farm-based business was established in 1997. It uses local apples, many from a managed producer group of organic farmers, hence about 60% of the cider is organic. Cider is naturally fermented and finished in wood.

Cider
Sparkling Cider (Medium), 6% ABV
(bottled/draught)
Farmhouse Cider (Medium/Dry), 6% ABV
(bottled/draught)

Annual Production
8,000 gallons

Sales
No direct sales available

Outlets
Over 200 outlets, available extensively in
South Devon and nearby areas

W.G.F. Hunt & Son
Higher Yalberton Farm
Paignton TQ9 6PU
☎ (01803) 782309
enquiries@broadleighfarm.co.uk

Family farm producing traditional farm
cider from their own 18 acre orchards
and selling retail from the farm shop.

Cider
Dry/Sweet/Medium, 6% ABV
(bottled/draught)

Annual Production
4,000 gallons

Sales
Visitors welcome. Shop on site open
Monday-Saturday 9am-5pm, Sunday
10am-12pm

Directions
1 mile from Paignton, turn left off the
Paignton-Totnes Road at the Parkers Arms
pub into Stoke Road. 1 mile towards
Stoke Gabriel turn left into Yalberton
Road. Farm shop first house on right

Kennford Cider
Lamacraft Farm
Kennford EX6 7TS
☎ (01392) 832298

Charles Baker began making cider in
1945. Today both farm and cidermaking
are carried on by his grandson, Roy Baker.

Cider
Dry/Medium/Sweet, 7.5% ABV (draught)

Annual Production
1,400 gallons

Sales
Farm gate sales available 9am-9pm daily

Killerton Estate Cider
The National Trust (Enterprises) Ltd
Forestry Yard,
Killerton Estate
Budlake, Nr Broadclyst
Exeter EX5 3LW
☎ (01392) 881418
peter.davies@nationaltrust.org.uk

Killerton Estate Cider is produced on
the National Trust's Killerton Estate,
which is situated north east of Exeter.
The cider makes use of the apples
which come from five estate orchards,
also managed for their wildlife benefit.
The orchards contain over 50 different
apple varieties and include the local
'Killerton Sharp' and 'Killerton Sweet'
cider varieties. All the production work
is carried out by National Trust wardens
and volunteers.

Cider
Killerton Estate Cider, 6% ABV (bottled;
sheet filtered)

Annual Production
660 gallons

Sales
Visitors are welcome. Sales are from the
Killerton Estate shop (opening hours vary,
please check in advance)

Directions
Off Exeter-Cullompton Road (B3181)

Luscombe Cider Ltd
Luscombe Farm
Colston Road
Buckfastleigh TQ11 0LP
☎ (01364) 643036
enquiries@luscombe.co.uk
www.luscombe.co.uk

Luscombe Cider Ltd is a family business that has been making cider for over 25 years and apple juice for about 10. All produce is made without concentrates, additives, preservatives, artificial sweeteners, colourants or flavourings.

Cider
Organic Devon Cider (Dry), 4.9% ABV (bottled; pasteurised, carbonated/draught)

Annual Production
40,000 litres

Sales
No direct sales available

Outlets
Anchor & Hope, 36 The Cut, London (020 7928 4595)
Avon Inn, Avonwick (01364 73475)
Crown, 223 Grove Road, London (020 8983 5832)
Duke of Cambridge, St Peters Street, London (020 7359 3066)
White Hart Bar, Dartington Hall, Totnes (01803 847111)

Lyme Bay Winery
Shute, Axminster EX13 7PW
☎ (01297) 551355
sales@lymebaywinery.co.uk
www.lymebaywinery.co.uk

Lyme Bay Cider has recently celebrated its 10th birthday. Nigel Howard left his city career to follow his dream of making real West Country cider, and taking inspiration from the local coastline, the Lyme Bay

LYME BAY WINERY HAS BEEN IN PRODUCTION FOR OVER 10 YEARS.

Winery (originally called the Lyme Bay Cider Co) was established. Lyme Bay not only produces several draught and bottled ciders, it also produces specialist country wines and liqueurs.

Cider
Jack Ratt Scrumpy, 6% ABV (draught)
Jack Ratt Scrumpy (Medium Sweet), 6% ABV (bottled)
Jack Ratt Vintage (Medium Sweet), 7.5% ABV (bottled)
Jack Ratt Vintage (Dry), 7.5% ABV (bottled)
Lyme Bay Cider (Dry/Medium Sweet), 6% ABV (bottled; carbonated)

Annual Production
80,000 litres

Sales
Visitors welcome. The shop is open Monday-Friday 9am-5pm and Saturday-Sunday 10am-4pm and sells Lyme Bay

wines, Liqueurs, ciders, jams, chutneys, chocolates and apple juice

Directions
Off A35 from Honiton, turn right after Wilmington (at brown tourist signs). Follow road through Shute to Lyme Bays signs. Off B1392 from Lyme Regis, turn right towards Musbury then left at Musbury towards Whitford. Follow signs

Outlets
The Dairy Shop, Sidmouth, Devon (01395 513018)
Farm Food Shop, Totnes, Devon (01803 847514)
P.J. & S.B. Vinnicombe Ltd, Torquay, Devon (01803 832602)
Sundial Garden, Offwell, Devon (01404 831549)
Hollies Farm Shop, Tarporley, Cheshire (01829 760414)
Masons Arms, Seaton, Devon (01297 680300)

Mill Top
Great Close
Combeinteignhead TQ12 4RE
☎ (01626) 873291
richard@milltop.co.uk
www.milltop.co.uk

Mill Top's new orchards were established between 1996 and 1998 after the property and land were acquired by the present owners. The orchards are planted with the bitter sweet cider apple trees, Dabinett, Browns Apple, Mitchelin, Kingston Black and dessert apples such as Katy, Gala, Cox and Bramley. The old Devon farm orchards, from which Martin Jenny cider is produced, are situated close by in the parishes of both Stokeinteignhead and Combeinteignhead.

Cider
Kingston Black, 6.5% ABV (bottled; pasteurised/draught)

Mill Top Old, 7% ABV (bottled; pasteurised/draught)
Martin Jenny, 7% ABV (bottled; pasteurised/draught)
Sweet Annie, 4.5% ABV (bottled; pasteurised/draught)

Annual Production
10,000 litres

Sales
Visitors are welcome. Full off licence on site is open seven days a week 2-8pm

Directions
From the Penn Inn roundabout (Newton Abbot) take the Combeinteignhead road. In Combe take the Stokeinteignhead road past Wild Goose. Follow signs

Outlets
Wild Goose, Combeinteignhead, Devon

Ostler's Cider Mill
Eastacott Lane
Northleigh Hill
Goodleigh EX32 7NF
☎ (01271) 321241
www.ostlerscidermill.co.uk

Ostler's products are made from their own apples, grown in the North Devon countryside close to Exmoor. Cider has been made there for centuries and they are reviving a rural craft, producing crisp, clean strong ciders.

Cider
Ostler's Traditional (Dry), 6.5% ABV (bottled/draught)
Ostler's Vintage (Dry), 6.5% ABV (bottled/draught)

Annual Production
10,000 gallons

Sales
Visitors welcome. Please ring Peter Hartnoll in advance

Outlets
Local supermarkets and off licences

Palmershayes Cider
Palmershayes Farm
Calverleigh
Tiverton
EX16 8BA
☎ (01884) 254579
wendyfindlay@hotmail.com

Aubrey Greenslade's family has been producing cider at Palmershayes Farm for around 100 years. A mixed variety of cider apples, including Dabinett and Yarlington Mill, are used and two thirds are grown at Palmerhayes.

Cider
Still Scrumpy Cider (Dry/Medium/Sweet), 6% ABV (bottled; sterile filtered/draught)

Annual Production
3,500 gallons

Sales
Visitors welcome. Shop on site open 8am-10pm

Outlets
Rose & Crown, Calverleigh, Devon (01884 256301)
Various local off licences and farm shops

Reddaways Farm Cider
Lower Rixdale
Luton
Chudleigh TQ13 0BN
☎ (01626) 775218

Cider has been made at the farm for generations, using apples grown on the farm. This is a sideline to the main farming business. The cider is made and stored in wooden barrels in the traditional way.

Cider
Dry/Sweet Farm Cider, 6% ABV (draught)

Annual Production
1,000 gallons

Sales
Visitors welcome. Farm gate sales are available 9am-6pm daily or by appointment

Directions
Follow the signs from the village of Luton (approx 0.5 miles)

Outlets
Elizabethan Inn, Luton, Devon (01626 775425)
Swan Inn, Dawlish, Devon (01626 863677)

Reed's Cider
Broadhayes Sawmill
Stockland
Honiton EX14 9EH
☎ (01404) 831456

Reed's Cider was founded in 1970 and is made from locally grown apples bought from local farmers.

Cider
Dry (draught)

Annual Production
1,000 gallons

Sales
Visitors are welcome. Farm gate sales available 9am-5pm daily

Symons Farmhouse Cider
Borough Farm
Holbeton
Plymouth PL8 1JJ
☎ (01752) 830247

Cider has been made at Borough Farm since 1987. Apples are sourced locally from a number of traditional orchards. The cider is 100% fresh juice.

Cider
Symons Farm Cider (Medium/Dry), 6% ABV

Annual Production
1,400 gallons

Sales
Visitors welcome. Farm gate sales available but please phone ahead

Tays Cider
Reeds Barn Farm
Hawkchurch
Axminster
EX13 5UN
☎ (01297) 678321

Tays Cider was founded in 1984. The cider is made the old traditional way using wooden presses and matured in wooden oak barrels. It is made with no preservatives or colouring.

Cider
Dry/Medium/Sweet Cider (draught)

Annual Production
1,500 gallons

Sales
Visitors welcome. Farm gate sales available 9am-6pm

Directions
On the B3165 Lyme Regis to Crewkerne Road, 3 miles from the A35

Whiddon Farm Cider
The Barn
Lower Whiddon Farm
Ashburton
TQ13 7EY
☎ (01364) 652840

Whiddon Farm Cider is a very small producer founded in 1990.

Cider
Medium Cider, 6-6.5% ABV (draught)

Annual Production
500-1,000 gallons

Sales
Visitors welcome by appointment only

Directions
From Ashburton turn off the A38 at Alston Cross and continue for 0.5 miles. The second left turning is Lower Whiddon Farm

Outlets
Rugglestone Inn, Widecombe-in-the-Moor, Devon

Winkleigh Cider Company
Western Barn
Hatherleigh Road
Winkleigh
EX19 8AP
☎ (01837) 83560
winkleighcider@freeuk.com

Winkleigh Cider is situated in the heart of Devon. Winkleigh Cider has been produced at Western Barn since 1916 and offers a full range of bottled and draught ciders that you can try before you buy.

Cider
Sam's Dry, 6% ABV (draught)
Sam's Medium/Sweet, 6% ABV (bottled; sterile filtered, carbonated/draught)
Sam's Poundhouse, 6% ABV (bottled; sterile filtered, carbonated)
Autumn Scrumpy Medium Dry/Medium Sweet, 7.5% ABV (bottled; sterile filtered, carbonated/draught)

Annual Production
50,000 gallons

Sales
Visitors welcome. Shop on site open Monday-Saturday 9.30am-5.30pm

Directions
Take the Hatherleigh Road out of Winkleigh village. Winkleigh cider is 500 yards from the village outskirts

Outlets
Available in many pubs, shops and off licences throughout Devon

Wiscombe Cider
Wiscombe Park
Southleigh
Colyton EX24 6JG
☎ (07976) 585465

Tim Chichester has been making cider at Wiscombe Park since he was 16, more than 30 years ago now. He still believes in doing things the traditional way and everything is still done by horse and manpower. Some of the apples used are grown at Wiscombe Park, the others are bought from local farms. Two horses pull the large granite mill and the cider is pressed by a single 7 foot screw. The barrels are steamed out with a 12nhp Ruston Proctor steamer dating from 1898.

Cider
Wiscombe Suicider (Medium), 8% ABV (draught)
Merrymaker, 6% ABV (draught)

Annual Production
1,600 gallons

Sales
Visitors welcome, please ring in advance. No direct sales available

Outlets
Hare & Hounds, nr Honiton, Devon

Wholesaler
Merrylegs (01626 770845)

WISCOMBE CIDER'S HORSE POWERED GRANITE MILL USED TO CRUSH THE APPLES.

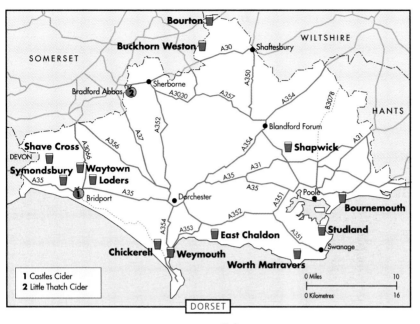

1 Castles Cider
2 Little Thatch Cider

0 Miles 10
0 Kilometres 16

DORSET

Dorset

Castles Cider
Crabbs Bluntshay Farm
Whitchurch, Canonicorum DT6 6RN
☎ (01297) 489064

sylviabluntshay@btopenworld.com

Although founded as recently as
1997, Castles Cider is steeped in
history, with a press dating from
1850, an apple mill dated circa
1890 and a 250-year-old cider cellar
under the farm itself. Malcolm
Castle uses a range of cider apples
from trees he grows himself and
now has a new orchard.

Cider
Castle's Dorset Cider, 7% ABV
(bottled /draught)

Annual Production
750 gallons

Sales
Visitors welcome. Farm gates sales available

Directions
From Bridport take the B3162 then follow
the signs for Broad Oak. Continue to Shave
Cross then turn left. Castles Cider is 800
yards down the lane on the left hand side

Little Thatch Cider
Little Thatch
Mill Lane, Bradford Abbas DT9 6RH
☎ (01935) 427111

Little Thatch is a new company formed
from years of experience brewing and
winemaking. The small volume of

cider produced is through using only Dorset local bittersweet cider apples. Still in its infancy, this company is spending its time on thorough research of the produce with sales being very much secondary to quality. The orchards that supply Little Thatch are in Long Burton, Dorset.

Cider
Little Thatch Rough Dry Cider, 6.5% ABV (bottled; pasteurised/draught)

Annual Production
3,000 litres

Sales
Visitors welcome. Farm gate sales available (cider vinegar also sold)

Directions
3 miles from Sherborne. Mill Lane is opposite the church in Bradford Abbas (go to end of lane and find only thatched house there)

Outlets
Village Shop/Off Licence, Bradford Abbas, Dorset
Antelope Hotel, Greenhill, Sherborne, Dorset (01935 812077)
Old Crown, Weybridge, Surrey

Essex

Delvin End Cidery
Blooms View, Delvin End
Sible Hedingham CO9 3LN
☎ (01787) 461229

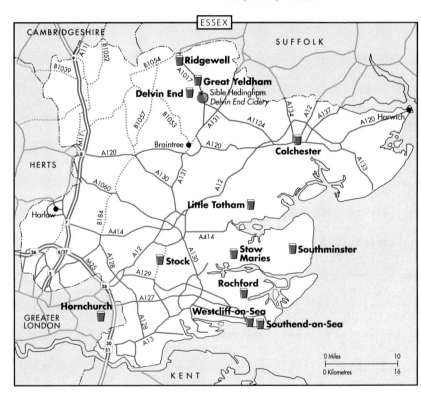

Delvin End Cidery has been making cider to sell since 2000 as there was a demand for a locally made cider. It is made in the traditional way by pressing locally grown apples in the autumn then allowing the apple juices natural sugars to slowly ferment over the winter months. There is no added water, sugar, colourings, flavourings, preservatives or carbonation.

Cider
Storm, 7% ABV (draught)
Cyclone, 7% ABV (draught)
Smiling Moose, 7% ABV
(filtered/draught)

Annual Production
1,500 litres

Sales
No direct sales available

Outlets
Swan Inn,
Little Totham, Essex
(01621 892689)
Bottle Hall,
Delvin End, Essex
(01787 462405)
Bell Inn, Castle
Hedingham, Essex
(01787 460350)
Waggon & Horses,
Great Yeldham,
Essex (07000 924466)
Also at most Essex beer festivals

Gloucestershire

Bland's Cider
Little Green Cottage
Ham, Berkeley
GL13 9QN
☎ (01453) 811004
vernon@bland.plus.com

Vernon Bland made his first cider at Frampton-on-Severn circa 1970.

Cider
Bland's (Dry/Medium /Sweet)

Annual Production
1,500 gallons

Sales
Visitors welcome. Farm gate sales available

Outlets
Falfield Post Office
Old Sodbury Post Office

Brains Cider
The Orchards
Edge Hills
Littledean
GL14 3LQ
☎ (01594) 822416

Cider has been made at Edge Hills for over 100 years and the family are now in their fourth generation. All cider is made from their own apples, Yarlingtons, Vilbere's and Foxwhelps and is available on draught from the barrel.

Cider
Dry, 5-6% ABV (draught)

Annual Production
300-600 gallons

Sales
Visitors welcome. Farm gate sales available but please ring first
(07887 678209)

Directions
At Cinderford take Littledean Hill Road to Foresters pub. Follow signs to Edge Hills

Brook Apple Farm Cider & Perry
24 Rendcomb
Cirencester
GL7 7HF
☎ (01285) 831479

Robert Cook has been producing cider and perry for eight years. The cider/perry is made at Scrubditch Farm, North Cerney where the farmer is a pig breeder so no pomace gets wasted.

Cider/Perry
Scrubditch (Medium), 8% ABV (bottled; pasteurised/draught)
Brook Apple Blend (Medium), 7% ABV (bottled/draught)
Bottle Fermented Perry (Dry), 7.2% ABV (bottle fermented)
Brook Apple Blend Perry (Dry), 7.5% ABV (bottled/draught)

Annual Production
1,200 gallons

Sales
Visitors welcome by appointment. Farm gate sales available

Directions
A435 Cirencester to Cheltenham Road, turn left if coming from Cirencester at the Bathurst, past North Cerney Church to Scrubditch Farm.

Outlets
Little Owl
Cheltenham
Gloucs
(01242 529404)

Crooked End Farm Organics/Popes Hill Orchard
Crooked End Farm
Ruardean GL17 9XF
☎ (01594) 544482
crookedend@supanet.com

The owners of Crooked End Farm Organics bought Popes Hill Orchard in 2003 with three friends. The orchard is now licensed organic (Soil Association). It is nearly 12 acres with old local varieties of cider

apples and perry pears. One of the owners (Howard Eason) grazes his flock of badger faced sheep there.

Cider/Perry
Crooked End Farm Cider, 6-7% ABV (bottled/draught)
Crooked End Farm Perry, 6-7% ABV (bottled/draught)

Annual Production
350 gallons

Sales
Visitors welcome. Farm shop open 8am-6pm Tuesday-Sunday

Directions
Eastern end of Ruardean village in the Forest of Dean off B4234.

Day's Cottage Apple Juice & Cider Co
Day's Cottage
Upton Lane
Brookthorpe
GL4 0UT
☎ (01452) 813602
applejuice@care4free.net
www.applejuice.care4free.net

Owned by David Kaspar and Helen Brent-Smith, Helen's family have lived on the farm for over 200 years, cider and perry making being traditional activities for the farm. The old stone wheel crusher and press are still in use. The main orchard was planted in 1912 and the current owners have continued the tradition and planted over 500 standard trees, including a 7 acre museum orchard of traditional Gloucestershire varieties. They are founder members of GOG (Gloucestershire Orchard Group) and are passionate about old orchards, local varieties, their preservation and celebration. They graft and sell many old varieties of apple and pear on a range of rootstocks suitable for farmland or the suburban garden.

Cider/Perry
Ciders include:
Morgan Sweet, Foxwhelp, Kingston Black
Perries include:
Blakeney Red, Malvern Hills, Brown Bess, Huffcaps
All ciders and perries are available draught but a small quantity of the entire range is also bottled

Annual Production
1,500 gallons (approx 400 gallons of this is perry)

Sales
Visitors are welcome. Please phone ahead as owners live on site and may not be available at all times (reasonable hours please). No shop on site but farm gate sales available

Directions
Brookthorpe is exactly half way between Gloucester & Stroud on the A4173. Look for Brentlands Farm on the OS map (Day's Cottage is part of Brentlands)

Outlets
Farmer's markets in Bristol, Stroud & Cirencester as well as direct from the farm

Wholesaler
Jon Hallam (01291 627242)

Harechurch Cider
White Lodge
Springfields, Drybrook GL17 9BW
☎ (01594) 541738
claire@margrett.fslife.co.uk

All Harechurch's cider and perry is 100% juice and fermented in oak casks using wild yeasts. Only local genuine cider apples and perry pears are used, grown on the Herefordshire/Gloucestershire borders.

Cider/Perry
Dry Perry, 6.5% ABV (bottle conditioned/draught)
Medium Perry, 6% ABV (draught)
Dry Cider 6.5-7% ABV (bottle conditioned/draught)
All ciders and perries vary from year to year depending on varieties available, single varieties and blends are also made

Annual Production
800 gallons

Sales
Visitors welcome. Shop on site open Saturday-Sunday 11am-6pm. Farm gate sales by appointment only

Hartlands Traditional Cider & Perry
Tirley Villa, Tirley GL19 4HA
☎ (01452) 780480

A family-run business passed down through three generations. Cider was originally started by Arthur Stranford, passed to Ray Hartland and then over to the present owner, Dereck, in 1982. Production moved to a larger site in 1994.

Cider/Perry

Dry/Sweet Cider, 6% ABV (draught)
Dry/Sweet Perry, 5.5% ABV (draught)

Annual Production

2,500 gallons

Sales

Visitors welcome. Farm gate sales available from 9am-6pm

Directions

From Tewkesbury head towards Gloucester on A38. Turn right onto B4213 to village of Tirley

Outlets

Available at various beer festivals during the summer

Wholesalers

Jon Hallam
(01291 627242)
Merrylegs (01626 770845)
National Collection of Cider & Perry
(01323 811411)

Hayles Fruit Farm Ltd

Hailes
Winchcombe GL54 5PB
☎ (01242) 602123
martin@hayles-fruit-farm.co.uk
www.hayles-fruit-farm.co.uk

Hayles Fruit Farm was planted in 1880 by Lord Sudeley. Now more than 100 years on it operates as a commercial venture run by the Harrell family, who have farmed at Hayles since 1950. The farm is now complemented by a farm shop, tearoom, caravan site, nature trail and coarse fishing.

Cider

Badgers Bottom (dry/medium dry), 7% ABV (bottled; pasteurised/draught)

Annual Production

600 gallons

Sales

Visitors welcome. Farm shop also selling home grown and local produce open daily 9am-5pm

Directions

Off the B4632 Winchcombe to Broadway road, behind Hailes Abbey

Minchews Real Cyder & Perry

Rose Cottage
Aston Cross
Tewkesbury
GL20 8HX
☎ (07974) 034331
www.minchews.co.uk

Since its launch to the public in 1993, Minchews have won many awards for both cider and perry. They are currently applying for an off licence and are committed to producing the highest quality ciders and perries through natural methods of fermentation; that is without the use of water, sugars, cultured yeasts or chemicals.

Cider/Perry

Dry Dabinett & Yarlington Mill Cider, 8.2% ABV (bottled; carbonated, pasteurised/draught)
Moorcroft Perry, 7.4% ABV (bottled; carbonated, pasteurised/draught)
Dabinett (draught)
Blakeney Red Perry (bottled/draught)
Kingston Black Cyder (bottled)
Sheeps Snout Cyder (limited quantity)
Malvern Hills Perry (bottle fermented)

Annual Production

1,500 gallons

Sales

Visitors welcome by appointment only. Farm gate sales available

Directions

600 yards along B4079 Bredon Road from Aston Cross

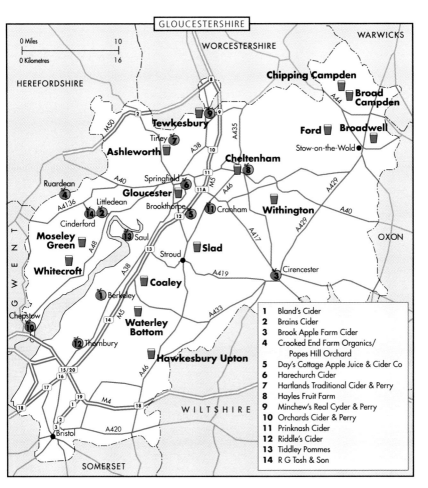

1	Bland's Cider
2	Brains Cider
3	Brook Apple Farm Cider
4	Crooked End Farm Organics/ Popes Hill Orchard
5	Day's Cottage Apple Juice & Cider Co
6	Harechurch Cider
7	Hartlands Traditional Cider & Perry
8	Hayles Fruit Farm
9	Minchew's Real Cyder & Perry
10	Orchards Cider & Perry
11	Prinknash Cider
12	Riddle's Cider
13	Tiddley Pommes
14	R G Tosh & Son

Outlets
Products available seasonally. Please check website for outlets

Wholesaler
Merrylegs (01626 770845)

Orchards Cider & Perry Co
Yewgreen Farm
Brockweir
NP16 7PH
☎ (01291) 689536
info@orchardsciderandperry.com
www.orchardsciderandperry.com

Orchard's first retail production was in 2000. They produce award-winning draught and bottled ciders and perries.

Cider/Perry
Wye Cider Medium Dry, 6.6% ABV (bottled; pasteurised, filtered/draught)
Farm House Cider (Dry), 6.7% ABV (bottled; pasteurised, filtered, carbonated/bottled)
Blakeney Red Perry, 6.4% ABV (bottled; pasteurised, filtered/draught)
Cannock, 5.4% ABV (bottled; pasteurised/draught)

As well as other single varieties and blends (varies from season to season)

Annual Production
1,500 gallons

Sales
Visitors by appointment only. Brockweir village shop sells all bottled stock

Awards
Hereford Cider Museum International Cider & Perry Competition 2004: Overall Champion for Cannock Perry

Outlets
Please see website

Wholesalers
Jon Hallam (01291 627242)
Free Miner Brewery, Cinderford, Gloucs

Prinknash Abbey Enterprises
Prinknash Abbey
Cranham GL4 8EX
☎ (01452) 812455
prinknash@waitrose.com
www.davidsemporium.co.uk/prinknash

Perry was made most years after World War II but solely for consumption by the monks and their guests. By the late 1960s many of the trees had suffered storm damage so cider apple trees were bought from Long Ashton and planted. It was not until 1996 that Prinknash Abbey commenced making cider for sale. Having had to abandon the old premises and the horse-drawn mill in order to satisfy health and environmental authorities an electric driven mill and press combination machine is now used.

Cider
Prinknash Cider Dry/Medium/Sweet, 6% ABV (bottled from casks)

Annual Production
1,200 gallons

Sales
Visitors are welcome. Cider is sold in the Abbey gift shop open 9am-5.30pm in the summer and 10am-4.30m in winter

Directions
On A46. 8 miles from Cheltenham, 7 miles from Stroud

Riddle's Cider
Oak Farm
Oldbury Lane, Thornbury BS35 1RD
☎ (01454) 202839

The Riddle family have been farming at Oak Farm since 1943 and making farmhouse cider since that date. Apples are grown in traditional orchards in the parishes of Thornbury, Oldham-on-Severn and Tytherington. These are grown without the use of pesticides or artificial fertilisers. The cider is produced using early 1900s machinery and stored in oak barrels.

Cider
Riddles Cider (Medium/Dry) (draught)

Annual Production
1,000 gallons

Sales
Visitors are welcome. Shop on sight open in daylight hours, closed Sundays. Free range eggs are also available

Directions
Halfway between Thornbury and Oldham-on-Severn on the Oldbury Power Station Road (Oldbury Lane)

Tiddley Pommes
39 Passage Road
Saul GL2 7LB
☎ (07748) 253834

Continuing the tradition at Priding Farm, Pete Smithies and family continue to make cider and perry

using traditional methods and
equipment. The cider house is a
chalet mounted on telegraph poles,
designed to give spectacular views
over the River Severn.

Cider/Perry
Tiddley Pommes Cider/Perry, 9% ABV
(draught)

Annual Production
1,000 gallons

Sales
Visitors welcome by appointment only.
Farm gate sales available at weekends
10am-4pm

Directions
Leave M5 at junction 13 and follow
signs for Frampton-on-Severn.
Continue through Frampton, cross the
canal and turn right through Saul. Turn
left at the phone box and follow signs
for Framilode. Turn left at River Severn
and the cider house is directly after
Priding Farm

R.G. Tosh & Son
Belvedere
Pleasant Stile
Littledean
GL14 3NT
☎ (01594) 823212

Ray Tosh has been making cider for 35
years. He has recently begun bottling the
cider but draught is also still produced.

Cider
Tosher's Tipple, 6% ABV
Dry/Medium/Sweet, 6% ABV

Annual Production
300-600 gallons

Sales
Visitors welcome but please phone first
to make an appointment

Hampshire

Mr Whiteheads Cider Company Ltd
The Old Granary
Inadown Farm
Newton Valence GU34 3RR
☎ (01420) 588433
mrwhiteheads.cider@virgin.net
www.mr-whiteheads-cider.co.uk

Angus Whitehead started the
company in late summer 2003 and
produced 50,000 litres of cider in the
first year. He has been making cider
since a teenager. All apples are
currently supplied by Blackmore
Estates near Selborne in Hampshire.
More products are planned to be
launched in the near future. All ciders
and perries are naturally produced.

Cider/Perry
Heart of Hampshire, 6% ABV (bottle
conditioned/draught)
Boxing Dog, 7.5% ABV (bottle
conditioned/draught)
Newtons Discovery, 3.8% ABV (bottle
conditioned/draught)
Cirrus Minor, 5% ABV (bottle
conditioned/draught)
Midnight Special Perry
(bottle conditioned)
Also a range of single variety ciders from
5.6-7.5% ABV
all bottle conditioned/draught

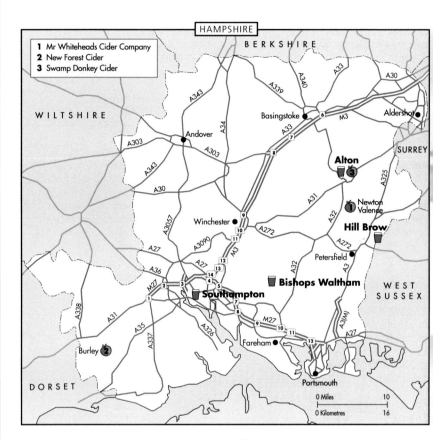

1 Mr Whiteheads Cider Company
2 New Forest Cider
3 Swamp Donkey Cider

Annual Production
50,000 litres

Sales
Visitors welcome. Farm gate sales available but please ring in advance as someone is not always there. Tours can also be organised

Directions
Just off A32 south of Alton

Outlets
Supplies to over 40 pubs in the region from the New Forest to London (mainly in Hampshire, Surrey and Sussex). Also visits Farmers Markets in the area every weekend

Wholesalers
Merrylegs (01626 770845)
Jon Hallam (01291 627242)

New Forest Cider
Pound Lane, Burley BH24 4ED
☎ (01425) 403589
newforestcider@msn.com
www.newforestcider.co.uk

New Forest Cider was founded in 1988 and uses local apples and cider fruit from Somerset and Hereford & Worcester. They have a display of vintage cider presses and a Normandy Calvados still on site as well as a travelling twin bed steam driven cider press which can be seen at their working weekend in mid October.

Cider/Perry
New Forest Perry, 7% ABV (bottled; carbonated, pasteurised/draught)
Kingston Black, 7.5% ABV (bottled; still or carbonated, pasteurised/draught)
Snake Catcher Dry/Medium/Sweet, 7.4% ABV (draught)
New Forest Farmhouse Blend, 6% ABV (bottled; carbonated, pasteurised)

Annual Production
12,000 gallons

Sales
Visitors welcome. Shop on site open 10am-6pm Easter-October half term, 10am-5pm other times. Also trade every weekend at Borough Market, London Bridge from a unique thatched trailer selling draught cider from the barrels

Directions
From A31 follow signs to Burley village, turn right at war memorial cross in centre of the village. New Forest Cider is 200m down on the left hand side behind the Forest Tea House

Outlets
Sheaf of Arrows,
4 The Square, Crawborne,
Wimborne, Dorset
(01725 517456)
Turfcutters Arms, Main Road, East Boldre, Brockenhurst (01590 612331)

Wholesalers
Beer Seller, Capricorn House, School Close, Chandlers Ford, Eastleigh, Hants (023) 8025 2299
Uttobeer, Borough Market, London Bridge

Swamp Donkey Cider
The Old Coach House
Draymans Way, Alton GU34 1AY
☎ (01420) 87800
swampdonkeycider@aol.com

Swamp Donkey Cider was started in 1996 by Anne and Barry Coe at the Hawkley Inn, which they still run. Production is now carried out at their barn in Hillbrow.

Cider
Swamp Donkey, 6% ABV (bottle conditioned/draught)

Annual Production
6,000 gallons

Sales
Visitors should go to the Jolly Drovers, Hillbrow (Swamp Donkey Cider is next door)

Outlets
Several including:
Hawkley Inn, Hawkley, Hants
Jolly Drover, Hillbrow, Hants

Herefordshire

Brook Farm Cider
Brook Farm
Wigmore
HR6 9UJ
☎ (01568) 770562
peter@brookfarmcider.freeserve.co.uk
www.brookfarmcider.co.uk

Peter Keam never intended to become a cider maker but after moving to Brook Farm in 1997 he thought it would be a shame to let the sheep eat all the apples in the orchard so he made a few gallons of cider the following year and one thing led to another.

Cider/Perry
Brook Farm Extra Dry/Dry/Medium Cider, 7.5% ABV (variable) (bottled; pasteurised)
Brook Farm Dry/Medium Perry, 6.5% ABV (variable) (bottled; pasteurised)
Brook Farm Medium Dry Cider, 7.5%

ABV (variable) (bottled; pasteurised & carbonated)
Brook Farm Draught Cider, 7.5% ABV (variable) (draught)
Brook Farm Draught Perry, 6.5% ABV (variable) (draught)

Annual Production
1,500 gallons

Sales
Visitors welcome but no farm gate sales at present

Directions
Turn off the A4110 at Wigmore immediately next to the telephone box near the garage. Brook Farm is at the end of the Bridleway on the left

Outlets
Orchard Hive & Vine, Leominster, Herefordshire
Shobdon Stores, Shobdon, Herefordshire
Spar, Craven Arms, Shropshire
Griffiths Garage, Leintwardine, Shropshire
Bats Stores, Watling Street, Leintwardine, Shropshire
CG Stores, Wigmore, Herefordshire

Butford Organics
Butford Farm
Bowley Lane
Bodenham HR1 3LG
☎ (01568) 797195
tuolomne@aol.com
www.butfordorganics.co.uk

Butford Farm is a mixed organic smallholding registered with the Soil Association. The cider is sold under the Butford Farm label and their first organic cider should be available in 2006. They started selling cider in 2001 and also sell organic pork, eggs, preserves and wine. They make 'Normandy Style' bottle conditioned ciders and perries as a range of draught and bottled (mostly sterile filtered) products.

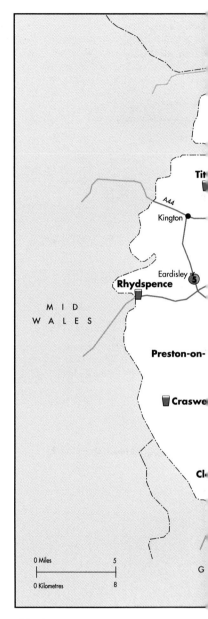

Cider/Perry
Méthode Normande Cider/Perry, 5-7% ABV (bottle conditioned)
Craft Cider & Perry (Dry), 6-7.5% ABV

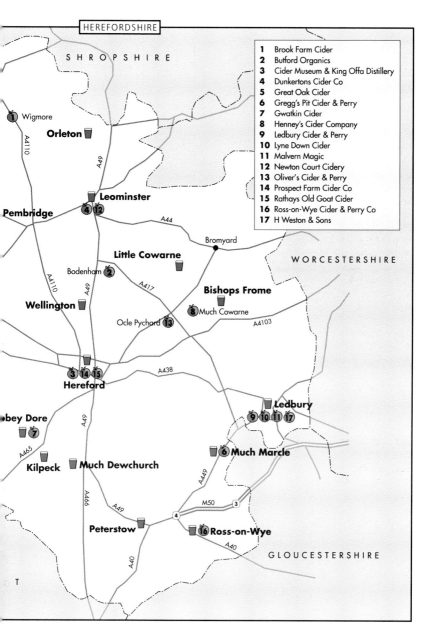

HEREFORDSHIRE

SHROPSHIRE

Wigmore

Orleton

A4110

A49

Leominster

Pembridge

A44

Bromyard

WORCESTERSHIRE

Little Cowarne

Bodenham

A4110

A49

A417

Bishops Frome

Wellington

Much Cowarne

Ocle Pychard

A4103

A438

Hereford

Ledbury

A49

bey Dore

A465

Much Marcle

Kilpeck

Much Dewchurch

A49

M50

Peterstow

Ross-on-Wye

A40

A40

GLOUCESTERSHIRE

T

1	Brook Farm Cider
2	Butford Organics
3	Cider Museum & King Offa Distillery
4	Dunkertons Cider Co
5	Great Oak Cider
6	Gregg's Pit Cider & Perry
7	Gwatkin Cider
8	Henney's Cider Company
9	Ledbury Cider & Perry
10	Lyne Down Cider
11	Malvern Magic
12	Newton Court Cidery
13	Oliver's Cider & Perry
14	Prospect Farm Cider Co
15	Rathays Old Goat Cider
16	Ross-on-Wye Cider & Perry Co
17	H Weston & Sons

(bottled; pasteurised)
Craft Cider (Medium), 6-7.5% ABV
(bottled; pasteurised)
Draught Cider/Perry,

6-7.5% ABV (draught)

Annual Production
1,400 gallons

Sales
Farm shop open 10am-5pm Friday-
Sunday and Bank Holidays

Directions
Butford Farm is 1.5 miles up Bowley Lane
from the A417 on the right hand side

Awards
CAMRA National Cider & Perry Awards
2004: Bronze for Draught Perry

Outlets
Orchard Hive & Vine, Leominster,
Herefordshire (01568 611232)
Hop Pocket, Bishops Frome,
Herefordshire (01531 640592)

Wholesalers
Jon Hallom (01291 627242)
Merrylegs (07776 013787)

**Cider Museum
& King Offa Distillery**
21 Ryelands Street
Hereford
HR4 0LW
☎ (01432) 354207
enquiries@cidermuseum.co.uk
www.cidermuseum.co.uk

The Cider Museum opened in 1981 and
obtained a licence to distil cider in 1984 –
the first such licence granted in over 200
years. The Museum portrays the history
of cider making worldwide and hosts an
International cider & perry competition
annually in May.

Cider
Cider Brandy, 40% ABV (bottled)
Cider Liqueur, 25% ABV (bottled)
Apple Apertif, 18% ABV (bottled)

Annual Production
2,500 litres of spirit

Sales
Gift shop on site which also
sells other quality ciders

Directions
West of Hereford on the
A438 Brecon Road

Outlets
Numerous including:
Alder Carr Farm, Creeting St Mary,
Ipswich, Suffolk
Chatsworth Farm Shop, Derbyshire
The National Collection of Cider & Perry,
Lewes, Suffolk

The following outlets are all in Herefordshire:
Mousetrap Cheese Shop,
Hereford/Leominster
Orchard Hive & Vine, Leominster
Pengethley Farm Shop, Ross-on-Wye
Truffles Delicatessen, Ross-on-Wye

Dunkertons Cider Co Ltd
Luntley, Pembridge
Leominster HR6 9ED
☎ (01544) 388653
dunkertons@pembridge.kc3.co.uk
www.dunkertons.co.uk

Dunkertons first began pressing in
1982 and became organic to Soil
Association standard in 1988. In

2005 they planted the largest perry pear orchard for a century or more in Herefordshire (153 ancient varieties covering 2.5 acres).

Cider/Perry
Traditional Dry/Medium Dry, 7% ABV (draught)
Medium Sweet/Sweet, 7% ABV (draught)
Blackfox, 7% ABV (bottled; carbonated)
Premium, 6.8% ABV (bottled; carbonated)
Dry (bottled; carbonated)
Perry (bottled; carbonated)

Annual Production
35,000 gallons

Sales
Visitors are welcome. Shop on site open Monday-Saturday 10am-6pm

Directions
A44 to Pembridge, left at New Inn, continue for 1 mile

Awards
Pomona Award 2005

Great Oak Cider
Roughmoor
Eardisley
HR3 6PR
☎ (01544) 327400

Great Oak is now solely a contract juice presser.

Annual Production
330 gallons

Sales
No sales available but visitors are welcome by appointment for a chat and 'house vat' sampling

Directions
A4111 (signed Kington), first village is Eardisley. Turn right at New Strand

GREGG'S PIT CIDER & PERRY RELY ON WILD YEASTS AND THERE ARE NO ADDED COLOURS OR ARTIFICIAL SWEETENERS.

Inn, 3rd property on the right after end of village

Gregg's Pit Cider & Perry
Gregg's Pit, Much Marcle HR8 2NL
☎ (01531) 660687
info@greggs-pit.co.uk
www.greggs-pit.co.uk

Gregg's Pit Cider & Perry is an award-winning, small scale producer of craft cider and perry. Their ciders and perries are made using traditional techniques from 100% juice of the fruit of their own orchard and a neighbour's adjacent orchards, managed to organic standards. They rely on wild yeasts and there are no added colours or artificial sweeteners.

Cider/Perry
Ciders include:
Brown's Apple & Kingston Black (dry)/Dabinett, Hangdown & Sweet Coppin (dry)/Brown's Apple & Dabinett (dry), Brown Snout & White Close Pippin (dry)
Perries include:
Thorn (dry)/Moorcroft (medium)/Gregg's Pit Aylton Red & Blakeney

(medium)/Brandy (medium)/Aylton Red, Blakeney & Brandy (medium)/Butt & Huffcap (medium)

Annual Production
800 gallons

Sales
Visitors are welcome. Farm gate sales are available by appointment only

Directions
OS Grid Reference OS662323

Awards
Big Apple Cider & Perry Trials, Putley: Champion Perry 1996, 1998, 2000-2004 International Cider & Perry Competition, Hereford: 1st Prize Perry 1996/1st Prize Best Presented Perry 2001/1st Prize Single Variety Cider 2004

Outlets
Numerous including:
Lough Pool Inn, Sellack, Herefordshire (01989 730236)
Scrumpy House, Much Marcle, Herefordshire (01531 660626)
Stagg Inn, Titley, Herefordshire (01544 230211
A Basket for All Seasons, Newent, Gloucs (01531 822940)
English Farm Cider Centre, Firle, Sussex (01323 811324)
Orchard Hive & Vine, Leominster, Herefordshire (01568 611232)

Wholesaler
Merrylegs (01626 770845)

Gwatkin Cider Co Ltd
Moorhampton Farm
Abbey Dore HR2 0AL
☎ (01981) 550258

The company was formed in 1991 and has grown from producing 100 to 15,000 gallons over that time. They have won CAMRA National

Champion twice for cider and once for perry as well as many regional awards. The cider is made in oak vats from 100% apple juice and is sold in both bottle and draught form.

Cider/Perry
Foxwhelp Dry, 7.5% ABV (bottled; filtered/draught)
Yarlington Mill, 7.5% ABV (bottled; filtered/draught)
Stokes Red, 7.5% ABV (bottled; filtered/draught)
Norman, 7.5% ABV (bottled; filtered/draught)
Blakeney Red, 7.5% ABV (bottled; filtered/draught)
Perries include:
Kingston Black/Thorn/Oldfield

Annual Production
15,000 gallons

Sales
Visitors welcome. Farm shop open from 10am-6pm daily and also sells wine, real ale and meats

Outlets
Local pubs

Wholesalers
Wye Valley Brewery
Merrylegs (01626 770845)
English Cider Centre

Henney's Cider
2 Tan House Court
Much Cowarne
HR7 4JE
☎ (01432) 820014
mike@henneys.co.uk
www.henneys.co.uk

Formerly known as Cheyney Lodge Cider Co, Mike Henney started producing in 2000 with the aim of making good quality bottled cider available to the mainstream cider market.

Cider
Frome Valley (Dry/Medium), 6% ABV
(bottled; carbonated, pasteurised)
Apple Blossom (Medium Sweet), 6% ABV
(bottled; carbonated, pasteurised)

Sales
No direct sales available

Outlets
Tesco (National)
Asda (National)
Waitrose (Local)
Booths (North West)
Spar (Midlands)

Wholesaler
Beer Direct
(01782 303823)

Ledbury Cider & Perry Company
The Old Kennels Farm
Bromyard Road
Ledbury HR8 1LG
☎ (01531) 635024
wilceoldkennelsfarm@btinternet.com
www.oldkennelsfarm.co.uk

Ledbury Cider & Perry Company have
been making cider since 1988 from their
own young apple orchards. Apple juice is
also pressed annually.

Cider/Perry
Old Kennels Farmhouse Cider (Medium),

7.5% ABV (bottled; sterile filtered,
carbonated)
Old Kennels Farmhouse Perry, 6.5% ABV
(bottled; sterile filtered, carbonated)

Sales
Visitors welcome. Farm gate sales
available anytime

Directions
Adjacent to Ledbury railway station

Outlets
Hop Pocket, Bishops Frome

Lyne Down Cider
Lyne Down Farm
Much Marcle
HR8 2NT
☎ (01531) 660543

Malvern Magic
Lower House Farm
Swinmore Trumpet
Ledbury
HR8 2SJ
☎ (07771) 904127

Rob Uren has been involved in
orchards since 1988 and naturally
progressed into cider making in
2000. He is currently operating as a
pruning contractor in Hereford,
which means a wide range of
orchards, giving him access to
vintage varieties of apples as well as
pears. All produce is fermented and
matured in oak.

Cider/Perry
Various blends:
Kingston Black Cider (Dry), 7% ABV
(draught)
New Meadow Perry, 7% ABV (draught)
Knotted Kernal, Strawberry Norman &
Brown's Dry Cider, 7% ABV (draught)

Annual Production
1,000 gallons

Sales
Visitors are welcome but no direct sales are available

Awards
The Cider Museum Hereford International Cider & Perry 2001: 2nd prize Class III Sweet Cider and 3rd prize Class II Medium Cider

Newton Court Cidery
Newton Court
Newton
Leominster HR6 0PF
☎ (01568) 611721
pandjstephens@aol.com

Newton Court Cidery first started producing in the autumn of 2000. All cider and perry is made only from organically grown fruit from Herefordshire including their own 15 acres of cider orchards.

Cider/Perry
Draught Cider Dry/Medium/Sweet, 7% ABV (bottled/draught)
Draught Perry Dry/Medium/Sweet, 7% ABV (bottled/draught)
Cider/Perry, 3-7% ABV (bottle conditioned; sparkling)

Annual Production
6,000-7,000 gallons

Sales
Visitors welcome. Cider and perry shop open Monday-Saturday 8am-6pm, Sunday 10am-1pm

Directions
Heading north on the A49 from Hereford take the B4361 towards Leominster off the Cadbury's roundabout. Go over the railway bridge and take the first left up Newton Lane

Outlets
Orchard Hive & Vine, Leominster, Herefordshire (01568 611721)
Hop Pocket, Bishops Frome, Herefordshire (01531 640592)

Wholesaler
Jon Hallam (01291 627242)

Oliver's Cider & Perry
Stanksbridge
Ocle Pychard HR1 3RE
☎ (01432) 820569
oliversciderandperry@theolivers.org.uk
www.theolivers.org.uk

Founded in 1999, Oliver's make distinctive cider and perry produced entirely within Herefordshire with the juice of fruit from unsprayed trees in the Three Counties, fermented by wild yeasts and matured in oak barrels.

Cider/Perry
Numerous including:
Table Cider (Dry), 7.5% ABV (bottled; sterile filtered)

Oliver's
Kingston Black
Single Variety • Dry Still Cider

Olivers Cider & Perry
Ocle Pychard, Herefordshire

75cl   7.8%vol

Kingston Black (Dry), 7.5% ABV (bottled; sterile filtered)
Three Counties Perry (Dry), 7.9% ABV (bottled; sterile filtered)
Three Counties Perry (Medium), 8.2% ABV (bottled; sterile filtered)
Coppy Single Variety (Dry), 7.8% ABV (bottled; sterile filtered)
Waterlow Dry Perry, 7.3% ABV (bottled; sterile filtered)
Cider Dry/Medium/Sweet, 6.7% ABV (draught)
Perry Dry/Medium, 7.3% ABV (draught)

Annual Production
7,000 litres

Sales
Visitors welcome by appointment only. Please phone before travelling

Awards
Royal Bath & West 2003/2004: 1st prize for dry perry
Arthur Davies Cup 2004 for outstanding cider & perry

Outlets
Numerous including:
Burley Gate Post Office, Herefordshire (01432 820201)
English Farm Cider Centre, Firle, Sussex (01323 811324)
Hop Pocket Wine Company, Bishops Frome, Herefordshire (01531 640592)
Orchard, Hive & Vine, 4 High Street, Leominster, Herefordshire (01568 611232)

Wholesalers
Jon Hallam (01291 627242)
The Ciderman, Isle of Wight (01983 730108)
Winechooser Ltd, Brighton, Sussex (01273 690004

Prospect Farm Cider Company Ltd
Prospect Farm
Upper Dormington, Hereford HR1 4ED

☎ (01432) 851734
simontabbiss@msn.com

Prospect Cider was formed 3 years ago, although the main business of the company is apple juice extraction, with approximately 15,000 gallons a year being produced for landowners that want to make their own cider and apple juice. The company also produces apple juice, which is primarily distributed through local outlets.

Cider
Prospect Dry/Medium (bottled; carbonated, pasteurised, sterile filtered/draught)

Annual Production
1,500 gallons

Rathays Old Goat Cider
Rathays
Sutton St Nicholas
Hereford
HR1 3AY
☎ (01432) 880936
rathays@btopenworld.com

Rathays is a smallholding with a traditional unsprayed orchard and a herd of pedigree Angora goats. Apples are harvested without mechanisation, relying on the traditional combination of a long panking pole and gravity. They have plans to bottle their ciders in the near future.

Cider
Old Goat Dry Cider, 7.5% ABV (draught)
Yarlington Mill, 7.5% ABV (draught)
Tremlett's Bitter, 7.5% ABV (draught)
Ball's Seedling, 7.5% ABV (draught)
Michelin, 7.5% ABV (draught)
Brown Thorn, 7.5% ABV (draught)

Annual Production
200 gallons

Sales
Visitors are welcome at any reasonable time but please ring first to check. Farm gate sales are available

Directions
OS Grid Ref 528457

Awards
Catford Beer Festival 2004: Best Cider in Show

Outlets
Beer festivals

Wholesalers
Merrylegs (01626 773650)
Jon Hallam (01291) 627242

Ross-on-Wye Cider & Perry Co Ltd (Broome Farm Cider)
Broome Farm
Peterstow
HR9 6QG
☎ (01989) 769556/(07841) 839991
woodsbarn@aol.com
www.rosscider.com

Ross on Wye Cider Co was formed in 2003 to increase sales and production of Broome Farm Cider, which has been made on the Johnson farm for more than 20 years. The farm has both modern bush orchards and traditional standard orchards, which include over 70 varieties of cider and perry trees.

Cider/Perry
Many different ciders and perries available draught, bottle conditioned or pasteurised

Annual Production
4,000 gallons

Sales
Visitors welcome. The Cider Cellar is open 10am-6pm most days, please ring first especially during winter. It also holds tastings, barbecues and sells cream teas in the summer

Outlets
Bell Inn, Skenfrith, Monmouthshire (01600 750235)
Victory (Spinning Dog Brewery), Hereford, Herefordshire
Orchard, Hive & Vine, Leominster, Herefordshire
Truffles, Ross-on-Wye, Herefordshire
Pengethley Farm Shop, Peterstow, Herefordshire

Wholesalers
National Collection of Ciders & Perries, Sussex
Merrylegs (01626) 773650
Jon Hallam (01291 627242)

H Weston & Sons Ltd
The Bounds
Much Marcle
Ledbury HR8 2NQ
☎ (01531) 660233
tradition@westons-cider.co.uk
www.westons-cider.co.uk

Westons is situated deep in the heart of the Herefordshire countryside, nestled amongst cider and perry pear orchards. Founded in 1880 and still family owned, Westons is the last of a crop of large scale independent cidermakers in Herefordshire. Its ciders are distributed nationally. The Westons site boasts historic oak vats, the award-winning Henry Weston garden, the Bottle Museum Tearooms, shire horse dray rides, a traditional and rare breeds farm, a children's playground and the Scrumpy House Restaurant and Bar.

Cider/Perry
Over 50 ciders are perries are available including 1st Quality Draught, Traditional

Scrumpy, Old Rosie Scrumpy and
Herefordshire Country Perry

Annual Production
2,000,000 gallons

Sales
Visitors welcome. The Visitors Centre is
open Monday-Friday 9am-4.30pm,
Saturday-Sunday 10am-4pm

Directions
Travel on the A449 from Ledbury, at
Much Marcle crossroads turn right.
Westons is 0.75 miles on the right

Isle of Wight

Godshill Cider Co
The Cider Barn
High Street
Godshill PO38 3HZ
☎ (01983) 840680

Godshill Cider Company has been
pressing cider for 30 years.

Cider
Farmhouse Dry, 6% ABV (bottled;
carbonated)
Rumpy Pumpy Scrumpy, 6% ABV
(bottled; carbonated)
Farmhouse Sweet, 6% ABV (bottled;
carbonated)
White, 8.4% ABV (bottled; carbonated)

Annual Production
3,500 gallons

Sales
Visitors are welcome. The Cider Barn is
open every day from 10am-5pm

Directions
On the High Street in Godshill (the main
road running through the village)

Rosemary Vineyard
Smallbrook Lane, Ryde PO33 2UX
☎ (01983) 811084
info@rosemaryvineyard.co.uk
www.rosemaryvineyard.co.uk

Conrad Gauntlet has been making cider

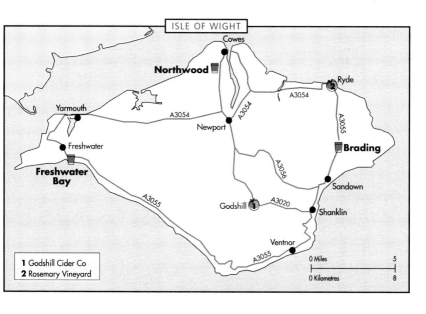

at Rosemary Vineyard for over nine years and is hoping to expand production. Some apples are grown on the premises. Entry is free to the vineyard and free tastings are available of all products.

Cider
Dry Cider, 5% ABV (bottled)

Annual Production
1,000 litres

Sales
Visitors welcome. The Vineyard is open to the public for tours etc, please phone for opening hours

Directions
From Ryde take the A3055 towards the Tesco store, then turn right at Westridge Garage. Continue along Smallbrook Lane then turn right onto the signed track for the Vineyard

Outlets
A few local outlets are supplied such as Co-op's in West Cowes and Freshwater

Kent

Badgers Hill Farm
Chilham CT4 8BW
☎ (01227) 730573

Badgers Hill farm was founded in 1985. It is an open farm with a garden centre and keeps many unusual animals. The cider is matured in oak casks.

Cider
Pippin (Dry/Medium/Sweet), 8.5% ABV (draught)

Annual Production
1,500 gallons

Sales
Visitors welcome. Shop open 10am-5pm

7 days a week March-October, Friday-Sunday October-December, Closed January-February

Directions
On A252, quarter of a mile from A28 junction. Half a mile from Chilham train station

Biddenden Vineyards
Little Whatmans
Gribble Bridge Lane
Biddenden
Ashford TN27 8DF
☎ (01580) 291726
info@biddendenvineyards.com
www.biddendenvineyards.com

A nationwide distribution of their draught ciders via wholesalers has helped Biddenden become one of the UK's largest regional producers. Biddenden Vineyards was started by Richard Barnes in 1969 and diversified into cider in 1978. Their ciders are made from the juice of farm pressed Kentish culinary and dessert apples.

Cider
Strong Kentish Cider (Dry/Medium/Sweet), 8% ABV
Monks Delight Mulling Cider, 7.5% ABV (with spices and honey)
Special Reserve Cider, 13% ABV

Annual Production
157,000 gallons

Sales
Visitors are welcome, tours available – please see website for more details. The on site shop is open Monday-Saturday 10am-5pm, Sunday 11am-5pm (closed Sunday in January and February)

Directions
Situated 1.5 miles outside the village of Biddenden, just off the A262 (Biddenden to Tenterden Road)

Castle Cider Co
Nestlewood
Wickhurst Road
Weald TN4 6LY
☎ (01732) 455977

Founded in 1987 by Tim
and Richard Davies.

Chafford Cider
Chafford Rise
Fordcombe TN3 0SH
☎ (01892) 740437
chris@ballenden.fsnet.co.uk

Chris Ballenden started
Chafford Cider in 1982 and
uses apples from his
own orchard.

THE CRIPPLEDICK CIDER
CO USES A TRADITIONAL
METHOD OF CIDER
PRODUCTION.

Cider
Cider varies depending on year, 8% ABV
(draught)

Annual Production
700 gallons

Sales
No visitors, cider not available direct from
producer

Outlets
Middle Farm National Cider Collection,
Firle, Lewes, Sussex

Crippledick Cider Co
Mount Ephriam Farms
Hernhill
☎ (01227) 750817

The Crippledick Cider Company is run by
P.B. Spillet and G. Clifford-Cox in their
spare time. They stick to a traditional
method of cider production, no added
yeasts, just natural fermentation, racked
over once or twice then left to mature.
They have been making cider for
pleasure and their own consumption for
the past 20 years.

Cider
Crippledick Cider
Dry/Medium,
6% ABV (bottle
conditioned/draught)

Annual Production
300 gallons

Sales
Not available direct

Outlets
Dove, Dargate, Kent
Three Horseshoes,
Staple Street, Kent

Double Vision Cider Co
Marlpit Farm, Wierton Road
Boughton Monchelsea
Maidstone ME17 4JW
☎ (01622) 746633
doublevision@tiscali.co.uk

Double Vision Cider has moved to new
premises at Marlpit Farm in March 2004,
having been in Staplehurst for many
years. Double Vision is famous
throughout Kent and East Sussex and is
produced using traditional Kent apples
and is unfiltered. Plans are afoot to bottle
the cider and sell it further afield.

Cider/Perry
Double Vision, 7.3% ABV (draught)
Double Vision Dry, 7.3% ABV (draught)
Perry, 7.3% ABV (draught)

Annual Production
5,000 gallons

Sales
Visitors welcome. Farm shop open
Tuesday-Saturday 10.30am-5pm, Sunday
11am-1pm. Mail order service also offered

Directions
1 mile east of Linton crossroads
on the A229

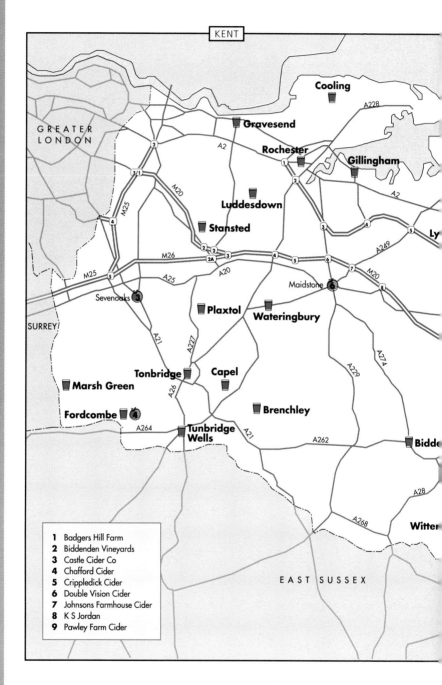

KENT

GREATER
LONDON

Cooling

A228

Gravesend

Rochester

Gillingham

A2

Luddesdown

M20

Stansted

M25

M26

M25

A25

A20

A249

Maidstone

M20

Sevenoaks

SURREY

Plaxtol

Wateringbury

Tonbridge

Capel

Marsh Green

A26

Brenchley

Fordcombe

A264

Tunbridge
Wells

A21

A262

Bidde

A28

Witter

EAST SUSSEX

A268

1 Badgers Hill Farm
2 Biddenden Vineyards
3 Castle Cider Co
4 Chafford Cider
5 Crippledick Cider
6 Double Vision Cider
7 Johnsons Farmhouse Cider
8 K S Jordan
9 Pawley Farm Cider

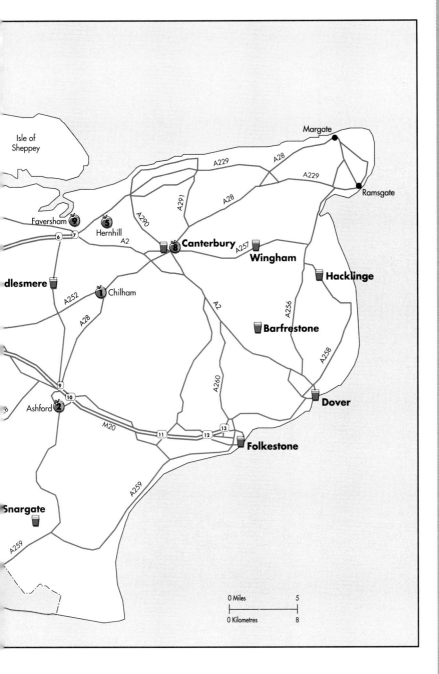

Outlets
English Farm Centre, Firle
The Bitter End, Tonbride Wells
Red Lion, Snargate
Man of Kent, Rochester
Perry Hill Orchard, Hartfield, East Grinstead

Wholesalers
Crouch Vale Brewery,
Essex (01245 322744)
A.V.S. Casks,
Kent (01474 537767)
East West Ales,
Kent (01892 825236)
Merrylegs (01626) 773650

Johnsons Farmhouse Cider
Cowstead Farm
Lower Road
Isle of Sheppey
ME12 3RL
☎ (01795) 665203

Paul Johnson started making cider 10 years ago and has won several awards. He is currently making cider with organic cider apples from south east England single varieties and a small amount of Huff Cap perry. It is a working sheep farm with a small orchard of cider apples that he planted himself. He has plans to bottle the ciders in the near future.

Cider/Perry
Marsh Monkey,
8.3% ABV (draught)
Gobbledegook,
8.3% ABV (draught)
Yarlington Mill
(draught)

Porters Perfection (draught)
Kingston Black (draught)

Annual Production
Less than 1,500 gallons

Sales
No direct sales at present but they will be available in the near future

Outlets
Ferry House Inn, Harty, Kent
Ship on Shore, Sheerness, Kent
Red Lion, Badlesmere, Kent
Many beer festivals including Great British Beer Festival, Peterborough, Reading, Canterbury

K.S. Jordan
Neals Place Farm
Neals Place Road
Canterbury
CT2 8HX
☎ (01227) 765632

KENTISH STILL CIDER 500ml
Sweet 8% vol
from Neals Place Farm
Neals Place Road, Canterbury, Kent Tel: 01227 765632

Neals Place Farm make apple juice, farmhouse jams, ciders and also have pick your own strawberries and raspberries.

Cider
Dry/Medium/Sweet, 8-13% ABV (bottled)

Annual Production
1,500 gallons

Sales
Visitors are welcome. Farm shop open seven days a week from June to September 11am-7pm

Directions
1 mile out of Canterbury City Centre on A290 to Whitstable. Farm is on the left behind Kent College

Pawley Farm Cider
Pawley Farm
Painters Forstal
Faversham
ME13 0EN
☎ (01795) 532043

The current owners (the Macey family) began making cider in the late 1970s as a hobby, which has grown into a steadily increasing business. The fruit used is mainly Bramley and Cox but includes several other varieties of dessert apple. The blend of culinary and dessert apples, traditional for Kent, produces a crisp and mature cider. The cider is matured in oak casks prior to being bottled.

Cider
Dry/Medium/Sweet/Spiced, 7.5% ABV (bottled; pasteurised)

Annual Production
1,400 gallons

Sales
Visitors welcome. Farm gate sales available but please phone first

Outlets
Farming World, Brenley Corner, Faversham, Kent
Macknade Farm Shop, Faversham, Kent
Ardennes Restaurant, Faversham, Kent
Goods Shed, Station Road, Canterbury, Kent
Timberbatts, Bodsham, Kent

Middlesex
(Middlesex details see Gt. London map)

Hounslow Cider Co-operative
Flat 6
394 Hanworth Road
Hounslow
TW3 3SN
☎ (020) 8570 3781
simon.stevenson@adh.nhs.uk

The Hounslow Cider Co-operative is three friends collecting local fruit, enhanced by cider apples brought (or begged) from Somerset. Production started as a 1 gallon experiment in 2000, with a steady increase ever since. Quantity produced, however, is limited by the size of premises.

Cider/Perry
Hounslow Heath Crab (Little Pincher), 6% ABV (draught)
Isis, 7-8% ABV (draught)
Muddy Perry, 5% ABV (draught)

Annual Production
50-100 gallons

Sales
No direct sales are available

Awards
Twickenham Beer Festival 2004: Cider of the Festival

Outlets
Due to limited volumes produced, most goes to CAMRA beer and cider festivals

Norfolk

Banham Cider
White Lodge
Grove Road
Banham NR16 2HG
☎ (01953) 887366
www.cidershed.co.uk

Banham Cider was founded by former art teacher Ryan Burnard over 15 years ago. He makes his cider with varieties such as Dabinett, Red Streak, Taylor and Yarlington Mill.

Cider/Perry
Farmhouse Sweet/Medium/Dry, 5.5% ABV (draught)
Rum Cider (Sweet), 7% ABV (draught)
Perry (available occasionally), 6.2% ABV (draught)
Some single varietal ciders also available

Annual Production
5,000-6,000 gallons

Sales
No direct sales at present, please phone for details

Outlets
Fat Cat, Norwich, Norfolk
Ribs of Beef, Norwich, Norfolk
Alexandra Tavern, Norwich, Norfolk
Coach & Horses, Norwich, Norfolk
The Shed, Norwich, Norfolk (01603 413153)

Crone's
Fairview
Fersfield Road, Kenninghall NR16 2DP
☎ (01379) 687687
info@crones.co.uk
www.crones.co.uk

Cabinet maker Robert Crone started making cider as a hobby in 1984, and Crone's became a full time business in 1989. Crone's make traditional cider from a blend of dessert apples, cookers and cider apples, using only organic fruit and without the use of chemicals or concentrates. The

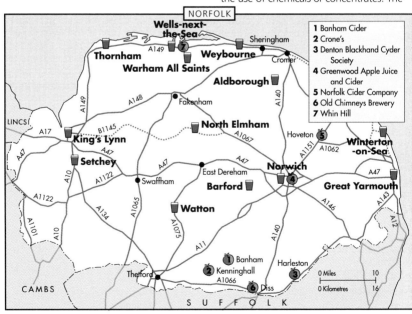

NORFOLK

1 Banham Cider
2 Crone's
3 Denton Blackhand Cyder Society
4 Greenwood Apple Juice and Cider
5 Norfolk Cider Company
6 Old Chimneys Brewery
7 Whin Hill

freshly pressed apple juice is fermented with natural yeasts and the resulting cider is matured and allowed to clear naturally without the use of finings (and therefore suitable for vegans).

Cider/Perry
User Friendly, 6.2% ABV (bottled; pasteurised/draught)
Original, 7.5% ABV (bottled; pasteurised/draught)
Special Reserve, 7.5% ABV (bottled; pasteurised/draught)
Norfolk Perry (occasional)

Annual Production
1,500 gallons

Sales
By appointment only. All ciders can be supplied in unpasteurised form in 10, 22.5 and 50 litre containers or pasteurised in 75cl glass bottles

Awards
Champion Cider of the Year 1998: Silver for Special Reserve

Outlets
Numerous including:
Take 5, 17 Tombland, Norwich, Norfolk (01603 763099)
Banham Barrel, The Appleyard, Banham, Norfolk (01953 888593)
Odd One Out, 28 Mersea Road, Colchester, Essex (01206 513958)
English Farm Ciders, Middle Farm, Firle, Lewes, East Sussex (01323 811324)
Ashlyns Farm Shop, Epping Road, North Weald, Essex (01992 525146)

Wholesaler
Rainbow Wholefoods (01603 630484)

Denton Blackhand Cyder Society
Ivy Farm, Darrow Green Road
Denton, Harleston IP20 0AY
alan@squirrell.org.uk

A private society based on Denton village, which was founded in 2000 and has 44 families as members. They press on two days per year using a historic mill and press which were rescued from a Norfolk barn just before it was demolished.

Cider/Perry
Poachers Perry, 6.5% ABV
World War I, 6.5% ABV
Blondie, 6.5% ABV
Oak Apple, 6.5% ABV
Half 'n' Half, 6.5% ABV

Annual Production
450 gallons

Sales
Visitors welcome by appointment. No cider sold to the public

Greenwood Apple Juice & Cider
The Ashes, Carleton Rode
Norwich NR16 1NN
☎ (01953) 860356
boc@greenwoodsapple.freeserve.co.uk

Formed in 1997, Greenwood use apples grown in their own orchards with their cider being made predominantly from dessert apples. They also offer a pressing service during the apple season (for a small charge).

Cider
Dry, 8% ABV (bottled; pasteurised/draught)
Medium, 6% ABV (bottled; pasteurised)

Annual Production
1,000 gallons

Sales
Visitors are welcome. Farm gate sales available 9am to 7pm daily

Directions
B1113, 14 miles south of Norwich

Awards
Norwich & Norfolk CAMRA Beer Festival 1998: Winner in cider category
Norwich & Norfolk CAMRA Beer Festival 1999: Runner up in cider category

Outlets
Ketts Tavern, Norwich
Local beer festivals

Norfolk Cider Company
The Apple Shop
Wroxham Barns, Hoveton NR12 8QU
☎ (01603) 783040
www.norfolkcider.co.uk

Norfolk's oldest established cider makers. The company uses an original 19th-century Norfolk mill and press, which can be seen in action at various shows around Norfolk and the south and east of England.

Cider
Kingfisher Farm Cider Dry/Medium Dry/Medium/Sweet, 7.5% ABV (bottled/draught)

Sales
Visitors welcome. The Apple shop is part of Wroxham Barns Craft Centre and is open seven days a week throughout the year. Please ring the shop beforehand on 01603 784876 to guarantee opening times

Outlets
Trafford Arms, Norwich, Norfolk (01603 628466)
Rosary Tavern, Norwich, Norfolk (01603 666287)
Black Horse, Earlham Road, Norwich, Norfolk (01603 624682)
Ribs of Beef, Norwich, Norfolk (01603 619517)
Also available throughout Norfolk and Suffolk in pubs, restaurants and village shops

Old Chimneys Brewery
Hopton End Farm, Church Road
Market Weston, Diss IP22 2NX
☎ (01359) 221013

Old Chimneys Brewery is a small scale cider producer established in 2001. The cider is very much a sideline to the main business of real ale production.

Cider
Dry/Sweet Cider, 7% ABV (bottle conditioned)

Annual Production
100 gallons

Sales
Visitors welcome by appointment. Brewery shop is open Friday 2-7pm and Saturday 11am-2pm

Directions
0.25 miles off B111, just south of Hopton

Whin Hill Cider Ltd
The Stables, Stearman's Yard
Wells-next-the-Sea NR23 1BT
☎ (01328) 711033
jim@whinhillcider.co.uk
www.whinhillcider.co.uk

Whin Hill Cider was founded in 1994 with the planting of 1,000 cider apple and 60 perry pear trees at nearby Stanhoe. They have been operating from the present site in an 18th-century barn in Wells since 1999. The apples are pressed at the orchard but the fermentation and bottling is carried out in Wells. 140 additional perry pear trees were planted in 2005. No artificial sweeteners or preservatives are used.

Cider/Perry
Numerous available including:
Dry (Bottle Fermented), 7.3% ABV (bottle conditioned)
Dry (Still), 7.1% ABV (draught)
Medium Sparkling, 7% ABV (bottled; carbonated, pasteurised)

Medium Still Perry, 6.5% ABV (bottled; pasteurised/draught)

Annual Production
5,000 gallons

Sales
Visitors welcome. Shop on site open weekends 10.30am-5.30pm Easter-October (at other times please phone first). The shop offers free tasting of their cider and apple juice

Directions
On the main public car park in Wells, off Freeman Street, near the Ark Royal pub

Outlets
Three Horseshoes, Warham, Norfolk (01328 710547)

Northamptonshire

Windmill Vineyard
Windmill Hill Farm
Hellidon
Daventry NN11 6HZ
☎ (01327) 262023

Doreen and Thomas Hillier-Bird planted their vineyard and orchard in 1978 and

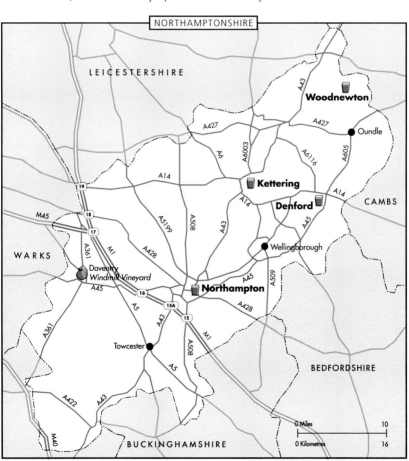

NORTHAMPTONSHIRE

LEICESTERSHIRE

Woodnewton

A43

A427

A427

Oundle

A6

A6003

A6116

A605

A14

19

A14

Kettering

A14

18

Denford

CAMBS

M45

17

A5199

A508

A43

A45

Wellingborough

WARKS

A361

M1

A428

A45

A509

Daventry
Windmill Vineyard

Northampton

A45

16

A5

15A

A428

A43

15

A361

A5

M1

A508

Towcester

BEDFORDSHIRE

A422

A43

A5

M40

BUCKINGHAMSHIRE

0 Miles   10
0 Kilometres   16

it was opened to the public for guided tours and tastings in 1995. They now sell an enterprising range of ciders and perries, selling all they produce from the on site shop. Wild crab apples are blended with their own apples to provide some tannin for a fuller-bodied flavour. They are also one of the few producers of 'cyser', an ancient drink that the Hillier-Birds make by fermenting apple juice with honey from their own colonies. The Windmill Tower is used for tastings of ciders and wines, with customers enjoying views over six counties.

Cider/Perry
Scrumpy Apple, 8.5% ABV
Millers Fancy, 7.5 ABV
Windmill Perry, 8.5% ABV
Windmill Pyeder (a blend of apple and pear juice)
Pippin Cyser (apple juice fermented with honey)

Annual Production
1,000 litres

Sales
Visitors welcome. Shop on site open Wednesday-Sunday 12-6pm. Shop also sells wines, vinegars and meads. Tours available

Directions
5 miles south of Daventry, signposted from the A361 and A425

Oxfordshire

Upton Cider Company
Upton Fruit Farm
High Street, Upton
Didcot
OX11 9JE
☎ (01235) 850808
fitchettupton@ukonline.co.uk
www.uptoncider.co.uk

Upton Cider Company's 10 acre traditional cider orchard was planted in 1970 to supply the Taunton Cider Company with apples to make Blackthorn. In 1983 they started to make their own distinctive cider, which is produced solely from their own organic apples.

Cider
Upton Dry/Medium/Sweet, 7% ABV (bottled /draught)

Annual Production
1,400 gallons

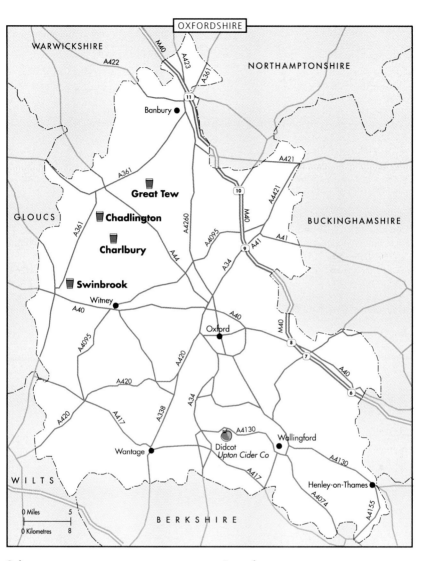

OXFORDSHIRE

Sales
Visitors welcome. Shop on site open Friday-Sunday (April-October) 12-5pm. It also sells organic apples, plums and nuts when in season

Directions
On the A417 at Upton, near Didcot. Between the villages of Blewbury and Harwell

Awards
CAMRA Tasting Committee 2004: National Silver Champion Cider for Upton Sweet

Outlets
Bell, Bell Lane, Aldworth, Berks (01635 578272)

Shropshire

All apples used are from Shropshire.

Mahorall Farm Cider
Mahorall Farm
Nash, Ludlow S78 3AH
☎ (01584) 890296
christhefarmer@yahoo.co.uk
www.farmcider.co.uk

Founded in 2000, this small family farm produces hand pressed ciders using a 160-year-old single screw press.

Cider
Dry, 6-8% ABV (bottled/draught)
Medium Sweet, 6.5% ABV (bottled)

Annual Production
1,500 gallons

Sales
Visitors welcome. The modest farm shop is open 9am-5pm and sells ciders

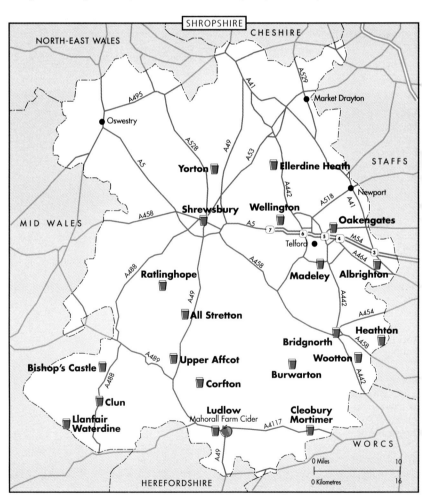

and fruit syrups. Brief cider talks/tours are available for small groups by appointment

Directions
Approx 7 miles from Ludlow via Cleehill Village (A4117) and 4 miles from Tenbury Wells (A456). Off B4214 Clee Hill to Tenbury Wells Road, near village of Hope Bagot

Outlets
Wharfside Bar, Stirchley, West Midlands
Crown Country Inn, Munslow
Discovery Centre, Craven Arms
Little Beer Shoppe, Ludlow, Shropshire

Somerset

Ashill Cider
Ashill Farm
Ashill
Nr Ilminster
TA19 9HE
☎ (01823) 480513

Cider has been made from the orchard since the 1920s and the present owner has been there since 1982. The scrumpy produced is organic as no sprays or fertiliser are used.

Cider
Dry/Sweet Scrumpy, 6% ABV (draught)

Annual Production
1,400 gallons

Sales
Farm gate sales available 9am-6pm Easter-end October

Directions
A358 Taunton-Ilminster, turn off at signpost for Ashill Village. In centre of village by pub & church

Avalon Vineyard/Pennard Cider
The Drove
East Pennard
Shepton Mallet
BA4 6UA
☎ (01749) 860393
pennardorganicwines@mail.com
www.pennardorganicwines.co.uk

Pennard cider has been in production since 1985 and has had organic certification since 1987. They also make English grape wine, organic fruit wines, mead, apple juice and raspberry liquer.

Cider
Dry/Medium/Sweet, 8.3% ABV (draught)

Annual Production
1,500 gallons

Sales
Visitors welcome. Shop on site, open 9am-6pm all week (please phone to check)

Directions
Turn west at Wraxall on A37, 5 miles south of Shepton Mallet, follow cider signs

Outlets
Heritage Fine Foods, High Street, Glastonbury, Somerset

Black Mac Cider
The Orchards
Stembridge
Martock
TA12 6BP
☎ (01460) 241736
mcgrouther@ntlworld.com

Formerly Black Toad Cider of Drayton, Black Mac has been producing at the present site since 1999 using traditional (organic) straw-pressing methods on an ancient twin screw press. The cider is fermented in oak barrels and many apple varieties are used.

Cider
Dry/Medium/Sweet, 6.7-8.2% ABV
(varies by year)

Annual Production
600 gallons

Sales
Visitors welcome. Farm gate sales available, please phone first. Cider available in quart, 4 pint or gallon plastic bottles

Directions
Opposite Kingsbury Primary School in the parish of Kingsbury Episcopi. 10 miles north-west from Yeovil, 3 miles north of A303

Outlets
Sold only at Farmers' Markets (mainly Frome & Glastonbury)

Bridge Farm Cider
Bridge Farm
East Chinnock
Yeovil
BA22 9EA
☎ (01935) 862387

Nigel Stewart started making cider in 1986 under the name of Sandford Cider in Dorset. He moved to Bridge Farm in 1990 and produces some very fine ciders that regularly win prizes at agricultural shows in the south west. Only fresh juice from cider apples is used, all of which are either grown in his own orchards or harvested by himself locally.

Cider
Bridge Farm Cider (Dry/Medium/Sweet), 7% ABV

Annual Production
3,000 gallons

1 Ashill Cider
2 Avalon Vineyard/Pennard Cider
3 Black Mac Cider
4 Bridge Farm Cider
5 Broadlands Fruit Farm
6 Broadoak Cider
7 Burrow Hill Cider & Somerset
  Cider Brandy Company
8 Chestnut Farm Award Winning Cider
9 Crossman's Prime Farmhouse Cider
10 Derrick's Cider
11 Dobunni
12 Ernie & Gertie's
13 Hecks Farmhouse Cider
14 Henry's Farmhouse Scrumpy
15 Parsons Choice Cider
16 Perry's Cider
17 Rich's Farmhouse Cider
18 R J Sheppy & Son
19 Thatcher's Cider
20 Torre Cider
21 West Croft Cider
22 West Monkton Cider (formerly Lanes)
23 Wilkin's Farmhouse Cider & Perry

Minehead

Porlock

Luxborough

Bis

D E V O N

0 Miles   10

0 Kilometres   16

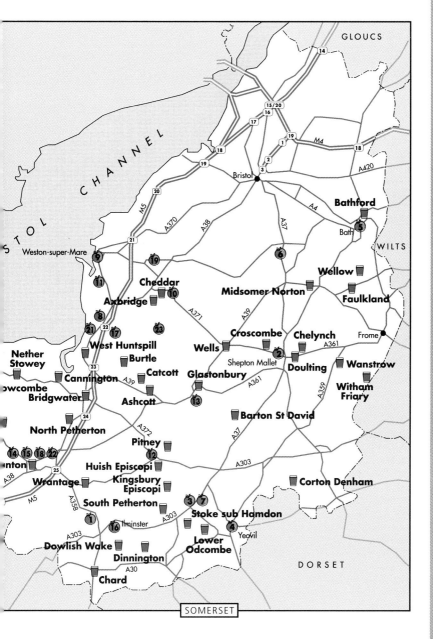

GLOUCS

14

15/20
16

17

19
1

M4

18

18

A420

2

3

Bristol

A4

Bathford

Bath
5

WILTS

18

19

20

M5

21

A370

A38

A37

Weston-super-Mare
9

19

6

Wellow

11

Cheddar
10

Midsomer Norton

Faulkland

Axbridge

8

A371

A39

Croscombe

Chelynch
A361

Frome

21 22 7

23

West Huntspill

Wells

Shepton Mallet
2

Doulting

Wanstrow

Nether
Stowey

23

Burtle

Catcott

Glastonbury

A361

Witham
Friary

owcombe

Cannington A39

Ashcott

13

A359

Bridgewater

Barton St David

24

North Petherton

A372

Pitney

A37

12

A303

Corton Denham

14 15 18 22

nton

25

Huish Episcopi

Kingsbury
Episcopi

Wrantage

A358

M5

South Petherton

1

A303

3 7

Stoke sub Hamdon

4 Yeovil

16 Ilminster

Dowlish Wake

Lower
Odcombe

DORSET

Dinnington

A30

Chard

A303

Sales

Visitors welcome, tours available. Shop on site open May-September, seven days a week 10.30am-6.30pm. The rest of the year Friday-Saturday only 10.30am-6.30pm

Directions

Just off the A30, south west of Yeovil. Bridge Farm is a short drive off the main road

Awards

Devon Show 2003 & 2005: Champion Cider

Outlets

East Chinnock Post Office, Somerset (01935 862157)
Mandeville Arms, Hardington Mandeville, Somerset (01935 862418)

Broadlands Fruit Farm

Box Road
Bath BA1 7LR
☎ (01225) 859780

Cider has been produced for over eight years at Broadlands Fruit Farm. A mix of Gloucestershire cider apples and perry pears are brought in from a supplier north of Gloucester.

Cider/Perry

Dry/Medium Cider, 5.5% ABV (draught)
Perry, 5.5% ABV (draught)

Annual Production

1,400 gallons

Sales

Visitors welcome. Shop on site open Tuesday-Saturday 9am-5pm, Sunday 10am-4pm (closed Mondays). The shop also sells plants, apple juice, pickles, preserves etc

Directions

From Bath take the A4 towards Chippenham. Broadlands Fruit Farm is 3 miles from the city centre on the left

Broadoak Cider

The Cider Mill
Clutton Hill Farm
King Lane
Clutton BS39 5QQ
☎ (01275) 333154 (Office)/(01761) 453119 (Mill)

Brian Brunt has been making cider at Clutton Hill Farm for 25 years and it has grown into one of the country's biggest independents thanks to a broad base of traditional, keg and bottled ciders. The white ciders are made from culinary apples, the others from Herefordshire and Somerset apples grown locally.

Cider

Various including:
Moonshine, KB, Broadoak Sweet/Medium/Dry, Pheasant Plucker, Classic Gold, Red Oak, Blackout, Mega, Crimson King (Strength varies from 5.9-8.4% ABV)

Annual Production

750,000 gallons

Sales

Shop on site 9am-5pm Monday-Friday (ring Mill Fridays)

Directions

From Bristol take the A37 to Shepton Mallet. From Bath take the A36 in the same direction. Turn off at signpost marked for Clutton then sharp left at top of Clutton Hill. Clutton Hill Farm opposite Cuckoo Lane

Burrow Hill Cider & Somerset Cider Brandy Company

Burrow Hill
Kingsbury
Martock
TA12 5BU
☎ (01460) 240782
apples@ciderbrandy.co.uk
www.ciderbrandy.co.uk

Traditional cider makers who make farmhouse cider from the farm's 150 acres of orchard and apple distillers who also produce 3, 5 and 10 year old cider brandy.

Cider
Burrow Hill, 6.5% ABV (bottled; pasteurised)
Burrow Hill Draught, 6.5% ABV (draught)
Burrow Hill, 8% ABV (bottle conditioned)

Annual Production
100,000 gallons

Sales
Visitors welcome. Farm shop open 9am-5pm every day except Sunday

Directions
1 mile from the centre of Kingsbury Episcopi (follow brown signs)

Outlets
Local pubs

Chestnut Farm Award Winning Cider
Chestnut Farm
Edithmead
TA9 4HB
☎ (01278) 785376

A family run business, the current owners are the 5th generation to make cider here. Featured on an early series of Rick Stein's 'Food Heroes'.

Cider
Dry/Medium, 6.5% ABV (draught)

Annual Production
2,500 gallons

Sales
Farm gate sales from 10am-4pm winter and 10am-8.30pm summer

Outlets
Occasionally sell at ploughing matches, vintage rallies and agricultural shows

Crossmans Prime Farmhouse Cider
Mayfield Farm
Hewish
Weston-Super-Mare
BS24 6RQ
☎ (01934) 834921

Ben Crossman uses a wide range of Somerset cider apple varieties to produce his traditional, unfiltered farmhouse cider.

Cider
Home Orchard Special, 7-7.5% ABV
Dry/Medium/Sweet, 6% ABV

Annual Production
5,000-8,000 gallons

Sales
Visitors welcome. Farm gate sales available Monday-Saturday 9am-6pm, Sunday 9am-1pm

Wholesalers
Jon Hallam (01291 627242)
RCH Brewery, Weston-Super-Mare, Somerset
Crouch Vale Brewery, Chelmsford, Essex

Derrick's Cider
Cheddar Valley Cheese Depot
Cheddar BS27 3QE
☎ (01934) 743113

Deep in Cheddar Gorge, the Derrick family business was established in 1870 as a cheese retailer and wholesaler. Cider was introduced in 1975. The current owner, A.J. Derrick, has been there for 31 years.

Cider
Country Bumpkin (draught)

Annual Production
600 gallons

Sales
Visitors welcome, shop open 9am-5pm all week

Directions
B3135 Cheddar Gorge

Dobunni Farm Cider
Dobunni Farm
Wick Road
Lympsham BS24 0HA
☎ (01278) 751593
iegibson@aol.com

The cider orchards were set up in 1974 and Dobunni has made cider for some 20 years and only make and sell traditional farmhouse cider. Dobunni is the home of the 'Somerset Orchard and Cider Project', a training operation. There is also a fishery and a farm shop.

Cider
Old Dobbie, 6% ABV (draught)

Annual Production
1,500 gallons

Sales
Visitors welcome by appointment. Farm shop open 10am-5.30pm

Directions
From junction 22 on M5; to roundabout, turn north on A38 and take first left turn to Brent Knoll. Take fourth turn on left (Wick Lane), go to T-junction and turn left. 300 metres to entrance on left

Ermie & Gertie's
Pitney House
Pitney, Langport TA10 9AR
☎ (01458) 252308
info@ermieandgertie.com
www.ermieandgertie.com

A small family-run business that was established in 2000 to provide a range of traditional, regional products, using only the very best and most natural ingredients available. They also make apple juice, fresh fruit sorbets and ice cream (with Guernsey milk and cream). Greeting cards and limited edition prints are also sold.

Cider/Perry
Whisky Barrel Finished (dry), 7-8% ABV (bottled/draught)
Yarlington Mill (dry), 7-8% ABV (bottled/draught)
Yarlington Mill/Crimson King Blend (dry), 7-8% ABV (bottled/draught)
Rum Barrel Finished (dry), 7-8% ABV (bottled/draught)
Dabinett (dry), 7-8% ABV (bottled/draught)
Morgan (medium dry), 5-6% ABV (bottled/draught)

Annual Production
250-500 gallons

Sales
Visitors are welcome but by arrangement only. Farm gate sales are available but please phone in advance

ERMIE & GERTIE'S PROVIDE A RANGE OF TRADITIONAL, REGIONAL PRODUCTS.

Directions
Opposite the church in Pitney village

Outlets
Lower Sea Farm Shop, Ilminster, Somerset
Olive Tree, Taunton, Somerset
Prockters Farm Shop, West Monkton,
Somerset
Shaftesbury Whole Foods, Shaftesbury,
Dorset
Williams Supermarket, Somerton,
Somerset

Hecks Farmhouse Cider
9-11 Middle Leigh
Street
BA16 0LB
☎ (01458) 442367

Established in 1896, Hecks make around
20 single variety ciders and perries as well
as apple juice.

Cider/Perry
Sweet/Dry/Medium Cider, 6.5% ABV
(bottled; pasteurised /draught)
Kingston Black, 7% ABV (bottled;
pasteurised/draught)
Hangdown, 7% ABV (bottled;
pasteurised/draught)
Dabinett, 7% ABV (bottled;
pasteurised/draught)
Hendre Huffcapp Perry, 6.5% ABV
(bottled; pasteurised/draught)

Annual Production
12,000-15,000 gallons

Sales
Visitors are welcome. Farm shop selling
cider, perry, apple juice, pickles, chutneys,
cheese and jams is open weekdays 9am-
5.30pm, Saturday 9am-5pm and Sunday
10am-12.30pm

Directions
Follow B3151 Somerton Road out
of Street and look for brown
tourist signs

Outlets
The Bell, Evercreech, Somerset
Halfway House, Pitney, Somerset
Barton Inn, Barton, Somerset
Heritage Fine Foods, Glastonbury,
Somerset
Truckle of Cheese, Glastonbury, Somerset

Henry's Farmhouse Scrumpy
Tanpits Farm
Bathpool
Taunton TA2 8BZ
☎ (01823) 270663

Cider making started around 1912 by
Harold Prings. Henry's now produce on a
larger scale and have planted their own
orchards. They use mainly their own
apples, no concentrates and try to make
the cider as natural as possible with no
additives.

Cider
Henry's Dry/Sweet, 6.5% ABV (draught)

Sales
Visitors welcome. Farm shop open
Monday-Saturday 8.30am-6pm

Directions
Take A38 Taunton to Bridgwater, in
Bathpool village turn left for canal car
park and left again

Parsons Choice Cider
Parsonage Farm
West Lyng
Taunton
TA3 5AP
☎ (01823) 490978

Parsons Choice have been making cider
for 15 years. The farm shop also sells
vegetables grown on the farm as well as
honey, jam etc.

Cider
Parsons Choice (Sweet/Medium/Dry),
6.5% ABV (draught)

The Morgan Sweet is fast disappearing from the West Country orchards. It ripens early and is the first apple used in cidermaking. Originally an eating apple, South Wales miners liked to eat them with their Caerphilly cheese.

PERRY BROS • DOWLISH WAKE • SOMERSET

500ml   6% Alc

Annual Production
3,000 gallons

Sales
Visitors are welcome. Shop on site open seven days a week 9am-6pm

Directions
On A361 between East and West Lyng

Perry's Cider
Cider Mills
Dowlish Wake,
Ilminster
TA19 0NY
☎ (01460) 55195
www.perryscider.co.uk

Founded in 1923 by William Churchill, the village blacksmith, and on his death in 1946 taken over by his nephews Henry and Bert Perry. Sadly they have now died but the business is still run by the Perry family. In addition to the cider mills and shop there is also a very interesting rural museum on site with a large collection of farming tools and wooden carts.

Cider
Traditional, 6% ABV (bottled; carbonated, pasteurised/draught)
Vintage, 6% ABV (bottled; carbonated, pasteurised/draught)
Single Variety (Redstreak/Dabinett), 6% ABV (bottled; pasteurised – still & carbonated)
Hogshead, 6% ABV (bottled; pasteurised – still & carbonated)
Premium Vintage, 6% ABV (bottled; carbonated, pasteurised)

Sales
Visitors welcome. Shop on site open Monday-Friday 9am-5.30pm, Saturday 9.30am-4.30pm, Sunday 10am-1pm. Shop also sells chutneys, jams, local produce and gifts

Directions
2 miles south of Ilminster, follow brown tourist signs

Awards
Royal Bath & West Show 2003/2005: Supreme Champion Cider winner

Outlets
Please see website

Wholesaler
Wylam Brewery, South Houghton Farm, Heddon on the Wall, Northumberland

Rich's Farmhouse Cider
Mill Farm
Watchfield
TA9 4RD
☎ (01278) 783651
jan@richscider.co.uk
www.richscider.co.uk

Cider has been produced at Rich's Cider Farm for over 50 years. Rich's has always been a family business, Jan Scott took over running the business in 1998 after Gordon Rich, her father, passed away and has since updated the visitors centre shop and pressing room and opened a shop in Cheddar Gorge at the Cheddar Gorge Cheese Co. Rich's also do a range of apple juice that is pressed and bottled at the farm.

Cider
Rich's Farmhouse Dry/Medium/Sweet, 6% ABV (bottled/draught)
Vintage Medium/Dry, 7.2% ABV (bottled; pasteurised)
Legbender Sweet/Medium/Dry, 6% ABV (bottled/draught)

Annual Production
75,000 gallons

Sales
Visitors welcome. Shop on site is open seven days a week. Summer Monday-Saturday 9am-7pm, Sunday 10am-7pm. Winter Monday-Saturday 9am-6pm, Sunday 10am-6pm. The shop also sells apple juice, cider brandy, Somerset cheeses, pickles, jams, crafts and pottery

Directions
2 miles from junction 22 of the M5 on the B3139. 2 miles from Highbridge, 4 miles from Burnham-on-Sea

Outlets
Numerous local pubs & off licences including:
Lion's Club, Bridgwater, Somerset
Kings Head Inn, Cannington, Somerset
Foresters Inn, Dunster, Somerset
Legbender Cider Shop, Cheddar Gorge, Somerset

Wholesalers
Merrylegs (01626) 773650
Jon Hallam (01291 627242)
RCH Brewery, Weston-Super-Mare, Somerset
Blackawton Brewery, Saltash, Cornwall
Crouch Vale Brewery, Chelmsford, Essex

R.J. Sheppy & Son
Three Bridges
Bradford-on-Tone
TA4 1ER
☎ (01823) 461233
info@sheppyscider.com
www.sheppyscider.com

This family-run, traditional cidermakers has been in production since the early 1800s. The 370 acre farm has 47 acres of cider orchards and the cider museum on site provides a unique insight into the farming of yesteryear.

Cider
Farmhouse Draught, 6% ABV (draught)
Oakwood Draught, 6% ABV (bottled)
Kingston Black, 7.2% ABV (bottled)
Organic, 7% ABV (bottled)
Dabinett, 7.2% ABV (bottled)

LEGBENDER
FARMHOUSE CIDER
DRY

4 Litre
6% ABV

REAL FARM CIDER

FAMOUS IN CIDERLAND FOR 50 YEARS
Made traditionally with Somerset Cider apples
by Richs Cider of Watchfield, Somerset. Tel: 01934 744127

Annual Production
100,000 gallons

Sales
Visitors welcome. Shop on site open Monday-Saturday 8.30am-6pm, Sunday 11am-1pm

Directions
A38 between Taunton and Wellington, 2 miles off junction 26 of the M5

Thatchers Cider Company Limited
Myrtle Farm
Sandford
BS25 5RA
☎ (01934) 822862
info@thatcherscider.co.uk
www.thatcherscider.co.uk

Thatchers is an independent family company that has been crafting cider for over 100 years since William John Thatcher first started making it for his farm workers in 1904. It is now fourth generation, with Martin Thatcher being the Managing Director.

Cider/Perry
Thatchers Traditional, 6% ABV (draught)
Cheddar Valley, 6% ABV (draught)
Thatchers Heritage, 4.9% ABV (draught)
Thatchers Perry, 7.4% ABV (bottled; cold filtered)

Annual Production
3,000,000 gallons

Sales
Visitors welcome. Shop on site open Monday-Saturday 9am-6pm, Sunday 10am-1pm, Bank Holidays 9am-1pm

Directions
Leave M5 at junction 21 to A371 Weston-Super-Mare. At 2nd roundabout turn left marked to Wells which leads into Banwell, turn left to A368 marked for Bath – Sandford is the village a few miles along this road

Outlets
Available in local Bristol pubs as well as through Punch and Enterprise pubs. Also available in supermarkets

and shops such as Tesco, Sainsburys and Waitrose

Torre Cider
Torre Farm
Washford
Watchet TA23 0LA
☎ (01984) 640004

Torre Cider was founded in 1989. It has a farm shop and tearoom as well as animals and a play area for children.

Cider
Sheep Stagger, 7.4% ABV (bottled; pasteurised/draught)
Farmhouse, 6.5% ABV (bottled; pasteurised/draught)
Tornado, 8.4% ABV (bottled; pasteurised/draught)

Annual Production
15,000 gallons

Sales
Visitors welcome. Farm shop open March-October 10am-6pm, November-February 10am-4pm

Directions
Follow brown tourist signs from A39 Bridgwater to Minehead Road at Washford

West Croft Cider
West Croft Farm
Brent Knoll
Highbridge TA9 4BE
☎ (01278) 760762
erica@westcroftcider.com

Founded in 1994 by John Harris, West Croft Cider produces a high quality, traditional cider that is sourced by fruit grown on the farm and local suppliers.

Cider
Janet's Jungle Juice (Medium/Dry), 6.5% ABV (draught)

Morgan Sweet (Medium), 6.5% ABV (draught)

Annual Production
7,000-10,000 gallons

Sales
Visitors welcome. Shop on site open 10am-7pm (closed Wednesdays)

Directions
Situated in the middle of Brent Knoll where Brent Street meets the B3140. 5 minutes from junction 22 of the M5

Outlets
Coronation, Southville, Bristol (0117 940 9044)

Wholesalers
RCH Brewery, Weston-Super-Mare, Somerset (01934 834447)
Merrylegs (01626) 773650
Jon Hallam (01291 627242)

West Monkton Cider Co Ltd
Overton
West Monkton, Taunton TA2 8LS
☎ (01823) 412345
www.wmcider.co.uk

West Monkton Cider Company was formed in 2000 from the amalgamation of Lane's Cider and the Kingston Vale Cider Co. Now, 30 years after Gary Lane made his first (non-commercial) barrel of cider, he, along with Sales Manager Roger Clark, are developing the companies brands throughout the tourist areas of the south west, together with new products for the local on-trade.

Cider
Lane's Farmhouse, 5.8% ABV (draught)
Lane's Organic Dry, 5.8% ABV (bottled; carbonated)
Bonking Billy, 6% ABV (bottled; sterile filtered)
Rampant Rosie, 6% ABV (bottled; sterile filtered)

Harvest Gold, 6% ABV (bottled; sterile filtered)
Scratch, 5.8% ABV (bottled; carbonated, sterile filtered)
Golden Ritter (Medium Sweet), 5.8% ABV (draught)
Kingston Red (Medium Dry), 4.5% ABV (draught)

Annual Production
10,000 gallons

Sales
Visitors welcome but please phone first. Farm gate sales available but 5 gallons minimum or wholesale packs of cider in 6 x 2 litre, 12 x 1 litre or 12 x 500ml

Outlets
All products are widely available throughout the south west tourist area in off licences, farm shops, holiday camps etc

Wilkins Farmhouse Cider
Land's End Farm
Mudgley, Wedmore BS28 4TU
☎ (01934) 712385

Roger Wilkins is one of the best known cider characters in Somerset. He took over the family cider business (started by his Grandfather in 1917) in 1966.

Cider
Wilkins Dry/Medium/Sweet, 6.2% ABV

Annual Production
30,000 gallons

Sales
Visitors welcome, tours available. Shop on site open 10am-8pm and also sells cheeses and pickles

Directions
2.5 miles south of Wedmore on the B3151

Wholesaler
Jon Hallam (01291 627242)

Suffolk

Aspall
The Cyder House
Nr Debenham
Stowmarket IP4 6PD
☎ (01728) 860510
info@aspall.co.uk
www.aspall.co.uk

Founded in 1728 by Clement Chevallier, Barry and Henry are the 8th generation to own and run the business. Aspall also produces speciality vinegar and apple juice and has a strong organic slant as Peronnelle Chevallier (Barry and Henry's Grandmother) was a founder member of the Soil Association.

Cider
Aspall Dry Premier Cru, 7% ABV (bottled; carbonated, sterile filled)
Aspall Organic, 7% ABV (bottled; carbonated, sterile filled)
Aspall Draught, 5.5% ABV (bottled; carbonated, sterile filled/draught)

Annual Production
440,000 gallons

Outlets
In excess of 250 pubs in East Anglia and London

Castlings Heath Cottage Cider
Castlings Heath Cottage
Groton
Sudbury CO10 5ES
☎ (01787) 211737/211412
john.norton@nortonorganic.co.uk

Castlings Heath have been making cider for 20 years and only produce organic cider. One ingredient only is used in their cider – apples!

Cider
Dry, 6.5% ABV (draught)

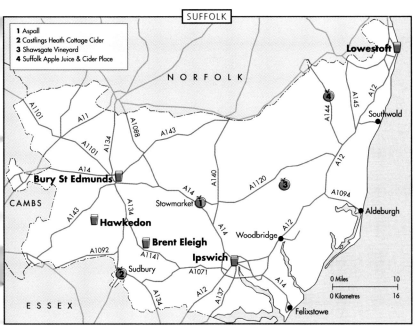

1 Aspall
2 Castlings Heath Cottage Cider
3 Shawsgate Vineyard
4 Suffolk Apple Juice & Cider Place

Annual Production
400 gallons

Sales
Visitors welcome but please ring first.
Farm gate sales available

Outlets
Cock, Brent Eleigh, Suffolk
White Horse, Edwardstone, Sudbury,
Suffolk

Shawsgate Vineyard
Badingham Road
Framlingham
IP13 9HZ
☎ (01728) 724060
tom@jarretts.co.uk
www.shawsgate.co.uk

Established in the mid 1970s,
Shawsgate produces a range of wines
as well as a cider every few years. The
cider sells out very quickly so it is
worth ringing in advance to check

availability. The next batch is
hopefully due for autumn 2005.

Sales
Visitors welcome. Shop on site open
April-November 10am-4pm. Winter
opening times are published in the local
press

Directions
Located on B1120 1 mile north of
Framlingham. Follow brown signs from
A12/B1119, A1120/B1120 or
B1119/B1120

Suffolk Apple Juice & Cider Place
Cherry Tree Farm
Ilketshall St Lawrence
NR34 8LB
☎ (01986) 781353

This small family firm was
established in 1980. All cider and
apple juice is made from local
apples, hand pressed on an 1864

'Suffolk Apple Juice & Cider Place'
Suffolk Apple Juice
Hand pressed at our Farm in a traditional manner

A naturally cloudy Pasteurised Juice - sediment may occur
consume within 10 days of opening - SHAKE BEFORE USE

'Suffolk Apple Juice &
Cider Place'
Cherry Tree Farm
Ilketshall St Lawrence
Nr Beccles Suffolk
Tel 01986 781353
(on A144 Bungay-Halesworth Rd.)

REFRIGERATE
ON OPENING
Contents: Apple Juice
Best Before See Cap
Min Contents   Litre

press and crushing mill. No
preservatives are used and ciders
are matured for 2 years before sale.

Cider
Dry/Medium/Sweet, 7% ABV (bottled)

Annual Production 20,000 litres

Sales
Visitors welcome. Shop on site
open 9am-1pm, 2-6pm. Closed

Wednesday, Friday and Sunday. If
shop is closed you can still phone
for an appointment for informal
sales. The shop also sells local jams
and pickles

Directions
Mid way between Bungay and
Halesworth on A144, 4.5 miles from both

Surrey

Coldharbour Cider
Leith Hill Place
Leith Hill
RH5 6LY
☎ (01306) 712140

A very small-scale craft cider
producer, established for 15
years. Only home grown organic
apples are used and the cider is
often sold out by Christmas.

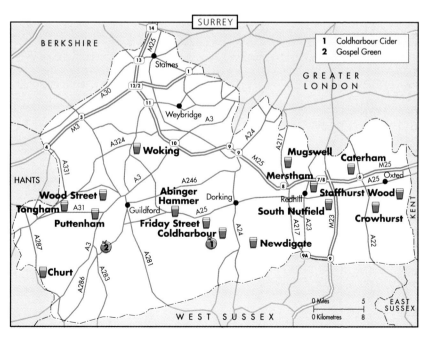

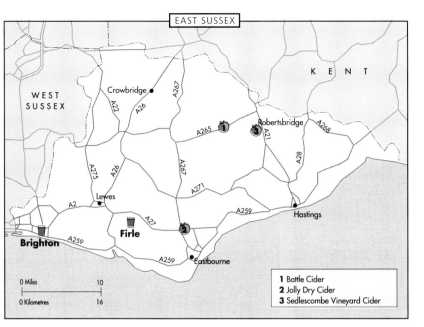

EAST SUSSEX

WEST SUSSEX

KENT

Crowbridge

A22
A26
A267

A265
1
3 Robertsbridge
A21
A268

A275
A26
A267

A28

Lewes
A2
A271

A259
Hastings

Firle
A27
2

Brighton
A259

A259
Eastbourne

0 Miles 10
0 Kilometres 16

1 Battle Cider
2 Jolly Dry Cider
3 Sedlescombe Vineyard Cider

Cider
Strong Farm Cider, 6% ABV (bottled)

Annual Production
1,000 litres

Sales
Please phone ahead for an appointment

Gospel Green
Gospel Green Cottage
Haslemere GU27 3BH
☎ (01428) 654120

Gospel Green have been making
champagne method cider since 1990
using local fruit, not cider apples.

Cider
Gospel Green, 8% ABV (bottled)

Annual Production
70hl (8750 bottles)

Sales
Visitors are welcome. Farm gate sales are

available but please call to make an
appointment

Directions
Signposted off the A283, half way
between Chiddingford and Northchapel

East Sussex

Battle Cider
Burnt House Farm
Burwash Weald TN19 7LA
☎ (01424) 429588
andy@battlecider.com
www.battlecider.com

Battle Cider is a dynamic young company,
which bases its products on traditional
cider making techniques and old English
cider apples. These are grown in one of
the few remaining orchards in East Sussex.

Cider
Dry/Medium/Sweet, 7.5% ABV (bottled;
pasteurised/draught)

Single Variety (Katy), 7.5% ABV
(bottled/draught)
Single Variety (Cox), 5.5% ABV
(bottled/draught)
Michelin/Dabinett, 7.4% ABV
(bottled/draught)

Annual Production
8,000 gallons

Sales
Visitors welcome (for guided tours). Shop
on site open seven days a week from
8.30am-5.30pm (01580 879385)

Directions
The farm shop and production are at
Ringden Farm, London Road,
Etchingham, East Sussex

Jolly Dry Cider
Wilmington House
Wilmington, Polegate BN26 5SJ
☎ (01323) 870445

Jolly Dry Cider started production circa
1993 to make use of fallen apples off of
very old eating and cooking apple trees.
They have a very small production run
requiring years of mellowing.

Cider
Jolly Dry, 7% ABV (draught)

Annual Production
235 litres

Sales
Visitors are welcome but no direct sales
are available

Outlets
Rose Cottage, Alciston
Middle Farm Cider Centre

Sedlescombe Organic Vineyard
Hawkhurst Road
Cripp's Corner
Sedlescombe TN32 5SA

☎ (01580) 830715
www.englishorganicwine.co.uk

Sedlescombe Organic Vineyard is an
independent family run business,
established in 1979, which has since
developed into England's leading organic
vineyard. Sedlescombe supplies an extensive
range of wines, liqueurs, country wines, fruit
juices as well as farmhouse style ciders.

Cider
Dry Cider Extra Strong, 7% ABV (bottled;
pasteurised)

Annual Production
666 gallons

Sales
Visitors welcome. Shop open daily from
10am-6pm

Directions
8 miles north of Hastings on
the B2244, 1.5 miles north of
Sedlescombe

West Sussex

Appledram Farm Products
Pump Bottom Farm
Birdham Road
Appledram
Chichester PO20 7EH
☎ (01243) 773828

Appledram Farm Products was
founded in 1981 to run in
conjunction with apple production on
site. There is a four day Blues festival
held every year at the end of June.
The Kencancook restaurant is next
door and many of the dishes often
contain Appledram Cider.

Cider/Perry
Appledram Dry/Medium/Sweet, 7% ABV
Appledram Perry, 6% ABV

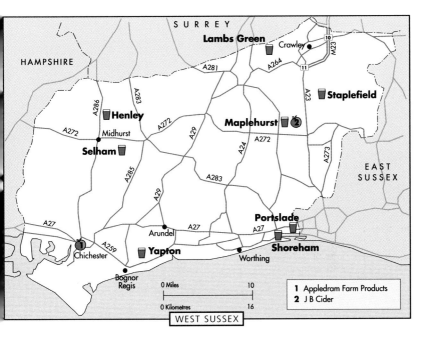

Annual Production
10,000 litres

JB Cider
The Orchard
Park Lane
Maplehurst RH13 6LL
☎ (01403) 891352

JB make cider in a traditional manner, from all types of apples. Their trees were first planted from 1985 onwards.

Cider
JB Dry/Medium/Sweet, 7.5% ABV (draught)

Annual Production
1,500 gallons

Sales
Visitors welcome. Farm gate sales available but please ring in advance

Directions
Once in Maplehurst turn right by the sign for the White Horse pub, the orchard is approx 200 yards on the left

Outlets
White Horse, Maplehurst
Evening Star, Brighton
Buckingham Arms, Shoreham
Beer Essentials, Horsham
Middle Farm, Firle, Lewes

Warwickshire

Hogan's Cider
North Lodge Barn
Haselor
Alcester B49 6LX
☎ (01789) 488433
allenhogan@onetel.com

Allen Hogan has been making cider for 10 years, the last 2 years commercially. Only 100% fresh pressed cider apple juice is used. The fruit is sourced locally – a limited amount from his own trees, the

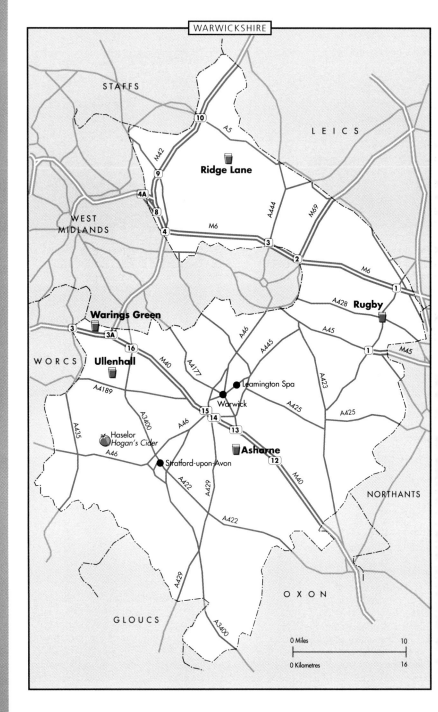

WARWICKSHIRE

STAFFS

LEICS

10

A5

M42

Ridge Lane

9

4A

8

WEST
MIDLANDS

4

M6

A444

M69

3

2

M6

1

A428

Rugby

Warings Green

3

3A

16

A46

A445

A45

1

M45

WORCS

Ullenhall

M40

A4177

A423

A4189

Leamington Spa

15

14

Warwick

A425

A425

A435

A3400

A46

Haselor
Hogan's Cider

13

Asharne

12

A46

Stratford-upon-Avon

M40

NORTHANTS

A422

A429

A422

A429

OXON

GLOUCS

A3400

0 Miles   10

0 Kilometres   16

majority from a 13 acre orchard in Leigh Sinton, near Worcester.

Cider
Hogan's Cider Medium/Dry, 7.5% ABV (bottled; sterile filtered, carbonated, pasteurised/draught)

Annual Production
900 gallons

Sales
Visitors are welcome. Please ring in advance. No direct sales available, however

Directions
Just off the A46 between Alcester and Stratford in the village of Haselor (OS124576)

Outlets
Stratford Farmers Market (0121 200 3115) Coach & Horses, Weatheroak Hill

(01564 823386)
Studley Cricket Club, Studley
(01527 853668)

West Midlands

Hamstead Brewing Centre
37 Newton Road
Great Barr
Birmingham
B43 6AD
☎ (0121) 358 6800
cider@hamstead-brewing-centre.co.uk
www.hamstead-brewing-centre.co.uk

A family owned and operated company that as well as cider produces wines and grape juices. They also produce wine with personalised labels, a large range of fruit presses and crushers and all ingredients/equipment for making wine, beer or cider at home.

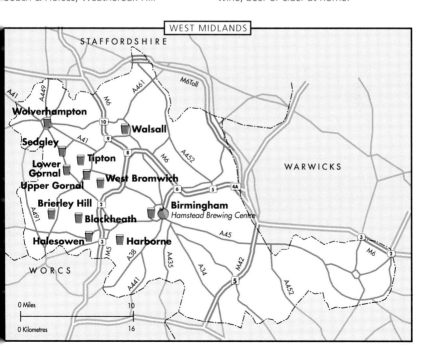

Cider
Wobblycob Traditional Original (medium dry), 7% ABV (bottled; filtered)
Wobblycob Single Apple Variety – Yarlington Mill (medium), 7% ABV (bottled; filtered)
Wobblycob Single Apple Variety – Michelin (medium dry), 7% ABV (bottled; filtered)
Wobblycob Single Apple Variety – Bulmer's Norman (medium), 7% ABV (bottled; filtered)

Wobblycob Traditional (medium sweet), 7% ABV (bottled; filtered)

Annual Production
5,000 litres

Sales
Visitors welcome. Shop on site open Monday-Saturday 9am-5.30pm

Wiltshire

Moles Brewery
5 Merlin Way
Bowerhill Trading Estate
Melksham SN12 6TJ
☎ (01225) 708842
www.molesbrewery.com

(See Thatchers, Somerset as they produce Black Rat for Moles)

Cider
Black Rat (Dry), 6-6.5% ABV
(bottled/draught)

Thornham Farm Shop T/A Tullor Ltd
Great Thornham Farm
Seend, Melksham SN12 6PN
☎ (01380) 828295
digby@digbyhawkins.freeserve.co.uk

Tullor Ltd is a small family run enterprise that had its first pressing in 2002. They use local cider apples and windfalls.

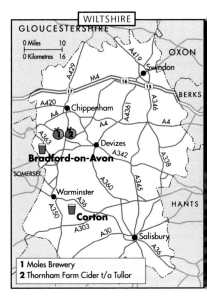

Cider
Morning Glory (Dry), 6.5% ABV (draught)

Annual Production
500 gallons

Sales
Visitors are welcome. Sales are mostly wholesale at present pending license

Directions
On A361 between A350 and Devizes

Worcestershire

Barbourne Cider
19 York Place, Worcester WR1 3DR
☎ (01905) 27151
rich@barbournecider.co.uk
www.barbournecider.co.uk

A small scale producer, making cider from locally grown apples, using traditional methods and equipment. Tupsley Court Cider is made from a mixture of hand picked bittersweet, sweet and sharp apples. The orchard they come from has 30 mature standard trees and was originally contracted to Bulmers in the 50s. So far they have identified Foxwhelp, Bulmers Norman and Major varieties and hope to identify the remaining trees this autumn. Barbourne Dry Cider is made from a blend of Somerset Redstreak, Major, Bulmers Norman and Browns Apple varieties and is available as draught or in bottles. They plan to produce some single varietal ciders for bottling and draught in 2006.

Cider
Tupsley Court (Dry/Medium), 6.7% ABV (draught)
Barbourne Dry Cider, 6.5% ABV (bottled/draught)

Annual Production
200 gallons

Sales
Visitors welcome but no shop on site. Please ring or email for further details

Outlets
Jenades Deli, 43 Upper Tything, Worcester (01905 731300)
Pershore Cricket Club, Defford Road, Pershore, Worcs

Barkers Real Cider & Perry
Moody Cow Cottage
Greenstreet Farm
Hallow WR2 6PY
☎ (01905) 640697/642731

Greenstreet Farm is a working cattle and sheep farm. John Barker started cider and perry making in 1996 and uses only his own unsprayed fruit from the farm's rejuvenated traditional Victorian orchards, planted in the 1850s.

Cider/Perry
Barker's Best Cyder (Dry), 5% ABV (draught)

Barker's Upsy-Daisy Real Perry (Medium Dry), 5% ABV (draught)

Annual Production
700 gallons

Sales
Visitors are welcome by appointment. Farm gate sales are available but minimum purchase is five gallons, please ring first

Directions
From Worcester A443 to Tenbury Wells, at Hallow (3 miles) turn by Royal Oak, after 30 yards take right fork then 2.5 miles to end of road

Awards
CAMRA National Cider & Perry Championship 2003: Bronze for Upsy-Daisy Real Perry

Outlets
Fox Inn, Monkwood Green, Nr Hallow, Worcs (01886) 889123

Wholesaler
Merrylegs (01626) 773650

Barnfield Winery and Cider Mill
Broadway Road
Broadway WR12 7HB
☎ (01386) 853145
wmbh@hotmail.com

Barnfield Winery and Cider Mill dates back to the late 1700's, the current owners took possession in 1986 and continued the long tradition of cider and wine production. There is a small museum, a café (currently available for pre-booked groups only) and a shop where the wines and ciders can be tasted for free and purchased in a variety of containers supplied from half a litre to 22 litres.

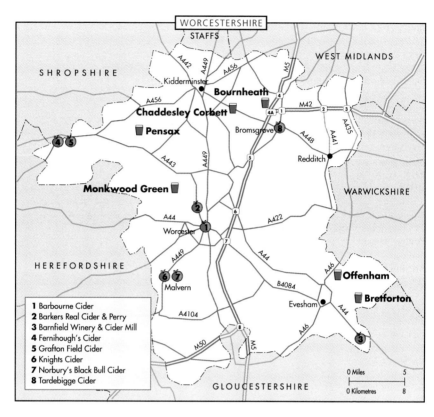

1 Barbourne Cider
2 Barkers Real Cider & Perry
3 Barnfield Winery & Cider Mill
4 Fernihough's Cider
5 Grafton Field Cider
6 Knights Cider
7 Norbury's Black Bull Cider
8 Tardebigge Cider

Cider/Perry
Dry, 6.5% ABV (draught)
Medium/Sweet, 6% ABV (draught)
Perry, 4.8% ABV (draught)

Sales
Visitors are welcome. Shop on site open
9.30am-8pm

Directions
On the outskirts of Broadway village
(nearest main road is A44) between
Oxford and Worcester

Fernihough's Cider
Ashdown
Worcester Road
Boraston, Tenbury Wells WR15 8LL
☎ (01584) 819632

The Fernihough's are a farming family,
the third generation on their farm in
Bewdley. Their first cider batch was in
1995 and after procuring a licence they
have been selling ever since. All apples
are sourced from local farmers.

Cider
Dry/Medium/Sweet, 4% ABV or 7.2%
ABV (draught)

Annual Production
1,500 gallons

Sales
Visitors welcome. Cider cellar
open every day 10am-8pm
except Thursday
(also sells rare breeds meat)

Directions
On the main A456

Awards
Tenbury Show: 1st for cider (for many years)

Grafton Field Cider
Grafton Field
Bockleton
Tenbury Wells WR15 8PT
☎ (01568) 750638
stavi.dog@velle.co.uk

A very small cider and perry producer that has been pressing for 10 years using local, unsprayed apples and pears.

Annual Production
200 gallons

Sales
Visitors are welcome. Farm gate sales are available, please ring in advance

Knights Cider Ltd
Crumpton Oaks Farm
Storridge, Malvern WR13 5HP
☎ (01684) 568887
enquiries@knightscider.co.uk
www.knightscider.co.uk

During the past 25 years Knights Cider has grown from a small family company making a few thousand gallons of traditional cider and having a cider apple orchard of 25 acres to become one of the country's largest independent commercial and traditional cider makers. Their cider orchards of various ages have increased to 200 acres. Specimens of old varieties are grown to save them dying out and experiments are being carried out to develop new varieties of trees for the future in conjunction with the National Association of Cider Makers.

Cider
Malvern Gold Medium Reserve, 6% ABV (bottled; carbonated, pasteurised)
Malvern Oak Dry Reserve, 6% ABV (bottled; carbonated, pasteurised)
Knights Traditional Medium Sweet/Dry, 6% ABV (draught)

Sales
Cider on sale at the shop, open Saturday-Sunday 10.30am-5pm

Directions
Approx 200 yards along B4219 off main Worcester to Hereford Road (A4103)

Outlets
Waitrose, Malvern
Malvern Gold and Oak available in approx 50 local outlets

Norbury's Cider
Holywell Farm Buildings
Storridge WR13 5HD
☎ (01886) 832206

Tom Norbury took over his family farm in 1981 but had been making cider there since 1979. All ciders and perries are made from a mixture of fruit either grown at Holywell Farm or bought from other local farms.

NORBURY'S BLACK BULL —MEDIUM DRY— CIDER 7% Vol 750ml

Cider/Perry
Medium Dry Cider, 7% ABV (bottled; carbonated/draught)
Medium Sweet Scrumpy, 7% ABV (bottled; carbonated/draught)
Perry (Medium Dry) (bottled)

Annual Production
5,000 gallons

Sales
Farm gate sales available during 'Pick your Own' season, Wednesday-Friday 2-5pm, Saturday-Sunday 10am-5.30pm

Directions
7 miles from Worcester on A4103 Worcester to Hereford road

Tardebigge Cider
Tutnall
Bromsgrove B60 1NB

☎ (01527) 877946
tardebiggecider@lineone.net
www.tardebiggecider.co.uk

Steve Cooper founded Tardebigge Cider in 2000 after planting his orchards in 1995.

Cider/Perry
Dry/Medium/Sweet, 6.5% ABV (bottle conditioned/draught)
Perry available occasionally

Annual Production
1,000 gallons

Sales
Visitors welcome. Farm gate sales available

Directions
Off B4096 near Bromsgrove

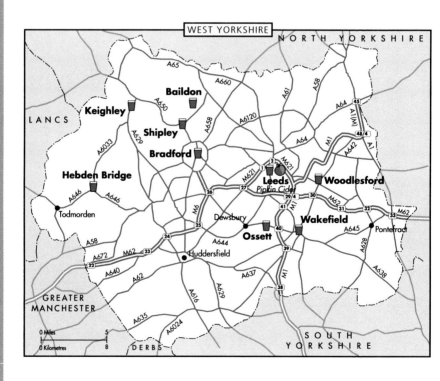

West Yorkshire

Pipkin Cider
Cherry Tree Cottage
Strait Lane
Huby LS17 0EA
☎ (01423) 734934

This very small cottage industry was set up by two CAMRA members in 1995 to bring a taste of the real thing to an area not usually associated with traditional cider. All of the varieties of apples used are sourced from local orchards in West Yorkshire. The business started life in the famous brewing town of Masham but moved to Huby in 2001. Most of the small output goes to various beer festivals both near and far. It also occasionally appears in pubs.

Cider
Pipkin Dry/Medium, 5.5-6.8% ABV (draught)

Annual Production
100-200 gallons

Sales
No direct sales available

Outlets
Fox & Hounds, Main Street, West Witton, North Yorks (01969 623650)
Grove Inn, Back Row, Holbeck, Leeds, West Yorks (0113 243 9254)

Cider Producers
Wales

Glamorgan

Gower Heritage Centre
Parkmill
Gower
Swansea
SA3 2EN
☎ (01792) 371206
info@gowerheritagecentre.co.uk
www.gowerheritagecentre.co.uk

The centre is based around an 800-year-old water-powered corn and saw mill with craft workshops, large tea rooms and a children's puppet theatre.

Cider/Perry
Medium Mill Cider, 8.4% ABV (sterile bottled/draught)
Medium Mill Perry, 6.4% ABV (sterile bottled/draught)

Annual Production
800 gallons

Sales
Visitors are welcome. Shop on site open 10am-5pm daily

Directions
A4118 from Swansea. Follow brown tourist signs

Gwynt y Ddraig Cider
Llest Farm
Llantwit Fardre
Pontypridd
CF38 2PW
☎ (01443) 217274

andrew.gronow@virgin.net
www.gwyntcider.com

They produced their first cider in autumn of 2001 and formed Gwynt y Ddraig Cider upon increased interest. This year they are producing oak conditioned farmhouse perry to compliment their oak conditioned ciders.

Cider/Perry
Haymaker Cider, 6.5% ABV (draught)
Barnstormer, 6.5% ABV (draught)
Black Dragon, 6.5% ABV (bottled; carbonated/draught)
Dog Dancer, 6.75% ABV (bottled; carbonated/draught)
Tremletts Bitter, 6.5% ABV (draught)
Foxwhelp, 6.5% ABV (draught)
Celtic Gold, 6.5% ABV (bottled/draught)
Yarlington Mill, 6.5% ABV (bottled/draught)
Gold Medal, 7% ABV (bottled; carbonated)
Grand Slam, 6.5% ABV (bottled/draught)

Annual Production
12,000 gallons

Sales
Visitors welcome. Please ring in advance

Directions
M4 junction 34, follow A4119 to Llantresant, turn right at first roundabout and follow A473 to

BILL GEORGE AND
'DREW' GRONOW
FOUNDERS OF GWYNT
Y DDRAIG CIDER.

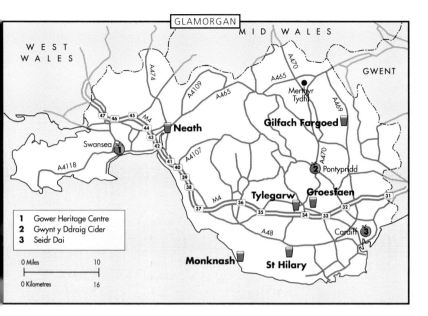

Pontypridd. Next village Llantwit Fardre, turn left by the Crown Inn, 100 yards up the hill then first right into Farm Lane

Awards

Reading Beer Festival 2003:
Silver for cider
Reading Beer Festival 2004:
Gold for cider

Seidr Dai

91 Black Oak Road
Cyncoed
Cardiff
CF23 6QW
☎ (029) 2075 8193
dave.matthews7@btinternet.com

Seidr Dai was founded in 2000 by Dave Matthews. It specialises in the production of perries and cider from Welsh varieties of perry pear and cider apple and is proud to produce only natural drinks – 100% juice with no added water, sugar or yeast. Dave founded the Welsh Cider Society in 2001 and is currently Secretary.

Cider/Perry

Berllanderi Green/Burgundy/Blakeney Red Perry, 6-8% ABV (draught)
Thorn/Nailer/Potato Pear Perry, 6-8% ABV (draught)
Welsh Gin/Hellen's Early/Pankers Pride (blend) Perry, 6-8% ABV (draught)
Breakwell's Seedling/Raglan's Rarest (blend) Perry, 6-8% ABV (draught)
Plus others

Annual Production

500 gallons

Sales

No direct sales available

Outlets

Usually sold at cider and beer festivals in south east Wales. No regular outlets but can sometimes be found at:
Clythe Arms, nr Abergavenny
Chapter Arts Centre, Canton, Cardiff

Wholesaler

Jon Hallam (01291 627242)

Gwent

Clytha Arms
Clytha, Abergavenny NP7 9BW
☎ (01873) 840206
www.clytha-arms.com

The Clytha Arms started to make perry
from their own pear trees and now also
use pears from a local orchard (with trees
up to 400 years old). The Welsh Cider
Society festival is hosted by the pub.

Perry
Clytha Dry Perry, 6% ABV (bottle
conditioned)

Annual Production
90 gallons

Sales
The perry is sold at the pub. Opening
hours are 12-3pm and 6-11pm except
Monday lunchtime

Seidr Mynediad Ysbyty
97 St Lawrence Park
Chepstow NP16 6DQ
☎ (01291) 627242

Jon Hallam's own cider and perry is a sideline
to his main business of cider wholesaling.

Cider/Perry
The range is changeable but often
includes:
Crab 'n' Dab (Dry), 6-7% ABV (draught)
Dabinett/Reinette D'Obry (Dry), 5.7-7.3%
ABV (draught)
Red Label Guyanese Style (Medium), 6%
ABV (draught)
Green Label Original Style (Medium), 6%
ABV (draught)
Deity Grade (draught)
Others that are rarely made include:
Slab Cake/Perry/Stunnem

Annual Production
Less than 200 gallons

Sales
No direct sales available

Springfield Cider
Springfield Farmhouse
Llangovan
NP25 4BU
☎ (01291) 691018
alan@springfieldcider.co.uk
www.springfieldcider.co.uk

Springfield Cider has its own
orchard containing 27,000 trees.
Cidermaking commenced in
2004. They also are breeders of
Andalusian Spanish horses.

Cider
Farmhouse, 6.6% ABV (draught)
Old Barn, 6.8% ABV (draught)
Sledgehammer, 8.4% ABV (draught)

Annual Production
1,000 litres

Sales
No direct sales available

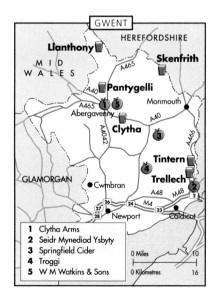

1	Clytha Arms
2	Seidr Mynediad Ysbyty
3	Springfield Cider
4	Troggi
5	W M Watkins & Sons

TROGGI

Modd Traddodiadol

Lower House Cottage, Earlswood, Monmouthshire NP16 6RH

Troggi
Lower House Cottage
Earlswood NP16 6RH
☎ (01291) 650653

This small company is named after the brook that runs through the picturesque Earlswood Valley – the Troggi or Trogglebrook. The company premises border the brook. Troggi (originally Troggi Seidr) was founded in 1986 and has from the outset produced single pressed, whole juice cider, which is pressed and fermented on the premises. Now more than half the production is of perry. Both cider and perry fruit are grown and additional supplies are obtained only from Monmouthshire orchards. Since 2002 a small proportion of both cider and perry are prepared for bottle fermentation using the traditional method.

Cider/Perry
Penallt Cider, 6.2% ABV (draught)
Kingston Black Cider, 6.1% ABV (bottle conditioned)
Yarlington Mill Cider, 5.9% ABV (bottle conditioned)
Tregagle Perry, 6.2% ABV (draught)
Broom Perry, 7.2% ABV (bottle conditioned)

Annual Production
3,500 litres

Sales
Visitors are welcome by appointment only. Cider and perry is, however, only distributed through wholesalers

Directions
Off the B4235 between Usk and Chepstow

Wholesalers
Jon Hallam (01291 627242)
Merrylegs (07776 013787)

W.M. Watkins & Sons
Upper House
Grosmont NP7 8LA
☎ (01873) 821237

The Company was set up in 2003 to make use of the traditional cider orchard on the farm. All cider is fermented and matured in oak barrels, mainly ex rum barrels.

Cider
Marketed as Ty Bryn Cider:
Rum Barrel Dry, 7.1% ABV (draught)
Oak Barrel, 7.1% ABV (draught)
Tom Putt, 6.3% ABV (draught)

Annual Production
400 gallons

Sales
No direct sales available, only wholesale

Mid Wales

Ralph's Cider & Perry
Old Badland Farm
New Radnor LD8 2TG
☎ (01544) 350304
ralph@oldbadland.fsnet.co.uk
www.ralphscider.co.uk

Ralph's Cider is a small family run business and Wales' longest established licensed cider and perry maker. Ralph Owen started making cider after the very hot summer of 1976 for his own consumption. Over the years production grew with demand from friends and neighbours. In 1986 he moved to Old Badland where there was a neglected orchard of White Norman cider apple trees. The orchard stands at 850 feet above sea level, is south facing and free draining. Restocking has taken place over the years with varieties suitable to the conditions. Fruit is also used from local orchards, making use of their apples and pears, which would otherwise go to waste. Ralph also holds a cider making festival in October where he demonstrates milling and pressing using scratters and screw presses.

Cider/Perry
Ralph's Dry/Medium/Sweet Cider, 6-8% ABV (bottled/draught)
Ralph's Dry/Medium Perry, 6% ABV (bottled/draught)

Annual Production
7,000 gallons

Sales
Visitors welcome. Farm gate sales available, please phone ahead

Directions
A44 to New Radnor. Between New Radnor and Kinnerton on the B4372

Awards
Welsh Cider Society Awards 2002-2004:
Champion Cider of Wales
Champion Perry of Wales (2004)

Outlets
Radnor Arms, New Radnor
Red Lion, Llanfihangl-nant-Melan
Stagg Inn, Titley, Herefordshire
Brecon Beacons National Parks Visitors Centre Tea Room & Restaurant, Libanus
English Farm Cider Centre, Lewes, East Sussex
Plus numerous other free houses throughout Wales

Wholesalers
Ystwyth Ales (01970 880659)
Merrylegs (07776 013787)
Jon Hallam (01291 627242)

Seidr o Sir (Welsh County Cider)
Y Betws, Betws Diserth LD1 5RP
☎ (01982) 570404
bettws_castle@yahoo.co.uk

Founded in 1999/2000 by Trefor Powell as a result of reading 'Johnny Appleseed' as a boy in New Zealand and then later meeting a neighbour in Wales wanting a home for her cider apples.

Cider
Cantrefdy (Medium), 8.3% ABV (draught)
Betws (Dry), 7.3% ABV (draught)
Blasedwy (Dry), 7.8% ABV (draught)
Colwyn (Sweet), 7.5% ABV (draught)

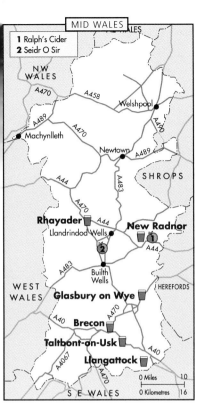

MID WALES

1 Ralph's Cider
2 Seidr O Sir

Founded in 2000, Abbey cider is made from unique cultivars only found around the Norman abbey in the village of St Dogmaels. It is thought that these cultivars were introduced by monks from Normandy and that the cider produced is therefore of the style of medieval Normandy.

Cider
Pig Aderyn (Medium),
5.5% ABV (draught)
Pen Caled (Medium),
5.5% ABV, (draught)
Abbot's Blend (Medium),
5.5% ABV (draught)

Annual Production
300 gallons

Sales
No farm gate sales. Cider is exclusively for cider festivals and local events in Pembrokeshire

Sudd Cwmpo Drosto
33 Coronation Avenue
Haverfordwest SA61 2RG
☎ (01437) 779245
betty-blue8d@hotmail.com

Annual Production
700-800 gallons

Sales
No direct sales available

Wholesalers
Jon Hallam (01291 627242)

West Wales

Abbey Cider
Rocklands
Pilot Street
St Dogmaels
SA43 3EY
☎ (07778) 967654
cooperrichardd@aol.com

Gethin ap Dafydd and Hannah Lumby started making cider in 2003 on a hobby scale by producing 20 gallons of cider made from a blend of eaters, cookers and crab apples. Output was increased to 200 gallons in 2004 by sourcing cider apples and perry pears from Monmouthshire.

Cider/Perry
JRT Cider (Dry), 6.4% ABV (draught)
Dappledown Cider (Dry), 6.5% ABV (draught)
Blakeney Red Perry (Dry), 6.8% ABV (draught)

Annual Production
200 gallons

Sales
No direct sales available

Toloja
Ty Gwyn
Dihewyd
Lampeter
SA48 7PP
☎ (01570) 471295
tolojacider@aol.com

Founded in 2004, Toloja Holdings encompasses not only the manufacture of cider, apple juice and perry but also the planting of a 100 tree museum orchard using only Welsh varieties of cider apple and pear trees. In addition Toloja are also registered breeders of rare breed animals. They hope to run residential courses in the ways of the country from growing vegetables, making preserves, keeping pigs and, of course, cider/juice making.

Cider
Merlins Mist Cider (Dry), 6.2% ABV (bottle conditioned/draught)
Queen Mab Cider (Dry), 7.5% ABV (bottle conditioned /draught)
Pendragon Cider (Medium), 5.8% ABV (bottle conditioned/draught)
Guinevere Cider (Medium), 5.8% ABV (bottle conditioned/draught)
Gallahad Cider (Sweet), 7.5% ABV (bottle conditioned/draught)
Lancelot Cider (Medium), 7.2% ABV (bottle conditioned/draught)
Igrayne Cider (Sweet), 7.5% ABV (bottle conditioned/draught)

Annual Production
620 gallons

Sales
No direct sales available

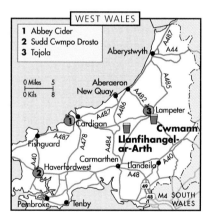

WEST WALES

1 Abbey Cider
2 Sudd Cwmpo Drosto
3 Tojola

Cider Producers
Channel Islands

Jersey

La Mare Vineyards Ltd
St Mary
JE3 3BA
☎ (01534) 481178
tim@lamarevineyards.com
www.lamarevineyards.com

Jersey history and its very close connections with France have meant there has always been a keen interest in cider making on the island. La Mare have recently launched a new bottle conditioned cider and hope to turn back the clock by returning land to cider apple trees for making cider and Jersey Apple Brandy. La Mare opened as a visitor attraction in 1976.

Cider
Cider, 6% ABV (bottled)
Pompette, 8% ABV (bottle conditioned)

Annual Production
30,000 litres

Sales
Visitors welcome. Shop open in visitors centre from 10am-5pm (admission charge applicable). There is also a shop in St Helens High Street open 10am-5pm

Directions
Signposted from St Mary

Outlets
Maison La Mare Shop, King Street, St Helen, Jersey
Lamplighter, St Helen, Jersey

Wholesaler
La Mare Wholesale Co
(01534 481178)

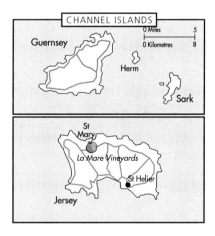

CHANNEL ISLANDS

Guernsey

Herm

Sark

St Mary

La Mare Vineyards

St Helier

Jersey

Welsh Perry & Cider Society

*The Welsh Perry & Cider Society, or 'Cymdeithas Perai a Seidr Cymru' as they say in Wales, was honoured with CAMRA's Pomona Award in 2003. Secretary **Dave Matthews** puts us in the picture:*

Welsh Cider History

Cidermaking as we know it today came over the channel with the Normans at sometime during the 12th Century, and swept across the border from Herefordshire into Wales by about the 14th Century. It became well established in the farming communities of the south-eastern part of the principality and in the region of mid Wales adjacent to the English border, but the harsh mountains prevented it spreading much further. Only the shelter of the Usk and Wye valleys allowed some orcharding to reach inland areas such as Brecon and Builth Wells.

In common with the cidermaking areas of England, cider in Wales went into decline with the industrialisation of agriculture just after the end of World War II. However, unlike England, no commercial Welsh cidermakers were left to continue the tradition. But the orchards remained, and in the 1980s the first of a new wave of craft cidermakers started to use the fruit from the old trees. In Monmouthshire, Mike Penney's *Troggi Seidr* started to produce both cider and perry with his Victorian machinery, whilst up in Radnorshire Ralph Owen's *Ralph's Cider* pressed local cider apples on an antique mobile twin-screw press.

A BOTTLE OF PERRY PRODUCED BY THE CLYTHA ARMS, BIRTHPLACE OF THE WELSH CIDER SOCIETY.

Society Beginnings

It was in 1999 that Alan Golding and I hit upon the idea of making cider, and so our company 'Seidr Dai' was born. By sheer luck, our first brew was a success, and our subsequent enthusiasm led us to form a national association. At that time there were cider associations for cidermakers, and of course CAMRA was there for the drinkers. Why not have a society that caters for both? And so the Welsh Cider Society was born at the Clytha Arms on a June evening in 2001, with Alan appointed as Development Officer, and myself as the Secretary.

Wales' perennial problem is its geography. The same mountains that stopped cidermaking spreading out of

Cymdeithas
S e i d r
C y m r u

(ABOVE) THE WELSH CIDER SOCIETY LOGO (BELOW RIGHT) THE CHAMPION WELSH PERRY TROPHY.

the south-east make it difficult for our national membership to get together. Luckily most of our members have email access, and our IT officers have constructed an excellent website.

Festivals and Championships

The best possible way to promote cider and perry is with a cider festival. The Welsh Perry & Cider Festival is held at the Clytha Arms, 6 miles east of Abergavenny, each Whitsun May Bank Holiday weekend. The first event in 2002 was a great success, and each successive year has seen an increase in the range of ciders and perries on sale, with great crowds of people filling the pub and its extensive grounds. One festival is not enough, and regional festivals are an excellent way of spreading the word – events in Gower, Cardiff, Pembrokeshire and Wrexham are also becoming established on the annual calendar.

The Welsh Perry & Cider Championships are held in tandem with the Welsh Perry & Cider Festival at the Clytha. Apart from being great fun (all of us cidermakers get to be the judges!), it's a simple but effective way of improving cider and perry quality. We all swap tips and hints with each other, plus tasting and marking your own cider blind can be a real eye-opener. The lucky winners to date are:

CIDER
2002 – Ralph's Cider
2003 – Ralph's Cider
2004 – Ralph's Cider
2005 – Gwynt-y-Ddraig Cider

PERRY
2002 – Seidr Dai
2003 – Seidr Dai
2004 – Ralph's Cider
2005 – Gwynt-y-Ddraig Cider

Cider and Perry

With the Society only four years old, it's early days yet. Nevertheless, we're already beginning to achieve our aim of successfully promoting Welsh cider and perry. The number of Welsh cidermakers has risen sharply to around twenty (not including all of the hobbyists

who make the odd gallon or two), and the overall volumes produced are showing a proportional increase, as consumers discover and demand our products. As a bit of a purist, it pleases me to report that all of our members produce natural ciders and perries, with none of that industrial processing that diminishes the flavour of the fruit.

Perhaps the greatest Welsh achievement to date comes from the Llantwit Lads at 'Seidr Gwynt-y-Ddraig'. Their blended Medium Cider carried off the Silver Award at CAMRA's National Cider and Perry Championships in 2003. In 2004, their appropriately named Gold Medal Cider won Gold, and they clinched the 2005 Perry Gold Award with their excellent Red & Green Longdon Perry. Some hat-trick.

Let's not forget Ralph's Cider, which took the 2005 CAMRA Cider Gold Award back to Radnorshire, with their 3B's Cider. So 2005 is the year of the Welsh Grand Slam, in cider as well as rugby!

Rare Varieties

Welsh cider and perry is similar to that made by our English cousins. Our only real unique selling point is the use of Welsh varieties of cider apple and perry pear – varieties that have been selected over the centuries to suit the local palate and climate. Some Welsh cider apples – *Frederick*, *Breakwell's Seedling* and

BILL GEORGE (LEFT) AND ANDY GRONOW (RIGHT) OF GWYNT-Y-DDRAIG CIDER BEING PRESENTED WITH CAMRA'S CIDER GOLD AWARD BY GILLIAN WILLIAMS IN 2004.

Perthyre – remain in commercial production and are readily available. Others, such as the *Broom Apple* of Monmouthshire, and *Pen Caled* from West Wales have had to be re-discovered, and propagated at Paul Davis' Dolau-Hirion Nursery at Llandeilo. *Frederick* is a fine apple, streaked bright red with hints of red in the flesh too. With its origins in Monmouthshire, its sharp-tasting juice will make an excellent apple jelly. Classified as a vintage variety, it is too sharp to be made into a single varietal cider, but is excellent when blended with some tannic bitter-sweet apples.

The perry pear trees of Monmouthshire are far more localised, often just a single example of a variety may be all that remains. We've rediscovered both *Burgundy* trees and the *Potato Pear* (yes, it looks like a spud growing on a tree!) at a number of locations, but other, rarer trees have no known name. I've tried to keep to the old conventions when giving names to these trees – *Berllanderi Green* (a green pear from Berllanderi Farm near Raglan), *Bastard St. Brides* (tiny and a 'bastard' to pick up!), *Chapman's Orange* – and these too are available from Dolau-Hirion, details on the website.

These Welsh varieties are now being sold and planted in orchards across Wales, ensuring their survival in the future, as well as providing an important habitat for all manner of wildlife. We've recently established our first Museum Orchard, which will act as a genetic bank, allowing future orchardists to take cuttings from all of the Welsh varieties of cider apples and perry pears.

The Future

As we stand, the future looks good for Welsh cider and perry. More and more people are planning to join the ranks of Welsh cidermakers, the number of Welsh cider festivals is set to increase, and rare varieties of Welsh apple and pear trees are regularly discovered and propagated. Membership of the Society continues to grow, and we now have members in England and even Hungary. You'd be welcome to join too, just log on to the website, www.welshcider.co.uk, or come along to the Welsh Perry & Cider Festival at the fabulous Clytha Arms.

Dave Matthews
SECRETARY,
WELSH PERRY & CIDER SOCIETY

Mantilly – World Perry Capital

Dave Matthews discovers one of Normandy's best-kept secrets

The medieval town of Domfront lies peacefully in southern Normandy. Not far away, the even sleepier village of Mantilly lies at the very epicentre of the world's most concentrated perry-making area. Every farm within kilometres of the village seems to have a mature perry pear orchard, and at blossom time the spectacle is one of the Seven Wonders of the Cider and Perry World.

Their perry (*poiré*) is somewhat different to the British style. Whereas our perry is typically dry and on draught, the Normans prefer to bottle-ferment theirs (leaving plenty of residual sweetness), suggesting it be served as an aperitif. An application for Appellation Control for Domfront Perry was progressing nicely back in 1999, until the great Boxing Day storms dealt the farmers a huge blow. Some perrymakers lost all of their trees, and most had a significant percentage blown over. Consider that these trees can attain the size of great oaks, can live for 300 years or more, but that new trees can take 30 years to produce their first significant crop, and you can imagine the devastation. In a race against time, many growers hired heavy machinery to raise and replant their fallen giants, but only a small proportion were saved in this way. After this delay, the Appellation Control is now in place, and Domfront perrymakers who qualify can charge a premium rate for their bottles. They must first pass a monthly inspection of premises, use at least 40% of pears of the 'Plant de Blanc' local variety, their perry must pass a stringent lab analysis, and it must get the thumbs-up from an appointed tasting panel.

PRODUCE FROM MANTILLY, NORMANDY

Another local speciality that has Appellation Control is the Domfront Calvados. Bottles carrying the legend *Appellation Calvados Domfrontais Contrôlée* give a guarantee of both origin and quality. Unlike other forms of Calvados, the Domfront version is made from a proportion of perry pears, and thus is a more subtle spirit, with fruitier and more floral notes. Most perrymakers around Mantilly produce a Calvados, but the exact recipe and proportion of perry to cider distilled differs from one to the next.

Let's take a little tour around Mantilly, starting in the village itself. In even-numbered years, at around July 14th, there's

PLANT BLANC PERRY PEARS (ABOVE LEFT). MADAME BRUNET WITH A FLUTE OF PERRY (NOTE THE PERRY PEAR TREE IN THE BACKGROUND) (ABOVE RIGHT).

a Perry Festival. At other times, pop into the *Petit Mantilly* bar for lunch and the odd bottle of Farmhouse Perry (*Poiré Fermier*). It's a tiny, friendly place, with a tiled floor and wooden tables and chairs. The three-course lunchtime Set Menu is great value for money, and can include a huge pot of boiled beef and whole vegetables. The *Poiré Fermier* on offer is from Michel Leroyer, who farms locally. It's a 4% abv brew that's served in a champagne flute, yellow-gold, with rising beads of bubbles. The aroma is enticing, and could almost be mistaken for an old champagne. The gentle fizz on the tongue doesn't hide the big, full-flavoured fruity/peary taste, and the finish is long and sweet.

A short drive through the pear orchards brings us to the perry farm belonging to the Lemorton family (La Baillée-Fêtu, 02 33 38 70 90). There's a beautiful, mature perry pear orchard, and a ground-floor cellar (with its timeless atmosphere and antique oak barrels) that doubles as a shop. They sell bottles of their cider, but charge a higher price for the *poiré*, since, as Monsieur Lemorton told us, "It's the local speciality!" The Lemortons are famed for their *Calvados Domfrontais*, which they distil from a mix of 70% perry and 30% cider. The youngest vintage is a 6-year old, and, as the vintages age, the prices rise until the 40-year old is nearly four times more expensive. They even have a 100-year old *Calvados Rareté*. When the Great Storm came, they had half of their 800 pear trees blown over, managing to pull up and save 20 of them. The surviving perry pear varieties enjoy names such as *Gaubert*, *Poire de Domfront* and *Rubesnard*. The most prized and famous of all is *Plant de Blanc*, which is often used to produce a single-varietal perry. British perry pears taste bad enough, but I was nearly sick after biting into a Norman pear. They have particularly high levels of tannins and acids, and the most astringent varieties are considered to have enough flavour to produce the *Calvados Domfrontais*.

A little further on, near the hamlet of Saint-Denis-de-Villenette, we are welcomed to our next perry farm by Madame Brunet (La Prémoudière, 02 33 37 23 27). She gives us a tour of the farm, starting with the steel mill. The pulped pears, she explained, are allowed to macerate for between 12 and 24 hours, before being squeezed on a twin-bed hydraulic press. The juice enjoys a slow fermentation at 5°C in fibreglass fermenters. Four perry pear varieties (*Plant de Blanc*, *Faussey*, *Blot* and *Gaubert*) are harvested over a three-month period, and blended one on top of the next using the flexibility of fermenters with adjustable floating lids. A typical starting gravity in October might be 1050, and by bottling time in January this may have dropped to 1030. A tiny bit of yeast works away in the bottle, dropping the gravity to around 1025, giving the gentle fizz. The 15,000 bottles produced each year have to be stored upright, so that excess gas can escape from around the cork, ready for sales to start in March. Perry is only one income stream for the Brunet family, and you could do a lot worse than take advantage of their farm B&B and Madame's wholesome home cooking.

Back on the road towards Mantilly, and we stop at the perry farm belonging to Monsieur and Madame Fourmand-Lemorton (Le Douët Gasnier, 02 33 38 71 63). Both have grandfathers who made calvados, and they take a break from perrymaking to show us around the orchard. In 1999 they lost half of their 150 perry pear trees, and only managed to rescue two by relifting. All of the fruit picking for their *poiré* is done by hand, since the degree of ripeness of the fruit, etc, is important. On the other hand, they harvest pears for their calvados by machine, since the fruit quality has far less impact upon the final product. Their calvados is distilled from 80% perry, one of the highest ratios in the area. They opened a bottle of perry for us to share in the orchard, and it was excellent. Pale yellow with rising bubbles, it had an aroma of pale fruit that was mellow and appealing. The taste started with a peary fizz, followed by a long medium-sweet golden and honeyed finish. This 4% abv perry was made entirely from the *Plant de Blanc* pear, and enjoyed some balancing acidity that also acts as a natural preservative.

Finally, let's pop over to Domfront itself, where we'll find a timber-framed bar in the town centre. *La Maison Normand* serves up local perry in badged *Poiré Domfront* champagne flutes – very civilised indeed. Down the street, Domfront Tourist Information (02 33 38 92 94) will willingly direct you towards the perrymakers. There's even a painting of a perry pear tree in blossom on the hanging sign!

For further Information

Domfront: see www.domfront.com
Perry: go to www.region-normande.com, Click on the following to reach Poiré producers listed under Syndicat des

Producteurs du Poiré Domfront:
1. Region Normande
2. box labelled Le Teilleul
3. Produits de Terroir on the left side menu
4. bottle icon beside Mantilly

Dave Matthews
SECRETARY, WELSH PERRY & CIDER SOCIETY

The Victorian Farmer and the Decline of Cider

The 19th century saw the virtual extinction of an ancient custom of farm cidermaking in mixed agricultural regions, and the creation of a new generation of large-scale commercial cidermaking firms.

There were a number of reasons for this. One was that the farmers themselves were becoming more and more specialised and saw the time and effort that went into making cider as a distraction. Another was the decline and final abolition of the practice of paying farm labourers part of their wages in cider. Still a third was that selling their best cider to brokers was becoming less profitable.

Historically, farming was best worked by a mix of crops, so if one failed there were others to fall back on. The yeoman farmer had his cattle and pigs, geese and chickens, barley and potatoes and more, as well as the obligatory orchard by the farmstead, providing him with fresh fruit and preserves for his family, with the bulk of his crop going for cider.

The apples were gathered up into tumps in late summer and left in the orchard to boost the sugar content, often until the first frosts. When the main corn harvest was safely gathered in, the apples were sacked and carted to the loft above the cider machinery so they could be easily tipped down a shute into the mill hopper and put through the mill, before being transferred to the press.

The juice from the first pressing made a cider of anywhere between 6-8 per cent alcohol by volume, which the farmer would sell to the local hostelry or to brokers who would take it to sell in the towns. The crushed pomace was removed from the press, put into a trough, covered with water, and left overnight. The pomace absorbed the water like a sponge and was pressed a second time the following morning, producing a cider with an ABV of 2-3 per cent. This was the farm workers' beverage.

Since this cider made up a percentage of his wages, it was important that the farmer had a

THE POMACE IS FORMED INTO ENVELOPES USING NYLON SHEETING AND A WOODEN MOULD. WHEN EIGHT LAYERS HIGH, THE PRESS IS SCREWED DOWN AND THE JUICE COLLECTED FOR FERMENTATION.

reputation for producing a good drop if he hoped to employ the fitter, younger workers who came to the annual hiring fair. The usual allowance was half a gallon for breakfast and half a gallon for lunch.

Throughout the century, this aspect of cidermaking became less and less important. Radical changes in farming methods pioneered in the 18th century by landowners such as Coke and Townsend were making an impact on crop production, and by the end of the century all manner of labour-saving machines were available to the farmer. The century also saw a largely depressed rural economy and a steady drift of workers away from the land to the new factories.

The 1887 Truck Act outlawed the payment of wages in kind and marked the demise of proper cider. It was becoming too much time and trouble. As one farmer was quoted as saying at the beginning of the 20th century, no doubt echoing the sentiments of many: "I pay them to make it and then I pay the buggers to drink it."

At the same time, sales of the better-quality first-pressed cider were becoming less profitable. At the end of the 18th century, apple juice from the press was 2d a gallon and the best cider 2s a gallon. A hundred years later and juice was 3d a gallon with good cider averaging a shilling a gallon. The brokers did good trade, but the quality of the cider suffered over long distances, especially in hot weather. The brokers were also prone to doctoring the cider to mask acetification, in some cases with lead powder, and thinning it with water to increase their margins. The growing urban populations, however, wanted to distance themselves from their peasant roots and were looking for more sophisticated products where quality was assured.

These different strands were drawn together towards the end of the century with the beginnings of a commercial industry exemplified by companies such as Whiteways, Bulmers, Gaymer, and Weston's. They saved the farmer the effort involved in cidermaking by buying his apple crop for cash. It freed time and workers for more profitable work and was altogether a lot less bother.

At the same time these new concerns offered urban drinkers the sterile, consistent product they demanded. In came standardization of containers and alcohol levels, preservatives, filtering, colouring, artificial carbonation, and one additive from the traditional labourer's drink, copious amounts of water.

The final nail in the coffin of old-style cidermaking was the flood of cheap wine pouring in from Australia at prices affordable to the masses. This obsession with wine at the expense of other drinks remains today. It is a pity, as many traditional ciders these days are capable of competing on an equal footing with wine, and unlike a bottle of wine we know what goes into a bottle of traditional cider – 100 per cent apple juice.

Stephen Fisher
NORFOLK CIDER COMPANY

Recipes

Kindly donated by Tom Oliver of Oliver's Cider and Perry

Chicken in Oliver's Perry with Pears

**1.75 kg (3½lb) chicken,
    jointed and carcass kept
700g (1½lb dessert pears
450 ml (3/4 pt) Oliver's dry
    perry
2 onions – 1 diced finely**

**4 carrots
85 ml (3fl oz) sunflower oil
25g (1oz) butter
bouquet garni
salt & pepper
450 ml (3/4 pt) water**

Make stock by putting the chicken carcass in a pan with the water, one onion, carrots, bouquet garni, salt & pepper. Bring to the boil and simmer for one hour, strain and reduce to 150ml (1/4 pint).

Heat half the oil in a heavy pan and brown the chicken pieces quickly. Remove into a casserole dish.

Add diced onion to pan and soften, add Oliver's Perry and stir to loosen chicken fragments from pan.

Heat carefully and pour over chicken with the chicken stock.

Cook with a lid on in a preheated oven 350°F (gas mark 4) for 45 minutes until tender.

Adjust the seasoning.

Quarter the pears, remove the cores, and slice the flesh (do not peel).

Fry them in the oil and butter until soft. Add to the casserole before serving.

Christmas Ham

An Easter tradition that has been hijacked for Christmas.

Soak a ham overnight and change water to remove salt if dry cured. I use an unsmoked ham, with or without the bone, from Happy Meats in Worcestershire. It is worth asking about the curing as it will tell you how much soaking is required.

Remove the ham and pat dry, removing rust from skin.

Each year, I alternate between 2 cooking methods:

METHOD ONE – SIMMER

For a 12lb ham on the bone, use
one pint Oliver's dry cider,
4 carrots in chunky pieces,
2 large onions stuck with cloves,
small fist of sweet hay,
large bunch of fresh herbs,
one clove of garlic,
2 tablespoons of molasses,
2 bay leaves and 12 peppercorns.
Place all in a large pan and bring to nearly boil, remove surface scum and simmer for 3 hours. Cover ham with liquid topping up with water as required.

METHOD TWO – BAKE

Bake in a huff paste –
1.5kg/3lb plain flour in one and a
half pints of water
OR in a double layer of tin foil around the ham, as in a tent, not letting the foil touch the meat.
Bake at 325°F (gas mark 3) for 20 minutes per 500g (1lb).

When cooked, remove ham from pan and drain (or remove from foil). Peel off skin. Score fat diagonally creating diamonds and then glaze. Insert a clove into each diamond. To make the glaze mix **3 tablespoons of runny honey, 2 tablespoons of dry mustard, 3 tablespoons of balsamic vinegar, with 2 tablespoons of molasses.**

In 375°F (gas mark 5) preheated oven, bake for 30 minutes.

Remove when golden glazed and let ham rest for 45 minutes if serving hot, or wait till cold.

Ham best if eaten within the next two weeks and keep cool at night covered in muslin. Vary ingredient quantities by taste.

(The huff paste is VERY messy but lots of fun on Christmas Eve!)

Crunchy Apple Cake
(as used by The Herefordshire Country Bakery)

BRAMLEYS or THE CATSHEAD CODDLING are the best apples for this cake, as they become fluffy when cooked.

250g (8oz) self-raising flour
100g (4oz) butter or marge
100g (4oz) soft light
** brown sugar**
200g (8oz) apples, peeled
** and roughly diced**

1 medium egg
1 tablespoon milk
2 tablespoons caster sugar
Half teaspoon cinnamon

Sieve the flour into a mixing bowl and rub in the butter or margarine with your fingertips until the mixture resembles fine breadcrumbs.

Stir in the brown sugar and apple, then add the egg and the milk to make a stiff mixture, with a reluctant dropping consistency.

Mix the caster sugar and cinnamon together and set aside. Put the mixture into a greased and floured cake tin and sprinkle the reserved sugar and cinnamon mix over the top.

Bake in the preheated oven (200°C, 400°F, gas mark 6) for 30-35 minutes.

Turn out and allow to cool on a cake rack. Do not try and cut this cake before it has completely cooled as it has a tendency to crumble.

A 30 x 45cm (11" by 17") baking tin will make 16 good size squares.

NB: All quantities are imperial measurements.

DIY Cidermaking

So why on earth would you want to make some cider or perry?

I suppose the most obvious answer being, also the reason you're holding this book, is that you like real cider. Taking that as read, because you just have, the next would be because it is an extremely rewarding and satisfying way to spend a balmy day in autumn. Next, it is remarkably easy, cheap and production is possible in any volume. I started with a gallon and now a few years down the way I produce up to a hundred gallons a year, and that limitation is purely down to the space I have available for storage.

Lesson 1

You may have noticed that I use the verb to produce, not brew.

You don't brew cider; you either make it or produce it. Brewing implies heating, as in a cup of tea. No heating is required, only a bit of muscle power.

I started making cider and perry in 2000, my handful of able assistants and I comprise Hounslow Cider Co-operative and every year we aim to increase production as more fruit becomes available to us. I have made a couple of trips to Somerset to source some cider apples. I also make meads, Methiglin and melomels for my own amusement. I've even had a go at a white wine pressed from grapes grown in a back garden in Hounslow.

The equipment needed goes from the basic kitchen-ware up to a few hundred pounds worth of dedicated machinery. More about kit later.

First things first.

Raw ingredients? Apples and pears obviously, that's it. Apple trees are everywhere and most of their bounteous gifts end up rotting on the ground. Shame!

Lesson 2

Don't buy fruit from supermarkets, it is washed, polished and in some cases irradiated, so all the natural wild yeasts that give ciders their depth of flavour and alcohol are removed.

The colour and size of apples is mostly irrelevant. The larger the apple, the more juice and hence cider you can get for your effort. However bear in mind that the larger apples often have the same amount of flavour as smaller ones but in a more diluted form. An important consideration with respect to the size of the fruit is that a lot of the flavours, especially the tannins are contained in the skin, so the higher the proportion of skin to juicy flesh the more flavoursome the end product.

The red fleshed ornamental apples can be used either alone or in a blend with

IF AT ALL POSSIBLE GET YOUR APPLES DIRECTLY FROM AN ORCHARD NOT THE SUPERMARKET.

other apples to give varying degrees of pink blush. If you want something with a little more character and depth of flavour you will need to get hold of either some actual cider apples or crab apples. These can be used blended with cooking and desert apples to produce an individual juice and hence cider. If you keep a record of the blend then you will be able to adjust the proportions to suit your palette next year. Basically if they taste horribly tannic then you're on to a winner.

If only cooking and dessert (eaters) apples are available you will end up with a Kentish style cider. For the best results you need a ratio of 2 cookers: 1 eaters.

Do not be put off by blemishes on the skin, some of the commonly used classic varieties of cider apples look like they've got a dose of the pox. As long as the skin is intact and there is no visible fungal growth then they will be fine. A bit of common sense goes a long way.

So where do you get all this fruit from? Back gardens, common land, heath land, local parks and even ornamental trees selected more for their blossom than fruit can produce a good crop. A study of local street and place names can put you on the right track. The number of Apple Lanes, Orchard Avenues, etc, even Perivale in NW London indicates the existence of pre-suburbia orchards that used to be common around our towns and cities nationwide. When housing was being laid out in the pre Second World War years of the twentieth century the builders had more consideration than these days. If there was a tree in the garden plot it was left. I am sure there are lots of these precious trees still out there undiscovered but well loved none the less for being inedible.

Lesson 3

Scrumping on private land is theft. So, ask and you will receive, especially with the promise of a share of the products.

Picking apples off the tree is a fool's game, but here is a tip. It only works well with small fruit on trees of reasonable stature. A supermarket carrier bag with one handle over your forearm, hold the branch with the bag behind the fruit, pick with the other and allow the fruit to drop into the bag. With larger trees, if they are in long grass a couple of weeks before harvest cut the grass. This sounds unnecessary, but believe me it helps. Pick up all the sound fruit from the ground and discard the unsound, then shake the tree or branch vigorously. Use a broom or garden rake to get at the top branches. In organised orchards they use long poles often with a crook on the end to shake down or knock off the fruit. This is termed "panking" and is traditionally done with long ash poles, especially for perry pear trees that can grow to huge heights.

On a recent visit to the legendary Naish brothers' farm in Somerset, I introduced a distinctly new fangled technique which was welcomed as much as a visit from the taxman. The idea is to gather the windfalls as above, then lay out a plastic decorator's dust sheet underneath the heavily laden bough. Shake/ pank the tree, let the fruit fall onto the sheet, gather up the edges and lift, all the fruit rolls together making it much easier to pick up the apples than otherwise. Mr Naish was not impressed but did grudgingly admit its efficacy. (Take your plastic with you; it is very dangerous to leave it in the environment. As Roy Harper says "leave this world as clean as when you came".)

Lesson 4

If the tree does not want to let go of the fruit it's not ripe yet.

Pears are a different matter though. Obviously you can use dessert pears but you will end up with a very thin, bland perry. Real perry pears are very rare, even in their last bastions of Somerset, Gloucestershire and Worcestershire. (Note to the cognoscenti – Yes I know there are some elsewhere in the UK, but don't tell everyone!) Some perry pears don't even look like pears, i.e. pear shaped, but look like little round apples hanging from a long stalk.

Whilst gathering pears please take special care. Pear trees are generally much more fragile than apple trees and can be easily damaged. They are also extremely long lived. The expression "plant apple trees for your children and pear trees for your great-grand children" is not an idle comment. Perry pear trees can have a productive life of over three hundred years and can be ten to thirty years old before they produce a good crop of fruit.

A second warning concerning pear trees and this comes from personal experience. Before grabbing hold of a pear tree, have a good look at it close up.

Some pear trees are armed and will defend themselves against unwary scrumpers. Three magnificent trees of my acquaintance are protected by very fine, very hard and extremely sharp thorns which vary from brittle little hairs to 3-5cm needles that have no problem whatsoever in going straight through thick pig-skin gardening gloves.

Pears contain oxalic acid granules in varying amounts; it is this that gives pears their gritty texture. Some pear juice can be very cloudy, even opaque. This can be unsightly but has little effect on flavour.

Once pears have been gathered they must be processed as soon as possible. If left around like apples they will very quickly spoil. Once pressed the fermentation container must be filled as too great an air-space above will lead to oxidation and increase the risk of bacterial and unwanted fungal contamination. If you have not got sufficient pears, press some apples and ferment the juices together. This is called a Pider.

Lesson 5

Pears lack the tannins which are present in apples. These not only produce the dryness of ciders but also have antibacterial properties so perries are more prone to bacterial contamination than ciders.

So, where were we? Oh, yes, making cider.

Apples – squash apples – squeeze juice – leave it for a bit. Simple?

Not quite that simple, but not far off.

At the most basic level the requirements are a knife, something to pulp the fruit (a rolling pin and elbow grease / a blender / food processor), a bucket, a funnel and a sieve. Then you need something to put your juice in such as a demijohn with an air lock (available from homebrew shops) or other suitable container that can be closed with a loose fitting bung and a bit of clean cloth. You already have your apples, gently rinse under running water to remove leaf detritus, etc. Do not scrub or peel the fruit as the wild yeasts that live on the skin are required to perform the fermentation of sugar to alcohol. Roughly chop the fruit, this makes pulping easier.

Lesson 6

Apple seeds do contain minute traces of cyanide; this will do you no harm at all unless you are planning on consuming about half a tonne of raw seeds in one go. But if you are concerned remove the pips as you chop the apples.

If you are using an old-fashioned blender you will need to add a small amount of water to the chopped fruit to get it going. This is the only water that should be added. Empty most of the pulp into a clean bucket, retaining enough to get the next batch going. Keep on pulping but pay attention to the temperature of the motor, resting it as required. Place the funnel in the neck of the demijohn and put the sieve in the funnel. Take a clean piece of cloth, I recommend off-cuts of non-patterned plain net curtain which can be purchased cheaply from fabric shops. It is important to use only fabrics that are no longer required. Once used for cider production they will be stained orange-brown, so don't use your mother's best linen pillow cases. You have been warned! Also it is wise to have dedicated clothing for cider making because if you are anything like me, you will end up splattered with juice and pulp.

Ladle in your pulp, twist the ends together to make a bag and squeeze and knead until you cannot get anymore juice out. This is tiring work, so have a glass of cider to hand to remind you why you're doing it. Once your container is full, put the air lock in or closely cover and leave in a cool dark place to ferment. If made at the most obvious time if year i.e. autumn then your cider will be ready early the following year and with galloping global warming giving warmer winters then it will be ready sooner. Do not be tempted to speed things up artificially by keeping it warm like beer as this will produce alcohol derivatives called esters and these will give you a nasty headache. Once fermentation has ceased the cider can then be racked off (transferred) into other containers. It is not essential but if you want a bright clear cider then transferring to another demijohn or bottling will help. Removing the yeast and sediment or lees also means it can be moved about without disturbing a sediment, do not worry, there will still be some yeast in suspension as a result of the racking off process to allow further fermentation.

Hygiene is not as crucial as in brewing beer but things do have to be clean and sterilisation is recommended if practicable. Sterilizer solutions and powders are available from homebrew shops. Do not use bleach or other chlorine based products, yes they will sterilize, but they will taint every thing with the taste of chlorine.

Lesson 7

The wild yeasts that live on the skin of the fruit may not just produce ethanol, some produce a cocktail of alcohols, ethanol is always the main one but others such as butanol can be produced in small amounts. Butanol is the one that causes a not uncommon side effect of cider drinking. That is, you're sat there happily chatting away quite coherently until its time to stand up, and then you discover that your legs don't work properly.

The sieve and funnel technique is only of use for small-scale production, in the next level of production we're getting on to specialised equipment such as fruit presses. These are expensive but can often be borrowed or hired (Check out local wine-making groups).

An alternative that I have never used but works very well is the old style of vertical drum spin dryers, these can be picked up cheap at car-boot sales, just give it a good clean before use to remove all traces of detergent. The last thing you want is foamy cider or worse still cider that makes you blow bubbles. Pulp the apples as before and either make a pressing sack or pillowcases can be used. Fill it up with pulp, ensure the load is

YOU WILL END UP NOT ONLY WITH A GREAT DRINK BUT ALSO A DEEP SENSE OF SELF-SATISFACTION.

evenly balanced, and set it going remembering to place the outflow in a collecting vessel.

An alternative to the blender is pounding the apples to a pulp in a metal bucket or dustbin using a piece of wood such as a fence post with flat headed nails in the end sticking out about 3-5cm. Various devices, called fruit crushers on the internet, are available for larger scale pulp production or scratting, as it is known.

A few ideas for more advanced practitioners

Traditionally apple pulp is, or rather was, pressed in cheeses built up out of a layer of barley straw with a layer of pulp on top pf it, the edges folded over and another layer of straw put on top, with the process continued to the depth required for pressing.

Small and medium-sized basket presses do not easily lend themselves to this method, but you can mimic the end product quite successfully. If you have access to freshly harvested clean barley straw then all well and good. If not, sterilized barley straw can be purchased from all good pet shops. This can then be cut up quite fine and added to the pulp for pressing. Do not use old, damp or musty straw as this will contain bacteria and fungi which will cause no end of faults in the cider and possibly make you very ill.

If you have access to only limited quantities of apples or just want to get more out of it, you may want to try this. Once you have pressed your pulp put the spent pomace into a sterilised container. Pour over freshly boiled water and mash up to the original consistency. Allow to cool and press again. It is recommended to pitch this with an activated brewing or wine yeast. This is because the sugar levels in this diluted pressing will be insufficient to act as an antibacterial so you want to get it fermenting straight away in order to get CO^2 levels up. Once fermented this is termed a ciderkin.

This does not comply with CAMRA's definition of a real cider but you will end up with an eminently drinkable beverage of about 3-5% ABV rather than the 6-8% of the full cider.

Making sweet and medium-sweet cider without the addition of sweeteners is a tricky business. Addition of sugar will stimulate further fermentation. It works in the short term but over any extended period of time it will naturally ferment back to dryness. Keeving is a process which makes this possible. I have never tried it but in theory it goes like this. You need lots of demijohns. Allow your cider to ferment for as long as required to get the original gravity down to the appropriate level or monitor sweetness by sampling. You want to start the process with a sweeter cider than you want as an end point. Then rack off your cider into a new demijohn without disturbing the sediment. Allow it to stand for a week or so and repeat the process until fermentation ceases. The basic aim of keeving is to remove the yeast without resorting to filtration, and hence stop fermentation at the point you require. Theoretically, once performed correctly then sugar can be added to give the required sweetness. Honey may be used however the legality of this is uncertain if you want to sell it. It used to be illegal but several commercial producers are now using it.

Artificial sweeteners should be avoided as they are very difficult to quantify for small volumes and they have horrible aftertastes.

Quantifying the alcohol by volume (ABV) of your cider can be done using a hydrometer to take the original gravity of the juice and then the specific gravity of the cider, a simple calculation of the difference between the two values gives a reasonable approximation. Other devices are available but are more expensive. Personally I favour the old-fashioned method of drinking a few pints and see how you feel, then making an educated approximation.

In order to sell your cider you will require a certificate for "Exemption from Registration by a Maker of Cider or Perry for sale" this can be claimed by completing form CP33 in HM Customs and Excise Notice 162 which can be found at: http://www.hmce.gov.uk. Return it to HMC&E, National Registration Centre, Portcullis House, 21 India Street, Glasgow G2 4PH (that well known cider producing region).

Simon Stevenson

The World's Best Cider Night Out?

Dave Matthews invites you to pop over to the Basque region of Northern Spain

The Basque region straddles the northern end of the France-Spain border, and enjoys an Atlantic Ocean coastline. Its people are fiercely independent, and proudly promote their unique culture and heritage. They're looking for political separation from Spain, and indeed genetic tests have shown that they're more closely related to the Welsh than to the people of mainland Europe. Their language, however, has no relation to any other, and is an indecipherable tongue liberally sprinkled with Xs and Zs.

The cidermaking region is the area of countryside just inland from San Sebastian (Donostia in Basque) in northeastern Spain. There are perhaps 70 ciderhouses (sagardotegias) each producing its own cider (sagardo). Production is centred around the village of Astigarraga, although the village centre itself is devoid of any cidery interest. Sagardotegias are rural destinations, which groups of Basques will visit for a social evening of eating and drinking. They vary from those offering basic wooden tables and chairs down to the ultra-traditional with no tables or chairs, and not even any plates (you balance your food on a hunk of bread!). Of course they all sell great cider.

A typical example is Gartziategi, a lovely sagardotegia just outside Astigarraga. In common with the other ciderhouses, it's only open during the draught cider season, approximately 20 January-20 April, and it's advisable to book ahead, especially at weekends. From the outside Gartziategi looks like any other farm, but stepping inside the difference is obvious. There's one long room, roughly divided into two areas. Wooden pillars hold up a beamed ceiling. The uncarpeted concrete floor is as bare and rustic as the unplastered stone walls. There are long wooden tables, but no chairs. But what really grabs your attention is the row of 11 huge chestnut cider barrels, arranged along one wall of the room, with each circular barrel end taller than a man. One of the barrels has a small brass tap in it, and we are allowed to serve ourselves as part of the all-in cost of the evening. A thin jet of cider shoots out five feet horizontally, landing (usually!) in your glass. Golden and foaming, it's a light and fruity cider with a slight bite to it. Gorgeous, and so perfect with food.

When the first course arrives, everyone stands beside one of the tables. There's no choice of what to eat: everybody has the same four courses, and the first is a melt-in-the-mouth cod omelette. Before you can finish it there's a shout of 'Txotx!' (sounds like 'church') from the proprietor Bitor Lizeaga, an impressively-bearded Basque. This means that it's time to try the cider from one of the other barrels, so you grab your glasses and join the queue.

Bitor fits a key into the tap and turns it on. Cider jets forth, and one by one the diners catch a sampler, moving their glasses upwards towards the barrel to allow the next customer to move their glass into position without interrupting the stream. This ritual punctuates the remainder of the meal until everyone has sampled each of the other 10 barrels. Each cider is different, some fruitier, some sharper, but each fresh and lovely.

The beauty of all this shuttling about during the meal, with people changing places at the tables, is that you get to talk to an awful lot of different people. With your British reserve dissolved by the cider, a group of locals become your new best friends, and you might also meet a group of French Basques who migrate over the border by the busload during the cider season.

The next course is cod with onions, followed by a superb steak cooked with salt over a flaming grill. There's another cry of 'Txotx', but this time Bitor heads for the front door (where's he going?), and everyone follows him outside. He turns left out of the farm, followed like the Pied Piper by his happy column of fans to his next-door neighbour's property. Here there are another couple of barrels to sample, and as you drink there's time to chat to Bitor. He makes about 100,000 litres of cider a year, using at least 50 different apple varieties. The exact formula is a secret, but at least 50 per cent of his apples are sharps or semi-sharps, a blend that is repeated across the whole of northern Spain. Sourcing apples can be a problem, and the Basque country may only provide half of his needs, so he must cast his net over Asturias and Galicia, and sometimes even to Normandy.

Back at the table a basket of walnuts has arrived, smaller and darker than their British equivalents, and less bitter too. Spring-loaded nutcrackers (cool!) make short work of the shells. The cheese on offer is Idiazabal, a Basque sheep's milk cheese similar to (but better than) a Manchego. It's served with quince jelly, a civilised custom rarely seen these days in Britain. This cheese/quince jelly/cider thing has to be one of the greatest food and drink combinations of all time. At this stage of the evening you might be entertained with some singing along to an accordion, or hear a recital of Basque poetry, both part of the ancient sagardotegia tradition.

A PARTY ENJOYING A NIGHT OUT AT A BASQUE CIDERHOUSE.

Outside the draught season (January to April, if you remember), you can still drink bottled cider from all the main sagardotegias. The bottled stuff is just as natural as the draught – the lack of filtration, pasteurisation and artificial carbonation allows the full flavour to be enjoyed. The way it's served would raise a few eyebrows if it happened in our local – the barman places a wide-rimmed glass on the counter and the bottle is poured from eye level. An inch or two of foaming cider is then drunk by the customer without delay. There's no better place to try this style of cider than in San Sebastian itself.

San Sebastian is a sprawling industrial city. However the jewel in its crown is the Old Town, a square mile of criss-crossing ancient and narrow streets set out in a medieval grid pattern. With hundreds of bars, some no bigger than a cupboard, it's the best place in the world for a bar crawl. Most of the bars offer Basque tapas (pintxos), which are basically a slice of French bread with a topping (the selection on offer is huge, and varies from bar to bar, perhaps stuffed red pepper, smoked salmon and onion, deep fried crab claw, prawn paté, blue cheese and parma ham, sardine purée, etc, etc) which is attached with a cocktail stick. When it comes to settling your bill, simply present your stick collection and pay accordingly. You could easily lose a couple of days wandering from bar to bar, grazing on the pintxos, sampling the ciders and discovering the Txakoli (the local white wine).

Tximista is a good example of the tiny and traditional type of bar, and you'll find it at one side of the Plaza de la Constitución. This square used to be the venue for bullfighting, and hosts a Cider Festival on the second Saturday of September. In recent years some urban imitations of the rural ciderhouses have sprung up around the city. In the Old Town you could try 'idreria Itxaropena (Embeltran, 16) with its draught Zapiain cider served from a fake barrel front. Perhaps better still, take a short stroll down the same street to Embeltran, 5, where you'll find Sagardotegia Donostiarra. Here there are three draught ciders on offer (Zelia, Zapiain and Astarbe) and one of the eating options is the traditional ciderhouse omelette-'n'-steak menu. Not bad at all, but for a truly great night out travel into the Basque countryside for the rural ciderhouse experience.

Basque Country information: www.euskadi.net
San Sebastian information: www.sansebastianturismo.com
Cider information: A list of cidermakers can be found at www.euskadi.net
Gartziategi: Baserria, 20115 Astigarraga. Tel 943/469674 www.gartziategi.com
Accommodation: In the Old Town, try 'txasoa, C/ San Juan 14, 20003 Donostia. Tel (00-34) 943/430086 Email itxasoa@euskalnet.net

Outlets

Key to Symbols

🛏	Accommodation
♨	Real Fire
Q	Quiet Pub
✿	Outdoor Drinking Area
🐷	Family Room
◖	Lunchtime meals
◗	Evening meals
⊟	Separate public bar
♿	Wheelchair accessible
⛺	Camping
🚆	Near railway station
⊖	Near underground or tram
♣	Traditional pub games
♦	Perry
🍺	Real Ale
P	Parking
✂	No smoking area
🍺	Oversized lined glasses

Key to Map

🍎	Location of Cider Producer
🥤	Location of Cider Outlet

Cider Outlets
England

Bedfordshire

Tudor Oaks
1 Taylors Road, SG5 5AB
(On A1 northbound S of Biggleswade)
⏵ 11-11; 12-3.30, 6.30-10.30 Sun
☎ (01462) 834133
www.tudoroakslodge.com

🍎 Westons

🍷 Westons

Oak-beamed pub and motel, once a farm, with seven real ales. Cider and perry dispensed from Manucubes hidden in a mock apple press with cool air blowing

through to keep it cold.
🅰Q🕮🛏🍺♿🏠P♻🍴

Wellington Arms
40-42 Wellington Street, MK40 2JA
⏵ 12-11; 12-10.30 Sun
☎ (01234) 308033
www.wellingtonarms.co.uk

🍎 Westons

🍷 Westons

Award-winning, former East Anglian Pub of the Year. A back-street local with an impressive choice of cider, perry, real ales and foreign beers Rolls and soup served at lunchtimes. 🕮🍺♣🏠🍴

Engineers Arms
66 High Street SG16 6AA
⏵ 12-11; 12-10.30 Sun
☎ (01462) 812284
www.engineersarms.co.uk

🍎 Westons

🍷 Westons

Welcoming village pub and East Anglia Pub of the Year 2003. It has nine real ales plus cider and perry direct from the barrel out of the cellar. 🅰Q🕮🏠

Chequers
High Street
MK44 1AW
TL013667
⏸ 5-11; 12-11 Sat; 12-10.30 Sun
☎ (01933) 356383

🍏 Addlestones, Westons

A traditional village pub with five real ales and two ciders. The small lounge is also used for meals on Friday and Saturday evenings and Sunday lunchtime. Yelden is on the Three Shires Way footpath and boasts impressive earthworks of an abandoned Norman castle.
🏚🌣🏵◑🅰♣📷P✂

Berkshire

Swan
9 Mill Lane
SL4 5JG
⏸ 5.30-11; 12-2, 5.30-11
　 Sat; 12-3, 7-10.30 Sun
☎ (01753) 862069

🍏 Addlestones

Out of Windsor town, in Clewer Village, this friendly pub serves real ales and Addlestones cloudy cider. 🏚🏵🚃♣📷P

Greyhound
92-96 Queen Street, SL6 1HT
⏸ 11-11; 12-10.30 Sun
☎ (01628) 779410

🍏 Westons

Wetherspoon pub near the station, sells cider from the cask as well as a range of real ales. Evenings tend to be busy with a younger clientele but afternoons quieter.
Q◑♿🚃 (Maidenhead) 📷✂

Rose & Crown
312 High Street
SL1 1NB
⏸ 11-11; 12-10.30 Sun
☎ (01753) 521114

🍏 Varies

💧 Varies

The oldest pub in the High Street. This friendly local offers a varying range of real ales, cider and perry. 🏵🗲🚃 (Slough) ♣📷

The Wine Company
93-95 Stoke Road, SL2 5BJ
⏸ 11.30-11; 12-10.30 Sun
☎ (01753) 797579

🍏 Varies (bottled)

Independent off-licence near town centre, north of A4. It stocks a large range of bottled beers and ciders.
🚃 (Slough) 📷P

Buckinghamshire

Eagle
High Street
HP7 0DY SU 9597
⏸ 11-11; 12-10.30 Sun
☎ (01494) 725262

🍏 Addlestones

Traditional and friendly 16th-century pub in a street of Grade II listed buildings. Home-cooked meals are served.
🏚Q🏵◑♣📷P

Village Hall
Gold Hill West, SL9 9HH
⏸ 11-11; 11-10.30 Sun

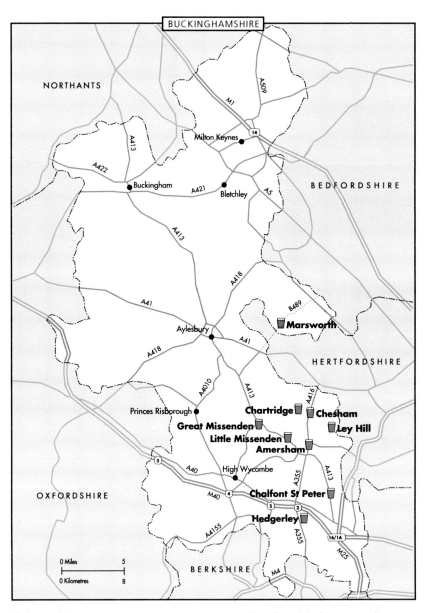

BUCKINGHAMSHIRE

NORTHANTS

BEDFORDSHIRE

Milton Keynes

Buckingham

Bletchley

Aylesbury

Marsworth

HERTFORDSHIRE

Princes Risborough

Chartridge

Chesham

Great Missenden

Ley Hill

Little Missenden

Amersham

High Wycombe

OXFORDSHIRE

Chalfont St Peter

Hedgerley

BERKSHIRE

0 Miles 5

0 Kilometres 8

☎ (01753) 887596

🍏 Addlestones

Faces Gold Hill Common. An upmarket, foodie pub providing a community meeting place. Meals are served 12-9.30 (12-6 Sun). A wheelchair ramp is available on request.
♿🐕🍺≼ (Gerrard's Cross) ♣🏠P♿↯

CHARTRIDGE

Bell
Chartridge Lane
HP5 2TF
⫸ 12-1 (3 Sat), 6-11; 12-3.30, 7-10.30 Sun
☎ (01494) 782878

🍎 Addlestones

Traditional village pub noted for mostly home-cooked food and an extensive menu. ⌂Q❀◑⊟🏠P

CHESHAM

Grape & Grain
84 Broad Street, HP5 3ED
⫸ 2-9.45 Mon-Wed; 12-9.45 Thu-Sat; 4-9.45 Sun
☎ (01494) 791319

🍎 Westons (draught), Varies (bottled)

Off-licence with a large variety of mostly bottled ciders. ⇌ (Chesham) ⊖

GREAT MISSENDEN

Black Horse
Aylesbury Road, HP16 9AX
⫸ 11-11; 12-10.30 Sun
☎ (01494) 862537

🍎 Addlestones

Patrons enjoy home-cooked meals and watching hot air balloons drifting by from a neighbouring field. Live music is staged about once a month. The large playground includes a mini assault course. ⌂Q❀◑♿⇌ (Gt Missenden) ♣🏠P

HEDGERLEY

White Horse
Village Lane, SL2 3UY
OS969874
⫸ 11-2.30, 5.30-11; 11-11 Sat; 12-10.30 Sun
☎ (01753) 643225

🍎 Westons

🝊 Westons

Old village pub serving seven ales from the barrel and two good ciders/perry (always available). The May beer festival features many ciders. A gem!
⌂Q❀◑⊟🏠P

LEY HILL

Swan
Ley Hill Common, HP5 1UT SP088021
⫸ 12-3, 5.30-11; 12-11 Sat; 12-3, 7-10.30 Sun
☎ (01494) 783075
www.swanleyhill.com

🍎 Addlestones

Built in the 16th and 17th-centuries, the Swan was originally three timber-framed cottages and claims to be the county's oldest pub. It was associated with the last ale request of condemned prisoners on their way to nearby gallows. Clark Gable, James Stewart and Glenn Miller visited during WWII from nearby Bovingdon Airfield. It has a smoking and no-smoking restaurant, lounge bar with oak beams and a real fire, and a snug complete the picture. Children are welcome at lunchtimes. No evening meals on Monday (or Sun Aug-Apr).
⌂Q☜❀◑♣🏠

LITTLE MISSENDEN

Crown
HP7 0RD
⫸ 11-2.30, 6-11; 12-3, 7-10.30 Sun
☎ (01494) 862571

🍎 Westons (draught), Thatchers (bottled)

This single-roomed pub near the River Misbourne displays interesting local photos of the past and present day. Other items include historic drinking-related plaques and farming equipment. The landlord's family have run the business for nearly 90 years. A small bar houses four handpumps, two of which are reserved for a variety of guest ales. Lunches are served Monday-Saturday. ⚒Q✫◖⑤♣🝙P

MARSWORTH

Red Lion
90 Vicarage Road, HP23 4LU
⮑ 11-3, 5 (6 Sat)-11; 12-3, 7-10.30 Sun
☎ (01296) 668366

🍎 Westons (draught & bottled)

A real village pub dating from the 17th-century and close to the Grand Union Canal. The saloon bar is plush, with a small restaurant, while the low-beamed public bar is split into drinking and games areas. Games include bar billiards, shove-ha'penny and skittles (by prior arrangement). A real fire and good atmosphere make for a wonderful retreat into yesteryear. Supervised children are permitted in the games area; dogs are welcome. Evening meals are served Tuesday-Saturday. Wheelchair access possible at the rear of the pub.
⚒Q🛏✫◖⊟⑤♣🝙P✂

Cambridgeshire

CAMBRIDGE

Bacchanalia
90 Mill Road, CB1 2BD
⮑ 11-8 Mon-Wed; 11-9 Thu-Sat; 12-3, 6-8 Sun
☎ (01223) 315034
www.bacchanalia.uksw.com

🍎 Varies

An off-licence stocking draught and bottled cider. It was formerly the Jug & Firkin. 🝙

Cambridge Blue
85-87 Gwydir Street, CB1 2LG
(off Mill Road)

⮑ 12-2.30, 5.30-11; 12-3, 5.30-11 Sat; 12-3, 6-10.30 Sun
☎ (01223) 361382

🍎 Cassels (summer only)

Welcoming, no-mobiles, no-smoking pub with a selection of seven real ales. Food is served at every session. ⚒Q🛏✫◖①⇶ (Cambridge) ♣🝙✂

Empress
72 Thoday Street, CB1 3AX
⮑ 11-2.30, 6.30-11; 12-2.30, 7-10.30 Sun
☎ (01223) 247236

🍎 Westons

Old fashioned, no-frills, back-street local with a good selection of beers. ⊟♣🝙

Live & Let Live
40 Mawson Road, CB1 2BA
⮑ 11.30-2.30, 5.30-11; 11.30-2.30, 6-11 Sat; 12-2.30, 7-10.30 Sun
☎ (01223) 460261

🍎 Cassels

Friendly back-street local with a selection of beers and an occasional guest cider. Food is served at every session. Q①⇶ (Cambridge) ♣🝙✂

Mill
14 Mill Lane, CB2 1RX
⮑ 12-11; 12-10.30 Sun
☎ (01223) 357026

🍎 Westons

Occupying an idyllic position opposite the millpond, The Mill was refurbished to a high standard during its previous incarnation as part of the Tap & Spile chain. It has oak floors, exposed brickwork and beams, wood panelling and more of a local feel than most city centre pubs. ①▶🝙

Red Bull
11 Barton Road, CB3 9JZ
⮑ 11-11; 12-10.30 Sun

☎ (01223) 300943

🍏 Westons

This de-modernised ale house has a long, narrow wooden-floored bar which widens at both ends into more lounge-like areas. Up to five real ales are also available. ⚐🅱️🕒✂️

Salisbury Arms
76 Tenison Road
CB1 2DW
🍺 12-3, 6-11; 6-11 Sat; 12-10.30 Sun
☎ (01223) 576363

🍏 Crones

A large, long bustling bar which used to be a CAMRA pub and is now owned by Charles Wells. 🕒🚆 (Cambridge) ♣🏠P✂️

MILTON

Waggon & Horses
39 High Street
CB4 6DF
🍺 12-2.30, 5-11; 12-3, 6-11 Sat; 12-3, 7-10.30 Sun
☎ (01223) 860313

🍏 Cassels

A bustling Elgood's pub which can be found at the northern end of the High Street. Darts, bar billiards and quizzes are played regularly. Food is served every session. ⚐🅱️🕒♣🏠P🍴

NEWTON

Queen's Head
Fowlmere Road
CB2 5PG
🍺 11.30-2.30, 6-11; 12-2.30, 7-10.30 Sun
☎ (01223) 870436

🍏 Cassels, Crones

Absolute gem of an unspoilt village pub, with Adnams beer served straight from the barrel. ⚐Q🅱️🕒🔲♣🏠P✂️

PETERBOROUGH

Coalheavers Arms
5 Park Street, Woodston, PE2 9BH
🍺 12-2 (not Mon-Wed), 5-11; 12-11 Fri-Sat; 12-10.30 Sun
☎ (01733) 565664

🍏 Varies

One-roomed back-street pub owned by Milton Brewery. Usually eight real ales are available including a mild. Cider is always available. Beer festivals in spring and autumn in the large garden always include extra ciders. Belgian bottled beers available. Q🅱️🚆 (Peterborough) 🏠🍴

Palmerston Arms
82 Oundle Road, PE2 9PA
🍺 12-11; 12-10.30 Sun
☎ (01733) 565865

🍏 Varies

🍷 Varies

Stone-built two-roomed pub owned by Batemans. Ten or more real ales, two ciders and a perry are all served by gravity from the cellar. There are always a mild and many micro-brewery beers, Belgian bottled beers and fruit wines. There is no juke box or TV. Mirrors adorn the walls and jugs hang from the ceiling. Local CAMRA Pub of the Year 2005. Q🔲♣🏠

STAPLEFORD

Longbow
2 Church Street, CB2 5DS
🍺 11-3, 6 (5 summer)-11 Mon-Thu & Sat; 11-11 Fri; 12-3, 7-10.30 Sun
☎ (01223) 566855

🍏 Cassels

Welcoming three-room pub offers a superb selection of ever-changing real ales and local cider. It has a games room and there is entertainment on Saturday evenings. Q🛏️🅱️🕒🚆 (Shelford) ♣🏠P✂️🍴

CAMBRIDGESHIRE

Cheshire

ASTON

Bhurtpore Inn
Wrenbury Road
CW5 8DQ
12-2.30 (3 Sat), 6.30-11;
12-10.30 Sun
☎ (01270) 780917

Varies

This large free house has been run by the same family for many years. Eleven real ales are normally on tap. The range changes regularly and includes the beer of the month. A mild ale is always served as well as a choice of 100 Belgian beers bottled and on tap. The imaginative food menu includes vegetarian options. A beer festival is held in summer. Current local CAMRA Pub of the Year. (Wrenbury) P

CONGLETON

Beartown Tap
18 Willow Street
CW12 1RL
12-2, 4-11; 12-11 Fri-Sat;
12-10.30 Sun
☎ (01260) 270990
www.beartownbrewery.co.uk

Varies

Welcoming local just yards from the Beartown Brewery. Opened in 1999, this was the brewery's first pub and such is the beer quality that it has won Regional CAMRA Pub of the Year in 2003 and 2004. Guest beers are usually sourced from other micros and there is generally another Beartown beer available. A good selection of Belgian beers are also stocked. Street parking can be found immediately outside the pub.

FRODSHAM

Helter Skelter
31 Church Street, WA6 6PN
11-11; 12-10.30 Sun
☎ (01928) 733361

Varies

Commonly called the Slide by locals, this one room pub can get very busy on weekend evenings. The bar occupies the right hand wall and is fronted by a standing area. Seating is arranged around the remaining walls, including a raised area to the rear. A bar snack menu is available together with interesting blackboard specials (no food Sun evening). Six handpumps dispense a range of reasonably priced ales, usually from micro-breweries.

NANTWICH

Black Lion
29 Welsh Row, CW5 5ED
4-11; 1-11 Fri-Sat; 1-10.30 Sun
☎ (01270) 628711

Westons

The date 1664 appears above the door of this old black and white half-timbered pub with candlelit tables in three adjoining rooms downstairs. There is a paved garden at the side for outdoor drinking and a heated conservatory. A friendly pub where the locals regularly play chess, it hosts a quiz night on Wednesday and live music at the weekend. The Shropshire Union Canal is nearby.

WHEELOCK

Commercial Hotel
2 Game Street, CW11 3RR
12-11; 12-10.30 Sun
☎ (01270) 760122

Westons

Welcoming family-run free house close to

bridge no 154 on the Trent and Mersey. It is popular with locals and visitors alike, particularly cyclists and boaters. The spacious interior, with three rooms and a public bar, reflects the pub's Birkenhead Brewery origins. Once known as the New Inn, this listed building dates back to the completion of the Trent and Mersey canal in 1777. Dogs are welcome here.
🏨🏠🍴♣🏠

Ship
SK11 0QE (off A64 near Danebridge)
OS652962
▮ 12-3, 7 (5.30 Fri)-11; 12-11 Sat; 12-10.30 Sun
☎ (01260) 227217

🍴 Varies

One of the rare regular Fuller's outlets in the area, this attractive 16th-century sandstone village inn is popular with locals, Walkers and diners and can become very busy on summer weekends. On the edge of the Dane Valley, the pub is divided into two bars, plus a small dining area and a further raised area where families can drink or dine. The pub has a good reputation for its imaginative menu. There is a beer festival on August bank holiday. 🏨Q🛏🌳🍴🏠P

Cornwall

Blisland Inn
The Green, PL30 4JF (off A30)
▮ 11.30-11; 12-10.30 Sun
☎ (01208) 850739

🍴 Varies

A friendly, rural community pub and real-ale mecca on the only village green in Cornwall. It was voted three times local CAMRA Pub of the Year and National

Pub of the Year 2001. Excellent food is served using local produce (booking recommended). There are usually six guest beers with at least two of them from Cornish breweries. The cider also constantly varies and usually includes a lesser-known concoction or two.
🏨Q🛏🌳🍴🏠P

Queen's Arms
TR13 9PD (off A394)
▮ 11.30-2.30, 6.30-11; 12-10.30 Sun
☎ (01326) 573485
www.thequeensarmsinn.co.uk

🍴 Varies

Comfortable and lively country inn in village centre in the shadow of the church. The enthusiastic landlord and his efficient staff offer a warm welcome to all, including families. The one long bar has an open fire at either end and a games room around the corner. A collection of plates hangs from the beams. Up to three guest ales usually available with draught cider on handpump. Separate smoke-free restaurant and outside tables include a few across the lane in a safe play area. Swingtime jazz staged on Thursday evenings. 🏨🌳🍴🏠P

Crown Inn
TR13 0AD (on B3303)
▮ 12-2.30 (closed Mon-Sat winter), 6-11; 12-3, 7-10.30 Sun
☎ (01326) 565538
www.crownlodges.co.uk

🍴 Westons

This large and friendly old granite free house was once a hunting lodge on the Trevarno estate and is thought to be about 250 years old. Although a single bar, there are several distinct drinking areas, a dining area, a beer garden and a separate room for the pool table. This is a community pub where conversation dominates although there is the occasional live entertainment and quiz night. The guest beers are varied frequently and favour Cornish breweries. Unusually, the ales are dispensed by gravity from the cellar, despite the array of four handpumps on the bar. Evening meals are served 7-10; Wednesday tends to be curry night while Sunday lunch is a roast. Accommodation is in lodges at the back of the pub. Q❶❀⇦❢P

FOWEY

King of Prussia
Town Quay, PL23 1AT
⇥ 11-11; 12-10.30 Sun
☎ (01726) 833694

● Cornish Rattler

Originally a 15th-century building which was rebuilt in 1887, now a welcoming community pub. It offers pleasant views across the river and harbour from the spacious upstairs bar. Meals are served 12-2.30pm and 6.30-9pm daily. All six bedrooms are en suite and no-smoking with views over the Fowey Estuary. ❶⇦Å❢

LOOE

Ship Inn
Fore Street, PL13 1AD
⇥ 11-11; 12-10.30 Sun
☎ (01503) 263124

● Cornish Rattler

Large and lively town-centre pub with live music including jazz on a Thursday. The pub consists of one main room with separate drinking spaces including a raised area towards the windows. Beer prices are competitive with many of the town's pubs and bars. Real scrumpy cider on handpump is supplied through St

Austell Brewery by the Cornish Cider Farm. ❶⛴⇦Å⇌ (Looe) ❢

PENZANCE

Alexandra Inn
Alexandra Road, TR18 4LY
⇥ 11.30-2.30, 5-11; 11.30-11
Sat & summer); 12-3.30, 6-10.30
Sun (12-10.30 summer)
☎ (01736) 365165

● Kerb Kisser

This pub near the seafront and the rugby ground has been tastefully modernised with bar carpeting and wooden structures much in evidence. The keen and friendly landlord cares for his ales (usually up to six), with the emphasis on Cornish brews and a distinct bias towards Skinners Brewery. There is usually a beer festival held in March. Good food on a limited menu includes the house speciality – Dinosaur Ribs! Q❀⇦⇌ (Penzance) ❢

STITHIANS

Seven Stars Inn
Church Road, TR3 7DH
⇥ 12-2.30, 7 (8 Fri)-11; 12-11
Sat; 12-10.30 Sun
☎ (01209) 860003

● Westons

Lively village local used by a good cross-section of the community, where euchre is enthusiastically played. The pub was purpose-built as an extension to a farmhouse to serve the drinking needs of local tin miners at the end of the 19th-century. The guest beers (up to two) are regularly changed by the landlord, who is a keen CAMRA member. The original bar and lounge have been opened out to form one drinking area, although the lounge end is now no-smoking. A more modern extension houses the pool table. Occasional mini beer festivals are held.

Good quality and value meals are available (no food Mon eve or Tue). ᴬQ◐✿🐾

Driftwood Spars
Quay Road, St Agnes TR5 0RT
▶ 11-11 (12 Fri-Sat); 12-10.30 Sun
☎ (01872) 552428

🍺 Westcountry

Former 17th-century mine warehouse and sail loft, now a vibrant family-run hotel and public house with micro-brewery. The pub is built of granite, slate and enormous ships spars, hence the name. The three-bar interior with beamed ceilings, lead-light windows and granite fireplaces is cosy and atmospheric. The décor is nautical, with a fine collection of ships' clocks; a wreckers' tunnel is also visible. The pub is warm and welcoming, popular with locals and tourists alike, with easy access to cliff walks and surfing. Excellent meals for all on an extensive, varied menu. Entertainment includes live theatre and music at weekends. Buses are a 10 minute walk away at Peterville.
ᴬQ✿☛🚲◐🅰🐾P

Cumbria

Cumberland Hotel
Townfoot, CA9 3HX
▶ 11-11; 12-10.30 Sun
☎ (01434) 381875
www.cumberlandarmsalston.co.uk

🍺 Westons

With four handpumps on the bar at least one of them will have a beer from a Cumbrian brewery as well as beers from other micro-breweries. Ideally situated at the bottom of the town, it is close to the narrow gauge steam railway and other local attractions including mines and museums. Q✿🚲◐👍🐾P

Black Dog Inn
Holmes Green
Broughton Road LA15 8JP
OS233761
▮ 5 (11 Fri-Sat)-11 winter;
11-11 summer; 12-10.30 Sun
☎ (01229) 462561
www.blackdoginn.info

🍎 Varies

🍺 Varies

Previously neglected, this warm, friendly country pub is a stalwart member of the Furness real ale scene, frequently winning local CAMRA awards. At least six ales and six ciders/perries are normally available. This snug pub provides a welcome retreat for walkers and tourists. The interior is split level, with exposed beams and open fires at both ends of the bar. There are two seating areas outside, one by a small stream. ᴬQ🚲✿🚲◐🐾P🍴

Prince of Wales
LA20 6BX
▮ 5-11 (not Mon-Tue); 12-11 Fri-Sat;
12-10.30 Sun
☎ (01229) 716238
www.princeofwalesfoxfield.co.uk

🍎 Varies

Two house breweries, Foxfield and Tigertops, service this traditional pub, providing beers from all over England, always including a mild. Continental beers are also sold on draught and in bottles. Themed mini beer festivals occur each year. This pub is located adjacent to a rural railway station and bus stop.
ᴬQ✿🚲🎆≥♣🐾P🍴

135

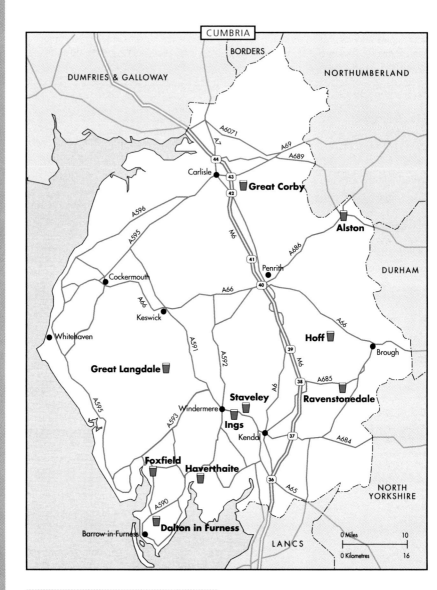

CUMBRIA

BORDERS

DUMFRIES & GALLOWAY

NORTHUMBERLAND

A6071

A7

A69

A689

44

Carlisle

43

42

Great Corby

Alston

M6

41

A686

Penrith

DURHAM

40

A596

A595

A66

Cockermouth

A66

A66

A591

Keswick

Whitehaven

Hoff

Brough

Great Langdale

A592

39

M6

38

A685

Staveley

Ravenstonedale

Windermere

A593

Ings

Kendal

37

A684

Foxfield

Haverthaite

36

A65

NORTH
YORKSHIRE

A590

Dalton in Furness

Barrow-in-Furness

LANCS

0 Miles   10

0 Kilometres   16

Corby Bridge Inn
CA4 8LL
🍺 12-11; 12-10.30 Sun
☎ (01228) 560221

🍎 Varies

🍺 Varies

A friendly, CAMRA award-winning local situated about half a kilometre east of Wetheral Station on the Carlisle to Newcastle railway. This Grade II listed pub has a three-room open plan layout. Games and a dining area are provided (no food Mon). Beer festivals have been held in May since 2002 with up to eight local beers available. ♨Q❀☎◖≋ (Wetheral) ♣🏠P⚡

Old Dungeon Ghyll
LA22 9JY
◗ 11-11; 12-10.30 Sun
☎ (015394) 37272
www.odg.co.uk

🍎 Westons

A basic walkers' and climbers' bar with benches – the hotel bar is more formal. Good value food is served. ♨❀☎◖⊟👤♣🏠P🍺

Anglers Arms
Old Barrow Road, LA12 8AJ
◗ 11.30-11; 12-10.30 Sun
☎ (015395) 31216

🍎 Westons

Just off the A590, opposite the Lakeside & Haverthwaite Steam Railway, the pub's dining area continues the theme with a miniature railway running along the wall. The main bar contains a collection of witches (watch out for Alice!), autographed sports memorabilia and a sunken games area. Meals are served daily with an emphasis on quality seafood and game. An upper function room helps to house the frequent beer festivals, augmenting the usual selection of up to ten real ales. ❀◖⊟♣🏠⚡

New Inn
CA16 6TA
◗ 11 (6.30 Mon)-11; 12-10.30 Sun
☎ (01768) 351317

🍎 Westons

There are records of licensees here going back to 1823, although the building is considerably older. Converted into a private dwelling in 1999, it made a welcome return as a village local in 2001. Flag flooring and oak furniture predominate but observation of the array of pump clips affixed to the black ceiling beams gives a clue to the main action. Good pub grub (not Mon-Tue) and occasional live music complete the picture. ♨Q❀☎◖👤👤♣🏠P⚡

Watermill Inn
LA8 9PY (off A591)
◗ 12-11; 12-10.30 Sun
☎ (01539) 821309
www.watermillinn.co.uk

🍎 Westons

Award-winning pub with a top bar, good-quality food and a large selection of real ales and foreign bottled beers. ♨Q👜❀☎◖◗ 🏠P⚡🍺

King's Head
CA17 4NH
◗ 11-11; 12-10.30 Sun
☎ (015396) 23284
www.kings-head.net

🍎 Varies

🍏 Varies (occasional)

Now recovered from serious flood damage in early 2005, the full range of ever-changing guest beers are flowing again. The cosy bar area is augmented by a no-smoking lounge and dining room (note the huge collection of water jugs) to the left and a games room to the right. The stream, which runs just across the road, passes the lawned garden. A red squirrel sanctuary. ♨Q❀☎◖👤♣🏠P⚡

Eagle & Child Hotel
Kendal Road
LA8 9LP
▮▶ 11-11; 12-10.30 Sun
☎ (01539) 821320
www.eaglechildinn.co.uk

🍺 Westons

🍺 Westons

The U-shaped bar area has an abundance of memorabilia on shelves around the walls. The upstairs function room, in the style of a medieval banqueting hall, can be hired. There are two gardens, one to the rear and the other next to the River Kent across the road. Buses to Ambleside and Kendal stop outside. 🏚🏡🚪🍴🕭🛏P

Derbyshire

Old Poets' Corner
Butts Road
S45 0EW
▮▶ 12-2.30, 5-11; 12-11 Fri-Sat;
   12-10.30 Sun
☎ (01246) 590888
www.oldpoets.co.uk

🍺 Varies

Friendly village pub serving good food, a wide range of real ales and country fruit wines. It is also popular with tourists and walkers because it lies between Chesterfield and Matlock. The views from the car park and outside seating area are outstanding. The pub has regular beer festivals, folk or acoustic nights on Sunday, poets' night every other Tuesday and regular live music including rock music from Crossfire, featuring the landlord. Local CAMRA Pub of the Season winter 2004.
🏚Q🏡🍴🛏Å♣🕭P✕

Derby Tup
387 Sheffield Road,
Whittington Moor, S41 8LS
▮▶ 11-3, 5-11; 11-11 Wed,
   Fri-Sat; 12-10.30 Sun
☎ (01246) 454316
www.tynemill.co.uk/derby/tup.htm

🍺 Varies

Friendly Tynemill pub with a range of real ales including offerings from micro-breweries. It also provides a range of bottled continental beers and malt whiskies. There is a regular quiz on a Sunday night. It is a frequent local CAMRA Pub of the Year winner (last time 2001) and recently received an award for having an entry in the Good Beer Guide for the past 21 years (1985-2005). Q🍴🛏♣♣🕭✕

Portland Hotel
West Bars, S40 1AY
▮▶ 10-11; 10-10.30 Sun (no alcohol
   before 12pm)
☎ (01246) 245410

🍺 Westons

One of two popular town Wetherspoon pubs serving a wide range of real ales. Known for its good value food, it includes a family dining area and a well-designed and pleasant beer garden. Food is served 10-10 each day. Ranges of drinks and special offers can differ between the two sites and the Portland has been known to run out of food and cider during busy periods such as bank holidays. Facilities include a toilet for the disabled. Q🏡🚪🍴🛏&⇌🕭✕

Rutland Arms
16 Stephenson Place, S40 1XL
▮▶ 11-11; 12-10.30 Sun
☎ (01246) 205857

🍺 Westons

Town centre split-level pub, popular with

all ages. Built c1700, it is right next to Chesterfield's famous crooked spire – some outside tables are available to take in the view. The pub stocks a wide range of real ales which changes frequently and it holds regular beer festivals which include guest ciders. Good value food is available. A quiz is held every Tuesday night. Local CAMRA's Pub of the Season autumn 2002. ⚄❀◑≈🍴

Spa Lane Vaults
34 St Mary's Gate
S41 7TH
◗ 10-11; 10-10.30 Sun
  (alcohol not served until noon)
☎ (01246) 246300

🍏 Westons (bottled)

This popular Wetherspoon's pub serves a wide range of real ales. It is known for its good value food (allowing family dining in the no-smoking area) and has a small outside drinking patio. Meals are served 10-10 each day.
Q❀◑≈🍴

CROMFORD

Boat Inn
Scarthin
DE4 3QF
◗ 12-3, 6-11; 12-11 Sat; 12-10.30 Sun
☎ (01629) 823282
www.theboatatcromford.co.uk

🍏 Varies (summer only)

Free house tucked away just off the market place. It has open fires, beamed ceilings and beer-barrel tables, which give it a cosy atmosphere and make it popular with walkers and tourists. There is a range of real ales and regular beer festivals, a quiz every other Sunday night and live music every Tuesday and the last Friday of the month. Local CAMRA Pub of the Season October 2004.
⚄Q❀◑⚗≈🍴P

DERBY

Alexandra Hotel
203 Siddals Road, DE1 2QE
SK361358
◗ 11-11; 12-3, 7-10.30 Sun
☎ (01332) 293993

🍏 Varies

Traditional real ale free house offering a guest cider, 10 or more real ales and at least five draught foreign beers. It has two rooms, one smoke free, plus patio and beer garden. Bed and breakfast accommodation is available.
Q❀🛏◑⚗≈ (Derby) 🍴P

Brunswick Inn
1 Railway Terrace DE1 2RU
SK362358
◗ 11-11; 12-10.30 Sun
☎ (01332) 290677

🍏 Westons

Grade II listed building constructed in the 1840s as a railwayman's pub. It is multi-roomed with flagstone floors, quiet downstairs with regular live music upstairs (jazz every Thursday). Home of the Brunswick Brewery (established 1991). Up to 16 real ales available from the Brunswick and independent brewers.
⚄Q❀◑⚗≈ (Derby) 🍴

Flowerpot
23-25 King Street DE1 3DZ
SK366353
◗ 11-11; 12-10.30 Sun
☎ (01332) 204955

🍏 Westons

Just up from the Cathedral and around Clockhouse Corner, this is one of Derby's premier real ale and cider outlets. A small roadside frontage leads to several interlinked rooms; from one the stillaged beer barrels can be seen and another provides the stage for a lively gig scene.
Q❀◑⚗

GLOSSOP

Globe
144 High Street West, SK13 8HJ
- 5-midnight (closed Tue); 5-12.30am Fri-Sat; 1-11.30 Sun
- ☎ (01457) 852417
- www.globemusic.org

🍏 Varies

🍺 Varies

This enterprising hostelry usually has three ciders and perries available. Music features strongly – the upstairs room hosts concerts by a plethora of artists at the weekend, while the downstairs room hosts folk on Monday and a resident band on Thursday. There is a popular quiz on Wednesday evening. There are usually seven beers available, always from regional or micro-breweries, with local producers strongly represented. The pub has a late licence but there is no entry after 10.45pm. Vegetarian snacks served at lunchtimes. ⊛◖⇌ (Glossop) 🏠

Star Inn
2 Howard Street, SK13 7DD
- 12-11; 12-10.30 Sun
- ☎ (01457) 853072

🍏 Varies

Friendly 'open all hours' pub across the road from the railway station. Six guest beers and two real ciders are brought from the cellar in jugs. ⇌♣🏠P

HOLBROOK

Dead Poets Inn
38 Chapel Street, DE56 0QT SK364455
- 12-2.30, 5-11; 12-11 Fri-Sat; 12-10.30 Sun
- ☎ (01332) 780301

🍏 Westons

In a delightful village five miles north of Derby, the pub features a low-beamed ceiling and nooks containing old bottles. There is a roaring fire in winter, four real ales are available and there are occasional poetry readings. ⋒Q◖♣🏠

Wheel Inn
14 Chapel Street
DE56 0TQ
- 12-2.30 (Thu-Fri), 6 (5 Fri)-11; 11-11 Sat; 12-10.30 Sun
- ☎ (01332) 880006

🍏 Thatchers

Several interconnected rooms include a restaurant at the rear with reasonably priced home-cooked food. Up to eight real ales are available and the patio is a delight in summer. Mini beer festivals are held and a micro-brewery has just opened on the site. ⋒⊛◖ 🏠P

ILKESTON

Durham Ox
25 Durham Street
DE7 8FQ
- 11-11; 12-10.30 Sun
- ☎ (0115) 932 4570

🍏 Westons

Back-street local was built as a town prison in 1760 and became a public house in the 19th-century. The cosy open-plan interior is divided into four distinct drinking areas, one with wooden settles, a real fire and old coal-mining photos. Real ales include Greene King IPA and Bass as regulars with up to three guests. It is situated close to local bus stops and is a 10 minute walk from the town market place on a back street between Bath Street and Chalons Way. A wide and varied clientele is found at this popular pub. Games include long alley skittles and dominoes. ⋒♣🏠P

Observatory
14a Market Place, DE7 5QA SK465426

◆ 11-11; 11-10.30 Sun
☎ (0115) 932 8040

🍺 Westons

Wetherspoon pub with a planetary theme, standing in the Market Square at the centre of Ilkeston. A good range of real ales is also available. ⌘◑♿🏠

KIRK IRETON

Barley Mow
Main Street, DE6 3JP (off B5023)
SK265502
◆ 12-2, 7-11; 12-2, 7-10.30 Sun
☎ (01335) 370306

🍺 Thatchers

Pub of great character with several rooms, real fire, stone floor, slate-topped tables and worn settles. Four real ales served from the cask via a small serving hatch. ⌂Q⌘⇋⊞▲♣🏠P⌁

MAKENEY

Holly Bush Inn
Holly Bush Lane, DE56 0RY SK353445
◆ 12-3, 5-11; 12-11 Fri-Sat;
   12-10.30 Sun
☎ (01332) 841729

🍺 Westons

Grade II listed building full of character with five separate drinking areas. Up to seven real ales are available on a rotating basis and occasional beer festivals are held. It is rumoured that Dick Turpin drank here. ⌂Q⥀⌘◑♿🏠P

OLD BRAMPTON

George & Dragon
Main Road, S42 7JG
◆ 12-4, 7-11 Mon; 12-11; 12-10.30 Sun
☎ (01246) 567826

🍺 Westons

Stone-built detached village pub on the

west side of Chesterfield with at least four beer festivals a year. There is a quiz every Tuesday night and a folk night the first Thursday of the month. Live music is a feature at weekends. Local CAMRA's joint Pub of the Season spring 2004.
⌂Q⌘⊞♣🏠P

PILSLEY

Chatsworth Farm Shop
DE45 1UF
◆ 9-5.30; 11-5 Sun
☎ (01246) 583392
www.chatsworth-house.co.uk/
shopping/farmshop.htm

🍎 Dunkertons, Sheppy's (bottled)

Excellent farm shop on the Chatsworth House estate. It sells a range of speciality food and drink, much of which is either produced on the estate or sourced locally. It stocks a range of bottled real ales, fruit wines and malt whiskies as well as a range of Dunkertons (including organic) and Sheppy's ciders. ▲🏠P

SHIRLAND

Hay
135 Main Road, DE55 6BA SK398587
◆ 4.30 (6 Mon)-11; 12-11 Sat;
   12-10.30 Sun
☎ (01773) 835383

🍎 Moles, Varies

Friendly local pub in the village of Shirland, which lies on the road between Chesterfield and Alfreton. It stocks a well-kept range of real ales, continental bottled beers and country fruit wines as well as at least one cider. There is a quiz every Thursday night. Q♣🏠P

SOUTH NORMANTON

Boundary
Lea Vale, Broad Meadows, DE55 3NA
SK445557

⬙ 12-11; 12-10.30 Sun
☎ (01773) 819066
www.theboundary.co.uk

🍏 Westons

A mile south of South Normanton, this large modern pub (built 1997) is tucked away on a housing estate. The enterprising landlord serves at least three real ales as well as cider. Occasional music evenings and beer festivals are also held.
⛱🏵🛏◑🍺♿♣📷P✂

SUTTON-CUM-DUCKMANTON

Arkwright Arms
Chesterfield Road, S44 5JG SK436714
⬙ 11-11; 12-10.30 Sun
☎ (01246) 232053
http://thearkers.mysite.wanadoo-members.co.uk

🍏 Varies (summer only)

Friendly mock-Tudor free house on the road from Chesterfield to Bolsover Castle. Well-kept real ales include offerings from micro-breweries and good value food is available (eve meals Mon-Fri only). There is also a grassed play area and patio tables outside. Local CAMRA Pub of the Year 2004. Wheelchair access is via the fire door. 🏨Q🏵◑🍺♿ (via fire door) 📷P

Devon

BRANSCOMBE

Fountain Head
EX12 3BG
⬙ 11.30-2.30, 6.30 (6 summer)-11; 12-2.30, 6.30 (6 summer)-10.30 Sun
☎ (01297) 680359

🍏 Green Valley

14th-century inn formerly a blacksmith's forge and cider house, which is now used as the lounge. It is popular with walkers.
🏨Q⛱🏵◑🍺♣📷P✂

EXETER

Green Valley Cyder Off Licence
Darts Farm, Clyst St George, Topsham, EX3 0QH SX977884
⬙ 9-5.30; 10-4.30 Sun
☎ (01392) 876658

🍏 Varies (bottled)

Off licence within the Darts Farm Shopping Village. Green Valley Cyder ha gradually extended its range of bottled ciders (and beers) over the past 15 years to its current considerable range. There i also an excellent restaurant and food ha on site. No smoking throughout.
🏵◑♿📷P✂

Well House Tavern
Cathedral Yard, EX1 1HD SX921927
⬙ 11-11; 12-10.30 Sun
☎ (01392) 22361
www.royalclarencehotel.co.uk/wellhouse.htr

🍏 Gaymers, Rich's

From outside this pub looks more like a wine bar than a traditional pub. Please c not be fooled; serious beer lovers will fir six handpumps and a real cider. The pub holds four seasonal beer festivals throughout the year with 12 beers on offer. Lunchtime meals served until 5.30pm. Occasional brewery trips and other outings are organised. 🛏◑🚉 (Exeter Central) 📷

HOPE COVE

Hope & Anchor Inn
TQ7 3HQ
⬙ 12-3, 6.30-11; 12-11 Sat; 12-3, 6.30-11 Sun
☎ (01548) 561294
www.hopeandanchor.co.uk

🍏 Varies

Large inn in a fishing village offering good quality food and accommodation.
🏵🛏◑📷

Powderham Country Store
Dawlish Road, EX6 8JQ
🕭 9-6 (5.30 Sat); 11-5 Sun
☎ (01626) 891883
www.powderham.co.uk

🍏 Varies

Retail site in the grounds of Powderham Castle.

Manor Inn
EX6 7RL OS844843
🕭 12-2, 6.30-11 (closed Mon); 12-2.30, 7-10.30 Sun
☎ (01647) 252304
www.themanorinn.co.uk

🍏 Grays, Westons

Small, friendly traditional country pub off B3193 between Dunsford and Chudleigh. It affords beautiful views over the Teign Valley and Dartmoor National Park. The food is good and makes use of local produce. No children under 14 allowed. ⚲Q✿◑⊞👤♣🖼P

Redwing
Church Road, EX8 5JT
🕭 11.30-3, 6-11; 11.30-11 Sat; 12-10.30 Sun
(01395) 222156

🍏 Thatchers

Friendly village free house with good food, traditional jazz on Tuesday and regular quiz nights. OLETP

Locomotive Inn
35-37 East Street, TQ12 2JP
🕭 Open all day Mon-Sun
☎ (01626) 365249

🍏 Westons

Cosy, friendly 17th-century inn in the town centre, with a long main bar connected to the pool and games room by an old sherry bar. Children and dogs are welcome. The pub serves real ale and has a mixed, friendly clientele. Sandwiches are available at lunchtime. ⚲⊞👤♣🖼🍴

Ye Olde Cider Bar
99 East Street, TQ12 2LD
🕭 Open all day Mon-Sun
☎ (01626) 354221

🍏 Varies

🍏 Westons

This atmospheric, traditional cider bar in the town centre is a real treasure and worth a detour for cider lovers. There is no beer, just an impressive range of ciders and country wines. Traditional pub games are played. Sandwiches, pies and pasties are available. ⚲Q👝✿🚇♣

Ship Inn
PL8 1EW
🕭 11-11; 12-10.30 Sun
☎ (01752) 872387
www.nossmayo.com

🍏 Thatchers

Former CAMRA Pub of the Year on the River Yealm and one with its own tidal moorings. Check with the pub regarding tides. The Ship is smoke-free and has an ethos of supporting local producers. ⚲Q✿◑👤♣🖼P✄

Maritime
19 Southside Street, The Barbican, PL1 2LD
🕭 11-11; 12-10.30 Sun
☎ (01752) 664898

🍏 Thatchers

Situated on The Barbican, one of the few outlets in the area selling both traditional cider and cask conditioned beer. ⚒◑🍎P

Prince Maurice
3 Church Hill, Eggbuckland
PL6 5RJ
⏸ 11-3, 6-11; 11-11
    Fri-Sat; 12-4, 7-10.30 Sun
☎ (01752) 771515

🍎 Thatchers

Former local CAMRA Pub of the Year, this two-bar pub still retains its village character. Look for it alongside the church and overlooking the village green in what was a village long before being swallowed up by Plymouth.
⚒Q❄◑♣🍎P

Providence
20 Providence Street, PL4 8JQ
⏸ 5 (4 Sat)-11; 12-10.30 Sun
☎ (01752) 228178

🍎 Thatchers

Quiet back-street pub, popular with locals and students. It is also a meeting place for the local Regiments of the Sealed Knot. There is no juke box – bring your own CDs. ⚒⅃♣🍎

SIDBURY

Hare & Hounds
Putts Corner, EX10 0QQ
SY141964
(on A375 between Sidmouth & Honiton)
⏸ 10.30-11; 12-10.30 Sun
☎ (01404) 41760

🍎 Wiscombe

Good food and sandwiches served in this quiet pub where the music is of the background variety only. A caravan site is just across the road. It is two miles from Sidbury village and served by the Exeter-Sidmouth-Honiton bus.
⚒🏕❄◑⅃⅃🍎P✂

SIDMOUTH

Dairy Shop
(incorporating Whites Bakery)
Church Street, EX10 8LY
⏸ 8.30-5 (Mon-Sat only)
☎ (01395) 513018
www.thedairyshop.com

🍎 Varies (bottled)

Grocery specialist and delicatessen selling a wide range of West Country products.

Dorset

BOURNEMOUTH

Porterhouse
113 Poole Road, Westbourne, BH4 8BY
⏸ 11-11; 12-10.30 Sun
☎ (01202) 768586

🍎 Varies

Cosy, Ringwood-owned pub with a bustling atmosphere, featuring a wood floor, oak panelling and hops adorning the bar. It sells the full range of Ringwood beers and an excellent choice of changing guests. A good selection of board games is available to while away the winter evenings. The pub was voted local CAMRA Pub of the Year six times in the last eleven years, as well as spring Pub of the Season 2004. Q⇌ (Branksome)♣🍎

BOURTON

White Lion
High Street, SP8 5AT
⏸ 12-3, 6-11; 12-3, 7-10 Sun
    (closed eve Jan/Feb)
☎ (01747) 840866

🍎 Thatchers

Traditional inn dating from 1763 with three flagstone bar areas separated by wood panel and glass partitions. This

popular village local serves regular and guest ales, often including Hop Back seasonal brews. Bar meals are available and top quality a la carte meals are served in the separate Bush restaurant. The large beer garden and children's play area is popular in summer. Accommodation in double and four-poster en-suite rooms is available.
🏚Q☸🍴◑◔♣🔌P

BUCKHORN WESTON

Stapleton Arms
Church Hill, SP8 5HS OS 757247
🍺 11-3, 6-11; 12-3, 6-10.30 Sun
☎ (01963) 370396

🍏 Varies

🍎 Westons

Popular, welcoming village pub at the hub of the community. Usually three guest ales are available, mostly from micros. Excellent home-prepared food, from bar snacks to full meals, is served in the large single bar or the two no-smoking dining areas. There is a large garden with a children's play area.
Q☸🍴◑♣🔌P

CHICKERILL

Lugger Inn
West Street, DT3 4DY
🍺 11-11; 12-10.30 Sun
☎ (01305) 766611
www.luggerinn.co.uk

🍏 Addlestones

Closed for 10 years, the pub has recently been extensively rebuilt as part of a housing project. Bearing little resemblance to the original, it now resumes its place as the only true pub in the village. It has a flagged bar area, restaurant and function room. Local beers feature prominently; the house beer comes from the Dorset Brewing

Company. Accommodation includes five holiday cottages. Wheelchair access is to the side. 🚲☸🍴◑◔♿🔌P

EAST CHALDON

Sailor's Return
DT2 8DN (1 mile S of A352)
🍺 11-11; 12-10.30 Sun
☎ (01305) 853847
www.sailorsreturn.com

🍏 Westons

This large, thatched inn on the fringe of a small hamlet provides a welcome break for ramblers on the nearby Dorset Coastal Path. It can be very busy on summer weekends. Inside is a large beamed bar at one end and a stone-walled dining room at the other with flagstone floors throughout. The food menu is extensive and renowned for its high quality and generous portions. Up to seven beers are offered in high season. A tented beer festival is held in late spring. ☸◑♣🔌P

LODERS

Loders Arms
DT6 3SA OS493942
🍺 11.30-3, 6-11 (11.30-11 summer Sat); 12-3, 6-10.30 (10-10.30 summer) Sun
☎ (01308) 422431
www.lodersarms.co.uk

🍏 Taunton

A charming inn standing in a pretty village on the River Asker Valley, a short drive from Bridport and the coast. The garden affords pleasing views of the surrounding hills which are etched with ancient field terraces. The pub comprises a long, beamed bar and a dining room at one end, with an enviable reputation for home-cooked food. Well supported by the locals, the pub has seven skittles teams. The caravan / camp site lies beyond the car park. Dogs welcome.
🏚☸🍴◑▲♣🔌P

SHAPWICK

Anchor
West Street, DT11 9LB (off B3082)
🍺 11-3, 6-11; 12-3, 7-10.30 Sun
☎ (01258) 857269

🍎 Addlestones

In the heart of the delightful Stour Valley lies the village of Shapwick and opposite the village cross is this 19th-century family-run pub. The main bar is light and open-plan with a central serving area and a small games room. Home-cooked meals are prepared to order with vegetarians catered for and local Dorset dishes a speciality. An annual beer festival is held in a marquee in the garden. A popular halt for walkers and cyclists on the Stour Valley Way in summer. 🏵🌓♣🏠P

SHAVE CROSS

Shave Cross Inn
DT6 6HW OS415980
🍺 11-3, 6-11 (11-11 summer); 12-3, 7-10.30 (12-10.30 summer) Sun
☎ (01308) 868358

🍎 Thatchers, Westons

A quintessential rural pub – stone built, stone-flagged, thatched and steeped in history. It was the resting place for pilgrims who had their heads shaved here to visit St White's shrine two miles away. The lovely garden has a new children's play area and the thatched skittle alley doubles as a family/function room. The house beer, Marshwood Vale, is from the Dorset Brewing Company. Local English and Caribbean food is served in the bar and dining room. CAMRA Regional Pub of the Year 2004. 🏠Q🌂🏵🌓♿▲♣🏠P

STUDLAND

Bankes Arms Hotel
Watery Lane, BH19 3AU

🍺 11-11; 12-10.30 Sun
☎ (01929) 450225

🍎 Varies

Built of Purbeck stone and covered in Virginia creeper, this famous pub overlooks the bay towards Bournemouth. A huge beer garden is across the lane from the pub. A range of nine ales is on offer including three from the Isle of Purbeck Brewery opened in 2003 which is next to the pub. Owned by the National Trust and run by the same family for many years, the pub hosts an annual beer festival in August. Superb food is served all day in summer. 🏠Q🏵🚲🌓▲🏠

SYMONDSBURY

Ilchester Arms
DT6 6HD
🍺 11.30-3 (not Mon), 6-11; 12-3, 6-10.30 Sun
☎ (01308) 422600

🍎 Taunton

A popular, stone-flagged pub situated at the heart of good walking country. In winter the low-beamed bar has a welcoming roaring fire burning in the inglenook. Home-cooked meals are served in the bar or dining room (booking recommended). Children are welcome in the skittle alley and the pretty stream-side garden. Two beers from Palmer are always available. 🏠Q🏵🌓♿▲♣🏠P

WAYTOWN

Hare & Hounds
DT6 5LQ
🍺 11.30-2.30 (not Mon), 7 (6.30 summer)-11; 12-2.30, 7-10.30 Sun
☎ (01308) 488203

🍎 Taunton

Attractive village local set in beautiful countryside, popular with walkers. On either side of the cosy bar is a children's room with a TV and a small restaurant. The garden, with lovely views, has a children's play area. The interesting menu uses mostly local ingredients including fresh fish. No food is served on Sunday evening or Monday. ♨Q❧❀◗🜂▲♣🏠P🍴

WEYMOUTH

Boot Inn
High West Street, DT4 8QT
🍺 11-11; 12-10.30 Sun
☎ (01305) 770327

🍏 Cheddar Valley

Weymouth's oldest pub is hidden behind the fire station. The wood-floor bar area leads to small rooms at each end with comfortable seating and warming fires. The full Ringwood beer range is supplemented with guest beers. The pub's popularity can lead to a spillage of customers onto the outside pavement where seating is provided in fine weather. An old-fashioned pub where conversation dominates. Local CAMRA Pub of the Year 2005. ♨Q❀🗲♣🏠🍴

WORTH MATRAVERS

Square & Compass
BH19 3LF (off B3069)
🍺 12-3, 6-11; 12-11 Sat; 12-3, 7-10.30 (closed winter eve) Sun
☎ (01929) 439229

🍏 Varies

🍏 Westons, Varies

Perched atop the Jurassic Coastline, this old Purbeck stone inn truly is a gem. Character flows from every nook and cranny, with a wealth of history stretching back 100 years. The tiny pub hosts beer and cider festivals, live music and eccentric events, all with spectacular views. Utterly unique and well worth seeking out – ring the landlord if you would like to camp. ♨Q❀▲♣🏠

Durham

BISHOP AUCKLAND

Grand
Holdforth Crest, South Church Road, DL14 6DU
🍺 6-11; 12-11 Fri-Sat; 12-10.30 Sun
☎ (01388) 601956
www.the-grand-hotel.co.uk

🍏 Westons

Out-of-town ale house dating from 1901 offering budget accommodation and up to six real ales. The cider is rotational from the Westons range. Parking is limited. ❀🗲≈ (Bishop Auckland) ♣🏠P🖫

DARLINGTON

Quaker House
1-3 Mechanics Yard, DL3 7QF
🍺 11-11; 12-10.30 Sun
☎ (07818) 848213
www.quakerhouse.co.uk

🍏 Varies

Award-winning ale house in the process of removing its keg products for cask, hence the first attempt at selling real cider. Up to 10 guest ales including the award-winning Ghost Ale, named after the pub ghost Ethel. ◖🍺🚻≈ (Darlington) 🏠

Railway Tavern
8 High Northgate, DL1 1UN
🍺 11-11; 12-10.30 Sun
☎ (01325) 464963

🍏 Thatchers

Built by the Stockton & Darlington Railway Company in 1827, just two years after they opened the service, the Railway was probably the first in the world to bear this name. A buoyant, well-run pub, consisting of a bar and lounge, it offers an excellent range of real ales including up to three guests. There is live music alternate Fridays. Have a pint where George Stephenson did. ♨❀🍺≈ (North Road) ♣🏠

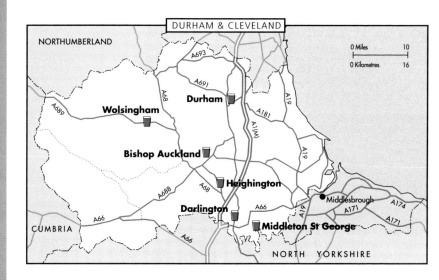

DURHAM

Tap & Spile
27 Front Street, Framwellgate Moor DH1 5EE

⏸ 12-3, 6-11 (closed Mon);
12-3, 7-10.30 Sun

☎ (0191) 386 5451

www.tapandspile.co.uk

🍎 Westons

Popular four-roomed village pub on the main road out of Durham City. Managed by an enthusiastic landlady, it has been a cider outlet for a number of years and offers a choice of guest ales. Regular buses from Durham City pass the door. Q⏻⏚⏚♣🍺P⏚

HEIGHINGTON

Bay Horse
28 West Green, DL5 6PE

⏸ 11-11; 12-10.30 Sun

☎ (01325) 312312

🍎 Westons

This late 17th-century pub has a long, narrow bar area, which is attractively furnished in country-cottage style complete with old photos, stuffed animals and bric-a-brac on exposed stone walls. It offers five real ales and the occasional beer festival is held. ♨♣🍺P⏚

MIDDLETON ST GEORGE

Fighting Cocks
Darlington Road, DL2 1JT

⏸ 11-11; 12-10.30 Sun

☎ (01325) 332327

🍎 Westons

L-shaped building, dating from early 19th-century. Locomotion No 1 driven by George Stephenson stopped here on the world's first passenger train journey on 27 September 1825. The pub puts a strong emphasis on its meals. It also offers three real ales and has a games room and attractive garden. ♨♣🍺P⏚

WOLSINGHAM

Black Bull Inn
27 Market Place, DL13 3AB

⏸ 12-11; 12.30-10.30 Sun

☎ (01388) 527332

🍎 Westons

Former coaching house in centre of village, popular with locals and visitors for its good food and accommodation. The cider began as an experiment and proved so popular it remained a regular fixture. Meals served 12-3 and 6-10. Weardale bus 101 runs from Bishop Auckland and Crook.

Essex

COLCHESTER

Bricklayers
27 Bergholt Road, CO4 5AA
11-3, 5.30-11; 11-11 Fri-Sat; 12-3.30, 6.30-10.30 Sun
(01206) 852008

Crones

Multiple CAMRA award-winning pub with separate public and lounge bars serving Crones cider on handpump. Being a flagship Adnams town pub, Adnams and guest beers are also available. (North Station) P

Odd One Out
28 Mersea Road, CO2 7ET
4.30-11; 12-11 Fri-Sat; 12-10.30 Sun
(01206) 513958

Varies

The ciders complement a wide range of real ales in this popular pub, which was local CAMRA's Pub of the Year 2004. Within walking distance of Colchester town railway and bus stations. Of the three ciders available the guest cider is generally stronger than the ones regularly available. Q (Colchester Town)

DELVIN END

Bottle Hall
Toppesfield Road, CO9 3LN TL756353
5-11 Tue-Sat (closed Mon); 12-10.30 Sun
(01787) 462405

Delvin End

Wonderful country pub in the middle of nowhere – from Sible Hedingham follow the back road through High Street Green, Bottle Hall is on the right. Storm cider is made in the same village and is always available, together with two or three local ales. The steak and chips is a must! P

GREAT YELDHAM

Waggon & Horses
High Street, CO9 4EX
11-11; 12-10.30 Sun
(01787) 237936
www.waggonandhorses.net

Delvin End

This friendly village local attracts all ages, from young people for a game of pool to families for Sunday lunch. The landlord is a real ale drinker. Ciders are local; the cidery is a couple of miles away so availability is never a problem. P

HORNCHURCH

J J Moons
46-62 High Street, RM12 4UN
10-11; 12-10.30 Sun
(01708) 478410

Varies

A 1990s Wetherspoon bar with a changing selection of ciders in up to three polybarrels or polypins on the bar. The pub also features a large and changing range of guest beers – up to 11 are available. There is a smoke-free family area at the rear and children can eat here until 6pm. The pub opens at 10am on Sunday for breakfast and soft drinks. Emerson Park station closes at 8pm. Q (Emerson Park) (Hornchurch) P

Swan
School Road, CM9 8LB
⏸ 11-11; 12-10.30 Sun
☎ (01621) 892689
john@theswanpublichouse.co.uk
www.theswanpublichouse.co.uk

🍎 Delvin End, Westons

🍎 Westons

CAMRA's National Pub of the Year 2002. The interior beams, unspoilt bar and wattle and daub walls ensure a cosy feel in this excellent country pub. As well as the one perry and four ciders, eight beers are available here. Both the cider and real ale are served by gravity. No meals served Monday, no evening meals Sunday. Two miles SE of B1022, between Tiptree and Goldhanger. ⏚❀◑ ⊟♿♣ ⌂P✄☐

White Horse
Mill Road, CO9 4SG TL737410
⏸ 12-3 (not Mon & Tues), 6-11;
  12-10.30 Sun
☎ (01440) 785532
www.ridgewellwh.com

🍎 Biddenden

Popular village local with a friendly landlord who is an active CAMRA member and cider enthusiast. The real ales and ciders are served straight from the cask. With a restaurant serving home-cooked food and new motel adjoining the pub, it is the perfect place from which to explore the north Essex countryside. ⏚❀⌀◑♿♣ ⌂P

Golden Lion
35 North Street, SS4 1AB
⏸ 12-11; 12-10.30 Sun
☎ (01702) 545487

🍎 Westons

This fine unspoilt friendly 17th-century pub is faced with Essex weatherboard and features stained glass windows. It can be lively on Friday and Saturday evenings. Inside the pub is adorned with the many local CAMRA awards it has won and also pump clips displaying the vast range of beers that have been on sale. Dogs are welcome but not children. ❀⇌ (Rochford) ♣⌂☐

Cork & Cheese
10 Talza Way, Victoria Plaza, SS2 5BG
⏸ 11-11; Closed Sun
☎ (01702) 616914
www.corkandcheese.co.uk

🍎 Thatchers

Central Southend's real pub, where shoppers, bank workers and punks happily mix among the breweriana and plastic beams. It can be found at ground level within the lower part of the shopping centre. Inside the pub is proud with the number of beers sold in the last 10 years – over 2,500. This pub is well worth a visit and much revered by the local CAMRA branch. ❀◑⇌ (Central / Victoria) ♣⌂

Station Arms
Station Road, CM0 7EW
⏸ 12-2.30, 6(5.30 Thu-Fri)-11;
  12-11 Sat; 12-4, 7-10.30 Sun
☎ (01621) 772225
www.pickapub.co.uk/thestationarms.htm

🍎 Westons

Unpretentious friendly weatherboarded pub recognised for the quality of its beer, hosting three beer festivals annually in January, May and August in the restored barn to the rear of the premises. Inside the pub is adorned with the obvious railway theme and also promotes community events as well as the weekly meat raffle. ⚞Q✿⟞≋ (Southminster) ♣🏠

STOCK

Hoop
21 High Street, CM4 9BD
�III 12-11; 12-10.30 Sun
☎ (01277) 841137
www.thehoop.co.uk

🍏 Wilkins

Recently extended pub which has a reputation for its good food and a selection of beers, wine and cider. The garden plays host to beer festivals which are the longest running of any pub in the area. Well served by the 100 bus running between Chelmsford and Billericay.
Q✿⟞♣🏠

STOW MARIES

Prince of Wales
Woodham Road, CM3 6SA OS830993
III 11-11; 12-10.30 Sun
☎ (01621) 828971
www.powstowmaries.co.uk

🍏 Westons

Restored village ale house with a reputation for the quality and range of the beers, hosting varied events from Burns Night to fireworks in November including pizza nights with home baked pizzas cooked in the pub's own Victorian bakery. Don't be put off by the Hull City FC memorabilia as inside is an equal amount of breweriana as the landlord is passionate about both.
⚞Q☕✿⟞🏠P

WESTCLIFF-ON-SEA

Cricketers Inn
228 London Road, SS0 7JG
III 12-11; 12-10.30 Sun
☎ (01702) 343168

🍏 Thatchers

Recently refurbished spacious pub which keeps its cider in the cellar and is not clearly on display in the serving area of the most southerly Grays & Sons house. Next door and connected is the music venue called 'Club Riga' which has bands on in the later part of the week. ⟞≋ (Westcliff/Victoria) 🏠

Gloucestershire

ASHLEWORTH

Boat Inn
The Quay, GL19 4HZ 819251
III (Closed Mon) 11.30-2.30, 7-11 Tues-Fri;
    11.30-3, 7-11 Sat; 12-3, 7-10.30 Sun
☎ (01452) 700272
www.boatinn.co.uk

🍏 Westons

An unspoilt gem on the bank of the Severn, it has been owned by the same family for 400 years. The beer from local micro breweries is served directly from the cask. A rare no-smoking pub. Rolls served at lunchtimes (not Wed).
⚞Q✿⟞P✄

BROAD CAMPDEN

Bakers Arms
GL55 6UR
III 11.30-2.30, 4.45-11; 11.30-11 Fri-Sat
    & summer; 12-10.30 Sun
☎ (01386) 840515

🍏 Thatchers

This Cotswold stone free house has exposed beams, an inglenook and an attractive oak bar counter. A superb hand-woven rug depicting the pub adorns one wall. The landlady's home-cooked food is popular in the dining room extension. Q❁◐ 🏠P

BROADWELL

Fox Inn
The Green, GL56 0UF
- 11-2.30, 6-11; 11.30-2.30, 6-11Sat; 12-2.30, 7-10.30 Sun
- ☎ (01451) 870909
www.pubs2000.com

🍏 Addlestones

A magnificent Cotswold stone pub on the village green. It has flagstone floors, log fires in winter and a large collection of jugs. The good value home-cooked food is available at all sessions. Aunt Sally is played in summer. No-frills camping permitted behind the pub. Well-behaved dogs on leads are welcomed. Q❁◐▲♣🏠P

CHELTENHAM

Cheltenham Motor Club
Upper Park Street, GL52 6SA
- 7-midnight; 11.30-3, 7-midnight Sat; 12-3, 7-midnight Sun
- ☎ (01242) 522590

🍏 Thatchers

Just outside the town centre with pedestrian access through Crown Passage from the A40 London Road, this friendly and welcoming club is open to all (regular visitors will be asked to join). The games room and bar are adorned with motoring paraphernalia and an extensive collection of pump clips. Sunday lunch is served. Q🏠P

Jolly Brewmaster
39 Painswick Road, GL50 2EZ
- 12-11; 12-10.30 Sun
- ☎ (01242) 772261

🍏 Varies

Built as a coaching inn in 1854, it has been sympathetically modernised and retains the feel of an old-fashioned local. Both smokers and dog owners are welcomed at the unusual horseshoe-shaped bar. There is a beer garden at the rear. Sunday lunches are a treat. ㎫❁♣🏠

Royal Oak
43 The Burgage, Prestbury, GL52 3OL
- 11.30-2.30, 5.30-11; 11.30-2.30, 5.30-11 Sat (11.30-11 summer Sat); 12-3.30, 7-10.30 Sun (12-10.30 summer Sun)
- ☎ (01242) 522344
www.royal-oak-prestbury.co.uk

🍏 Thatchers

The public bar features exposed beams and low ceilings, while the lounge serves as a dining room until 9pm. Fresh fish and Cotswold game are a feature of the menu. Annual cider festivals are held in the large garden that leads to a skittle alley and function room. The pub is close to the Cheltenham racecourse. Bus service A from Cheltenham stops nearby. ㎫Q❁◐⊟🏠P

Sudeley Arms
25 Prestbury Road, GL52 2PN
- 11-11; 12-10.30 Sun
- ☎ (01242) 510697

🍏 Westons

💧 Westons

This three-roomed pub is a five minute walk from the town centre and close to Cheltenham Town FC. The pub dates from 1826 and offers a friendly welcome. Q❁◐⊟🏠

CHIPPING CAMPDEN

Volunteer Inn
Lower High Street, GL55 6DY
- 11.30-3, 5 (6 Sat)-11; 12-3, 7-10.30 Sun
- ☎ (01386) 840688
www.thevolunteerinn.com

 Thatchers

This free house is a former local CAMRA Pub of the Year and has been run by the same family for over 20 years. The front lounge bar has a large bay window and stone fireplace. The rear bar is popular with youngsters. The River Cam runs at the end of the attractive rear garden and the courtyard is ablaze with hanging baskets. The pub is on the Cotswold Way. ▲Q❀☎◑ ⊟♣🐕

COALEY

Fox & Hounds
GL11 5EG
◑ 12-3, 7-11; 12-3, 7-10.30 Sun
☎ (01453) 890366

 Addlestones

A 300-year-old traditional Cotswold stone inn that has one cosy bar with a wood-burning stove. The function room has a skittle alley and a dining area with excellent home-cooked food at reasonable prices. The pub is renowned for its jazz, Irish and Cajun music evenings on Saturdays. ▲Q❀◑♣🐕P

FORD

Plough Inn
GL54 5RU (On B4966 5 miles W of Stow-on-the-Wold)
◑ 11-11; 12-10.30 Sun
☎ (01386) 584215
www.ploughinnatford.co.uk

 Varies

16th-century stone inn with low, beamed ceilings, flagstone floors and inglenooks. The restaurant has a good reputation. Horse racing chat is normal in the bar because the pub lies across the road from the stables of Jonjo O'Neill. This former local Pub of the Year has a garden play area. ▲❀☎◑ ⊟&♣🐕P

GLOUCESTER

Fountain Inn
53 Westgate Street, GL1 2NW
◑ 10.30 (11.30 Sat)-11; 12-10.30 Sun
☎ (01452) 522562
www.fountainglos.co.uk

 Addlestones

Tucked away down a passage from Westgate Street, this 17th-century inn stands where there has been an inn since 1216. The flower-bedecked courtyard is crammed in summer. Excellent home-cooked food served all day. Separate restaurant opens Thursday-Saturday evenings. Q❀◑&≠ (Gloucester) ♣🐕

Imperial
59 Northgate Street, GL1 4AG
◑ 11-11; 12-6 Sun
☎ (01452) 529918

 Thatchers

Smart one-bar pub with superb tiled Victorian frontage. Its name arose from the Imperial Gloucesters, later known as the Glorious Glosters, the famed county regiment. ◑≠ (Gloucester) ♣🐕

New Inn
16 Northgate Street, GL1 1SE
◑ 11-11; 11-1.45am Sat; 12-10.30 Sun
☎ (01452) 522177
www.newinnglos.com

 Moles

The New Inn is the finest medieval galleried inn in Britain and has been splendidly revived after years of neglect. The building dates from the 15th-century. Cider is only available in the real ale bar. Special weekend accommodation rates for CAMRA members. ❀◑🐕

HAWKESBURY UPTON

Beaufort Arms
High Street, GL9 1AU

〰️ 12-11; 12-10.30 Sun
☎ (01454) 238217
www.beaufortarms.com

🍏 Westons

Popular village local with both a public and lounge bar. It boasts a wonderful collection of brewery and local memorabilia. A no-smoking restaurant, skittle alley, function room and a pleasant garden add to the pub's appeal. Local CAMRA Pub of the Year 2004.
🏚Q🐾❀◑🍺🔥♣🏠P

MOSELEY GREEN

Rising Sun
GL15 4HN
〰️ 11-3, 6.30-11 (11-11 summer Sat);
12-3, 7-10.30 Sun
(12-10.30 summer Sun)
☎ (01594) 562008

🍏 Varies

The pub was built in the early 1800s to serve the mining community. In 1982 a balcony and skittle alley were added. A patio seating 50 was created in 1989 to celebrate 50 years of ownership in the same family. Further additions include a barbecue and children's play area. Family meals are always available. The pub has magnificent panoramic views of the Forest of Dean. ❀◑🏠P↙🍺

TEWKESBURY

White Bear
Bredon Road, GL20 5BU
〰️ 11-11; 12-10.30 Sun
☎ (01684) 296614

🍏 Thatchers

This lively pub has an L-shaped bar with a dartboard and pool table – its darts, crib and pool teams compete locally. The pub is close to the marina and is popular with river users.
❀🅰♣🏠P🍺

SLAD

Woolpack
GL6 7QA
〰️ 12-3, 6-11; 11.30-11 Sat; 12-10.30 Sun
☎ (01452) 813429

🍏 Varies

Popular 16th-century inn made famous by the late Laurie Lee, author of Cider with Rosie. The building has been thoughtfully restored with settles in the end bar, in which children are welcomed. No evening meals on Monday. Local CAMRA Pub of the Year 2004-2005.
🏚Q🐾❀◑🍺🏠P

WATERLEY BOTTOM

New Inn
GL11 6EF OS758964
〰️ 12-2.30, 6 (7 Mon)-11; 12-11 Sat; 12-10.30 Sun
☎ (01453) 543659

🍏 Thatchers

Beautiful free house in a small hamlet surrounded by steep hills. The pub has two bars and an attractive garden with a boules pitch. Children are welcome. The pub is signposted from North Nibley but a good map is a must for first-time visitors. 🏚Q❀◑🍺♣🏠P

WHITECROFT

Miners Arms
New Road, GL15 4PE
〰️ 12-11; 12-10.30 Sun
☎ (01594) 562483
www.minersarmswhitecroft.co.uk

🍏 Moles, Thatchers (draught & bottled)

🍶 Varies (summer only)

A traditional free house close to two coal mines. Quoits is played in the bar and there is a boules pitch in one of the gardens. The back garden is safe for

children. The Dean Forest Steam Railway passes the back of the pub. Three draught ciders always stocked, plus a perry in summer. Winner of the National Cider Pub of the Year 2005.
ꝲQ⟰⊕◖⊟⟱♣🐈P

WITHINGTON

King's Head
Kings Head Lane, GL54 4BD
⫧ 11-2.30, 6-11; 12-3, 7-10.30 Sun
☎ (01242) 890216

🍎 Varies

A true village local tucked away at the end of the lane. A warm welcome is assured from the landlady. No food served except for sandwiches that need to be ordered in advance. Children are welcomed in the lounge ante-room. Chedworth Roman Villa is close by.
ꝲQ⟰⊟♣🐈P

Hampshire

ALTON

Cavern Bar
Alton Community Centre, GU34 1HN
⫧ 7-11 (not Sat-Sun)
☎ (01420) 85057

🍎 Mr Whiteheads

Community Centre bar that welcomes visitors. Good for live music; open mic on Wednesday, jamming and blues on Thursday, punk and ska once a month on Saturday. One real ale pump usually has Triple FFF on tap but occasionally other micros are available. Selection of bottled beers also offered. ⟰◖⟱🐈P⤬

Railway Arms
26 Anstey Road, GU34 2RB
⫧ 11-11; 12-10.30 Sun
☎ (01420) 82218

🍎 Swamp Donkey

Close to the Watercress line and main station, this cosy pub is owned by the proprietor of Triple FFF Brewery. The front of the pub is under a striking sculpture of a steam locomotive. ⟰⇌ (Alton) ♣🐈

BISHOP'S WALTHAM

Hampshire Bowman
Dundrige Lane, SO32 1GD
⫧ 12-3, 6-11; 12-11 Fri-Sat; 12-10.30 Sun
☎ (01489) 892940

🍎 Mr Whitehead's (Apr-Nov only)

Country gem, hard to find but worth the effort. Good food and a changing range of real ales, usually five or six. Cider is usually from Mr Whitehead's but changes from time to time. ꝲQ⟰◖▲🐈P

HILL BROW

Jolly Drover
GU33 7QL (J of B2070 & B3006)
⫧ 11-2.30, 6-11; 12-3 Sun (closed eve)
☎ (01730) 893137

🍎 Swamp Donkey

Built in 1820 by a drover, this pub is halfway between Petersfield and Liphook. This family-run local has original beams, a huge log fire, an extensive menu (including Swamp Donkey sausages!) and four regular guest ales plus one from an independent brewery. The cider is pressed on the premises. ꝲQ⟰◖🐈P

SOUTHAMPTON

Bitter Virtue
70 Cambridge Road, SO14 6US
⫧ 10.30-8.30 (closed Mon); 10.30-2 Sun
☎ (02380) 554881
www.bittervirtue.co.uk

🍎 Varies (bottled)

🍐 Varies (bottled)

Small, friendly off-licence in a back street at the edge of the city centre. Numerous ciders and perries stocked including Breton Cider. There is also a huge range of bottled beers from many countries. Draught beers also sold. 🍺

Herefordshire

Abbey Dore Farm Shop & Cider Mill
Moorhampton Park Farm, HR2 0AL
⏰ 10-6 Mon-Sun
☎ (01981) 550258

🍎 Gwatkin (draught & bottled)

🍏 Gwatkin (draught & bottled)

This converted barn houses the farm shop associated with Gwatkin's cider mill. A wide range of Gwatkin ciders and perries is available both on draught and in bottle – the highly distinctive Foxwhelp should certainly be tried if it is available. Also sold are beers from local breweries, local country wines, Herefordshire apple juice, home-reared beef and lamb and a range of other produce. At the rear of the barn, the tasting room is a highly attractive recreation of a traditional cider house in which drinks can be served to pre-booked parties; simple wholesome catering can also be arranged. ♣🍺P

Neville Arms
HR2 0AA (on B4347)
⏰ 11-11; 12-10.30 Sun
☎ (01981) 240319

🍎 Gwatkin (bottled)

Large roadside house named after the Neville family, Marquesses of Abergavenny, who built the pub in 1907. The L-shaped bar has a games area with pool table and a separate restaurant. The front garden offers good views of the Golden Valley with the 12th-century Dore Abbey nearby.

Bottled local cider is available. All-day bar snacks are complemented by contemporary cuisine with a Sunday carvery in the restaurant. ⛺🐕🛏◐♣P

Hop Pocket Wine Co
Hop Pocket Craft Centre, WR6 5BT (on B4214, south of village)
⏰ 10-5.30 Tue-Fri; 12-5 Sun; Closed Tue in Jan/Feb; Open Mon in Nov/Dec
☎ (01531) 640592
www.hoppocketwine.co.uk

🍎 Varies (draught & bottled)

🍏 Varies (bottled)

Located in an expanding complex next to a hop yard, free cider tasting is offered every day. The restaurant serves draught cider in summer. 🍺

Cornewall Arms
Longtown, HR2 0PD
⏰ 11-11; 12-10.30 Sun
☎ (01873) 860677

🍎 Gwatkin (bottled)

A tiny, unspoilt pub of great character, resplendent with a serving hatch that (sadly) serves no real ale, but does offer local bottled cider. Of great interest to pub historians. Games include darts, table skittles and quoits. ⛺Q♣♣

Bull's Head
HR2 0PN SO278360
⏰ 11-3, 6-11; 11-11 Sat; 12-6 Sun
☎ (01981) 510616
www.thebullsheadcraswall.com

🍎 Westons

🍎 Westons

Refurbishment of this ancient cider house has been achieved without altering the main bar, with its sloping flagstone floor, peeling wallpaper and serving hatches where real ale is drawn direct from the cask. Two further rooms are provided for diners to enjoy the exciting range of food that has established a national reputation (weekend booking advisable). Ideally located for walking the nearby Hay Bluff and Offa's Dyke path, the pub offers both en-suite and hostel-type B&B and camping is permitted in nearby fields. ⚲Q❀🖛◑⊟🛆🛏

Barrels
69 St Owen Street, HR1 2JQ
⊪ 11-11; 12-10.30 Sun
☎ (01432) 274968

🍏 Thatchers

Once home to Wye Valley Brewery and still the brewery's flagship outlet, stocking most of the beer range. Voted local CAMRA Pub of the Year 2003, its four distinct rooms cater for all age groups. A pool table occupies one bar and another has a large-screen TV for major sporting events; otherwise conversation rules. Freed from brewery activities, the rear courtyard now provides a great outdoor drinking area and is the venue for the August bank holiday charity music and beer festival. ❀⊟≉♣

Brewer's Arms
97 Eign Road, HR1 2RU
⊪ 12-11; 12-10.30 Sun
☎ (01432) 273746

🍏 Thatchers

Small, locals' two-bar pub with games room at the rear with skittle alley, pool table and large screen TV. The pub is used by local anglers for weighing in. Pints are discounted on Wednesdays. ⛱❀⊟♣

Oxford Arms
111 Widemarsh Street, HR4 9EZ
⊪ 10-11; 12-10.30 Sun
☎ (01432) 272635

🍏 Thatchers

A 17th-century timber-framed building which, although much altered over the years, still looks and feels genuine. This small, two-bar pub, recently redecorated, has a separate pool room and a large garden. It enjoys a loyal community following, with live music some Saturday evenings. Basket meals and filled rolls are available. A large public car park can be found to the rear. ⚲❀◑⊟≉♣

Victory
88 St Owens Street, HR1 2QD
⊪ 11-11; 12-10.30 Sun
☎ (01432) 274998

🍏 Varies

🍏 Westons

Home of Hereford's Spinning Dog Brewery, the pub serves most of its beers and offers the city's best range of real ciders and perry. The main bar is of timber construction with bare wooden floors and the bar servery is in the shape of a galleon. The unusual nautical theme continues through to a large narrow bar and skittle alley to the rear. A key venue for local bands (Saturday and Sunday evenings) it holds mini beer festivals usually twice a year. ⚲⛱❀◑⊟≉♣🛏P

Red Lion
HR2 9DN SO446304
⊪ 12-2 (not Tue), 6-11; 12-3, 6-11 Sat;
   12-3, 7-10.30 Sun
☎ (01981) 570464

🍏 Westons

A welcoming pub in the centre of the village near the historic church and castle.

It is loosely divided into a lounge and public bar with pool table, all served from a central bar. Bar snacks and full meals are served at all sessions, including Sunday lunches for which booking is recommended. Children are welcome away from the bar. ✿◖◗♣🅿✝

LEDBURY

Brewery Inn
Bye Street, HR8 2AG
⊪ 11-11; 12-10.30 Sun
☎ (01531) 634272

🍎 Westons

On the right hand side of what once was the entrance to Ledbury Town Station stands the Brewery Inn, a fascinating and unspoilt 15th-century two-bar pub with traditional quarry-tiled floors. This well supported local has a snug bar which is probably the smallest in the country. Bar snacks available Monday to Friday lunchtimes. Limited free parking nearby. 🏚Q✿◖⇌♣

Prince of Wales
Church Lane, HR8 1DL
⊪ 11-11; 12-10.30 Sun
☎ (01531) 632250

🍎 Westons

🍷 Westons (summer only)

Tucked away in a beautiful narrow cobbled street, this superb 16th-century timbered pub comprises front and back bars and an eating area. Always bustling with locals and visitors alike, it holds a very popular folk jam session (Wed eve) and is popular for pub games. Good value home-cooked bar meals and Sunday roasts. 🏃✿◖⇌♣

LEOMINSTER

Black Horse
74 South Street, HR6 8JF

⊪ 11-2.30, 6-11; 11-11 Sat; 12-3, 7-10.30 Sun
☎ (01568) 611946

🍎 Addlestones

An enthusiastically run coach house to the south of the town centre. Once home to the Dunn Plowman Brewery and still noted for the range and quality of its beers, it has a basic public bar, a small narrow lounge area resplendent with 1980s décor and a separate dining area to the rear. Bar snacks and meals are served (not Sun eve), with Sunday lunches a speciality. Games include pétanque, table skittles and quoits. Car park access is via the narrow courtyard entrance. 🏃✿◖◗⊞▲⇌♣🅿

Black Swan Hotel
33 West Street, HR6 8EP
⊪ 11-11; 12-10.30 Sun
☎ (01568) 612020

🍎 Thatchers

An 18th-century hotel near the town centre with two bars and an eating area. The lounge is plush while the public bar is less so, but quieter. A further drinking area is used for eating at lunchtimes and there is a patio outside. Accommodation is en-suite, bed and breakfast. The food is mainly bar snacks. 🏚✿◖⊞⇌♣🅿

Orchard Hive & Vine
4 High Street, HR6 8LZ
⊪ 9.30-5.30 Mon-Sat (may close for lunch 1.30-2pm)
☎ (01568) 611232
www.orchard-hive-and-vine.co.uk

🍎 Varies (draught & bottled)

🍷 Varies (draught & bottled)

Opened in 1997, this first-rate specialist off-licence showcases a large range of cider and perry, with the emphasis firmly on local produce. As well as bottles, draught cider and perry is sold at most times of the year. There is also a judicious selection of high-quality bottled beers, fine wines and mead (including the owners' Meads of Mercia). This altogether splendid establishment is supported by a highly efficient mail-order operation (order by phone or on the internet). 📠

LITTLE COWARNE

Three Horseshoes
HR7 4RQ SO604509
🍺 11-3, 6.30-11; 12-3, 7-10.30 Sun
(closed Sun eve in winter)
☎ (01885) 400276
www.threehorseshoes.co.uk

🍎 Oliver's

💧 Oliver's

This pleasant country inn was, until 1900, a blacksmiths shop. Now open-plan, the single large bar serves a lounge, games area, a garden room and a restaurant as well as the gardens outside. Customers are a good mix of diners and locals, including those involved in nine various pub teams. A varied and interesting range of bar and restaurant meals is offered – booking recommended at weekends. 🏰Q🐾🛏️🕪👫♣📠P⌀

MUCH DEWCHURCH

Black Swan
HR2 8DJ (on B4348)
🍺 12-3, 5.30-11; 12-4, 6-10.30 Sun
☎ (01981) 540295

🍎 Dewchurch (summer only), Gwatkin (bottled), Westons (draught)

A most interesting and delightful 15th-century, heavily beamed pub complete with a priest hole. A small lounge leads into a dining room with open fire and to a public bar with a flagstone floor leading on through to a games room. Food is available every session and Sunday lunches are remarkably substantial. Thursday night

is folk night. The guest beers are mainly from regional breweries. Dewchurch cider is available on draught around Easter, while bottled cider from Gwatkin is always available. 🏰🐾🕪👫♣📠P

MUCH MARCLE

Scrumpy House
The Bounds, HR8 2NQ SO648331
🍺 11-3 Mon-Tue; 11-3, 7-11 Wed-Sat; 12-3.30 Sun
☎ (01531) 660626
www.scrumpyhouse.co.uk

🍎 Westons

💧 Westons

Restaurant and bar at the Westons cider mill, set behind attractive gardens. 🛏️🕪📠

Slip Tavern
Watery Lane, HR8 2NG SO651333
🍺 11.30-2.30, 6.30-11; 12-2.30, 7-10.30 Sun
☎ (01531) 660246

🍎 Lyne Down (bottled), Westons (draught)

💧 Lyne Down (bottled)

The pub name arose from a landslide in 1575 which buried the church and a herd of cattle (see plaque in entrance hall). The pub consists of a main bar with a real fire plus a dining area, set in an attractive garden. Folk music evenings are held on the first Thursday of the month, while Tuesday is games evening. The food (not served Sun or Mon eve) is mostly English, with some international cuisine. Well-behaved children are welcome in the dining area. The guest beer is often from Whittingtons. 🏰🐾🕪📠P⌀

Walwyn Arms
HR8 2LY (on A449 at B4024 junction)
🍺 12-2.30, 5-11; 12-11 Fri-Sat; 12-10.30 Sun
☎ (01531) 660758

🍎 Westons

A 17th-century village pub that for many years doubled as a butcher's shop and slaughterhouse. It now consists of a single large L-shaped bar, skittle alley and function room. Home-cooked, locally sourced traditional bar snacks and meals are served (no food after 6pm Sun). Live music is staged on the last Friday of the month. Families are welcome away from the bar. 🏚🐾🌸🍺♣🏠P✂

Boot
SY8 4HN (off B4361) SO494672
⏳ 12-3, 6-11; 12-3, 7-10.30 Sun
☎ (01568) 780228

🍎 Brook Farm

Popular 17th-century black-and-white village pub with distinctive and comfortable public bar, lounge and restaurant. A charity quiz is held monthly on a Tuesday. A large, attractive beer garden includes a children's play area and a barbecue. The home-cooked food ranges from bar snacks to à la carte with interesting daily specials. The guest beer is from mainly local breweries and Town Crier alternates with a second guest. 🏚Q🌸🍺♣🏠P

New Inn
Market Square, HR6 9DZ
⏳ 11-3, 6-11; 12-3, 7-10.30 Sun
☎ (01544) 388427

🍎 Westons (draught), Dunkertons (bottled)

This imposing and authentic old building faces the market square, where outdoor seating is available. Facilities include a public bar, resplendent with flagstone floor, large settle and large fireplace; a lounge bar, a separate eating and family

area and a downstairs restaurant. The heavily beamed interior is decorated with hop bines and a variety of traditional furniture, which gives a homely atmosphere. Games include shove-ha'penny. A wide selection of malt whiskies is also available.
🏚Q🐾🌸🍺🍺♣P

Broome Farm
HR9 6QG OS570250
⏳ Open most reasonable hours (please ring ahead)
☎ Shop (01989) 769556, restaurant and B&B (01989) 562824
www.broomefarmhouse.co.uk

🍎 Broome Farm (draught & bottled)

🍎 Broome Farm (draught & bottled)

You'll find a warm welcome at Mike Johnson's cider cellar, where a wide range of Broome Farm cider and perry is available to take away, either in bottles (often bottle fermented) or in containers filled straight from the cask. As with most small producers, what is available depends on what was pressed the previous season, but Mike's advice and tastings should ensure a wise choice. Opening times vary according to the exigencies of the cider business so it is always wise to ring before visiting. The restaurant has a growing reputation (always book in advance) and the cream teas are a treat – you can even stay the night in the bed-and-breakfast accommodation on site. 🍺🍺P

Yew Tree
HR2 9JT SO385414
⏳ 7-11; 12-3, 7-10.30 Sun
☎ (01981) 500539

🍎 Thatchers

A pleasantly eccentric and unspoilt single-bar drinkers' establishment in a quiet hamlet near the River Wye. Comfortable and welcoming, it supports boules, pool and quiz teams, while in the summer it is popular with fishermen and canoeists. The beer, which tends to alternate between local and regional breweries, is served from a cask behind the small bar. Usually open additionally on Saturday lunchtimes in summer; it also hosts monthly live music on Saturdays. ᴁQ❀Å♣🏠P

RHYDSPENCE

Rhydspence Inn
HR3 6EU (on A438)
🍺 11-2.30, 7-11; 12-2.30, 7-10.30 Sun
☎ (01497) 831262

🍎 Dunkertons (draught, summer only), Dunkertons (bottled)

This beautifully positioned 14th-century drovers' inn retains many original features. Located right on the Welsh border, half the pub grounds are in Wales! The emphasis now is on high-quality food and accommodation but drinkers are still welcome. An architectural gem, totally free from piped music and other distractions. ᴁQ❤❀🏠🌙🍴P✓

ROSS-ON-WYE

Crown & Sceptre
Market Place, HR9 5NX
🍺 10-11; 12-10.30 Sun
☎ (01989) 562765

🍎 Westons

A 17th-century drinking house positioned proudly on the old market place. It has recently been refurbished to a high standard, maintaining many traditional aspects. Scrubbed tables and sofas at the front of house give way to a long narrow bar with a clean refectory feel, plus a pool and games area at the rear. This pub

is popular with all, but the younger set dominates weekend evenings when it can get very loud and busy. Modern-style bar food and a children's menu is available all day. ᴁ❀🌙🍴

Truffles Delicatessen
High Street, HR9 5HG
🍺 9-5.30 Mon-Sat
☎ (01989) 762336

🍎 Varies (bottled)

Stockist of bottled cider from various Herefordshire producers (Broome Farm, Gwatkin, Oliver's) among many other good things.

TITLEY

Stagg Inn & Restaurant
HR5 3RL (on B4355)
🍺 12-3, 6.30-11 (not Mon); 12-3 Sun
☎ (01544) 230221
www.kc3.co.uk/stagg/info.html

🍎 Dunkertons (bottled)

Originally called the Balance Inn as wool would have been weighed here, it was renamed and refaced in 1833 by the diarist Eliza Greenly. Thanks to her, we have the large light rooms in use today at the front of this splendid inn. Nationally renowned food is prepared from ingredients carefully sourced from small, independent food producers, and the menu is interesting and varied. Outside the dining rooms, diners may elect to join local drinkers in the cosy beamed bar – or even eat al fresco in the garden in summer. Very popular – booking for food is essential. Q❀🌙🍴 🏠P

WELLINGTON

Wellington Inn
HR4 8AT (half a mile W of A49)
🍺 12-3 (not Mon), 6-11; 12-3, 7-10.30 Sun
☎ (01432) 830367

🍎 Westons

Thriving traditional village hostelry with a welcoming public bar, where wooden benches contrast with opulent leather sofas. A separate barn-style restaurant is popular with diners. Commended in the Tastes of Herefordshire 2004, food is a real speciality, with bar snacks, an elaborate lunchtime and evening menu and a carvery on Sunday. The bar has interesting local photographs, board games and newspapers. Guest beers are mainly from micro breweries and Westons First Quality cider is served. ♨️🍺🔔♣🔔P

Hertfordshire

ALLENS GREEN

Queen's Head
CM21 0LS
⏮️ 12-2.30 (not Mon-Tue), 5-11; 12-11 Sat; 12-10.30 Sun
☎ (01279) 723393
www.shirevillageinns.co.uk

🍎 Varies

🍎 Westons

Old McMullen's pub closed in 1995, was converted into separate house and pub and re-opened in June 2001. It is now the focal point of the village and has been kept deliberately traditional. Meals served all day at weekends.
Q🛋️🍺🔔♿♣🔔P✂️

BENINGTON

Lordship Arms
42 Whempstead Road, SG2 7BX
OS308227
⏮️ 12-3, 6-11; 12-3, 7-10.30 Sun
☎ (01438) 869665

🍎 Varies

Friendly, one-bar pub voted local CAMRA Pub of the Year 1997, 1999 and 2000. The pub features telephone memorabilia

and has a good selection of real ales. Curry nights every Wednesday are popular. It is hard to find: go three miles east of Stevenage via B1037. ♨️🍺🔔🔔P🔔

HITCHIN

Half Moon
57 Queen Street, SG4 9TZ
⏮️ 12-2.30, 5-11; 12-2.30, 5-10.30 Sun
☎ (01462) 452448

🍎 Varies

Former coaching inn on the edge of this historic market town. There is always a friendly welcome with cider and perry always available with a wider selection for beer festivals. Regular programme of events include curry and quiz nights – phone for details. Well-behaved dogs welcome. ♨️🍺🔔⇌ (Hitchin) ♣🔔P✂️

Sunrunner
24 Bancroft, SG5 1JW
⏮️ 11-11; 11-10.30 Sun
☎ (01462) 440717
www.sunrunner.co.uk

🍎 Thatches, Westons

🍎 Westons

Busy town-centre pub usually selling ciders or perries. The Wednesday folk night is always popular. A range of real ales and foreign beers are also available. Evening meals served on Tuesday and Thursday. 🍺🔔⇌🔔

OLD KNEBWORTH

Lytton Arms
Park Lane, SG3 6QB OS229202
⏮️ 11-11; 12-10.30 Sun
☎ (01438) 812312
www.lyttonarms-herts.co.uk

🍎 Varies

Popular large 19th-century pub designed

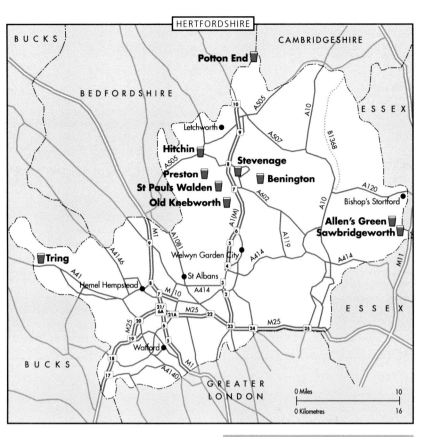

by Lutyens and adjoining the Knebworth House estate. It offers an extensive selection of food and hosts regular beer festivals. ⚒️🍺🐾⬅️◐⊞📷P🗓️

POTTON END

Plough
Plough Lane, HP4 2QS
🍴 11-3, 5-11; 11-11 Fri-Sat;
12-10.30 Sun
☎ (01442) 865391 / 876409

🍏 Addlestones

Lunchtime meals served 11-2.30 daily. Darts, cards and dominoes played. Children are welcome until 8pm.
⚒️🐾◐👶♣🗓️

PRESTON

Red Lion
The Green, SG4 7UD (Signposted from B651)
🍴 12-2.30, 5.30-11; 12-3, 7-10.30 Sun
☎ (01462) 459585

🍏 Varies

🍶 Varies

This attractive Georgian-style free house on the village green became Britain's first community-owned pub in the 1980s. The landlord was persuaded to stock real cider and perry for the first CAMRA cider and perry month and has never stopped since. Excellent home-cooked food using local supplies provides a varied menu (lunchtime meals 12-3 weekdays, no eve meal Tue). ⚶Q❀❄◑&♣🏠P

SAWBRIDGEWORTH

Gate
81 London Road CM21 9JJ
🍺 11.30-2.30, 6-11; 11.30-11 Fri-Sat; 12-10.30 Sun
☎ (01279) 722313

🍎 Varies

Small pub catering for the local community. Small car park is also used for the pub's beer and cider festival. Real cider is on sale most of the time, although the make varies. The main bar displays over 2000 pump clips showing the variety of ales that have been served over the past few years. ❄◑&⇌♣🏠P

STEVENAGE

Our Mutual Friend
Broadwater Crescent, SG2 8EH
🍺 12-11; 12-10.30 Sun
☎ (01438) 312282

🍎 Varies

🍎 Varies

Two-bar estate pub run by local CAMRA members. Beer festivals and live music sessions are held regularly. Local CAMRA Pub of the Season and Most Improved Pub of the Year 2002. Good pub food is served (12-3.30 Mon-Sat; 12.30-2.30 Sun roast). The pub is one mile off A1(M) J7, off A602 – turn right at roundabout with Esso garage close to football ground. Q❄◑⊟♣🏠P⊟

ST PAUL'S WALDEN

Strathmore Arms
London Road, SG4 8BT (on B656)
🍺 12-2.30 (Tue-Thu), 5 (6 Mon)-11; 12-11 Fri-Sat; 12-10.30 Sun

☎ (01438) 871654

🍎 Varies (summer only)

🍏 Varies (summer only)

Pretty country pub next to the Bowes-Lyon estate. The pub has recently been refurbished and offers good food and a fine selection of real ales, including many from micro-breweries. Q❧❄◑ Å♣🏠P⊟

TRING

Kings Arms
King Street, HP23 6BE
🍺 12-2.30 (3 Fri), 7-11; 11.30-3, 7-11 Sat; 12-4, 7-10.30 Sun
☎ (01442) 823318

🍎 Varies (draught & bottled)

Local CAMRA Pub of the Year for several years. Real cider is stocked for apple month and features in summer or on an occasional basis, especially at the August bank holiday beer festival. ⚶Q❄◑♣🏠✂

Isle of Wight

BRADING

Yarbridge Inn
PO36 0AA
🍺 11-11 summer; 11-3, 5-11 winter; 12-10.30 Sun
☎ (01983) 404212
www.yarbridgeinnn.co.uk

🍎 Varies

Previously known as the Anglers, this is a very pleasant single bar pub with an interesting selection of ever-changing ales. It provides a dining area and a menu including specials board and a choice of roast on Sundays. Outside is a safe area for children with an adventure playground and a paved area with parasols. There is plenty of railway memorabilia, its own model train and the

Brading to Sandown line at the bottom of the garden. ⊛◑▲⇌♣🖻P⊬🗂

Fat Cat
Sandpipers, Coastguard Lane, PO40 9QX
▶ 11-11; 10.30-10.30 Sun
☎ (01983) 758500
fatcats@btconnect.com
www.sandpipershotel.com

🍎 Varies

🍎 Varies

A real gem, tucked away within the Sandpipers Hotel and situated between Freshwater Bay and the Afton Nature Reserve. There is always an ever-changing range of ales on offer. This is a unique pub and well worth a visit, especially at the end of March for the biggest real ale festival on the island with 60 ales on offer. For the children there is an adventure playground and cosy playroom with games and amusements.
🛏Q🛇⊛🛏◑❶⅃♿▲♣🖻P⊬🗂

Travellers Joy
85 Pallance Road, PO31 8LS
▶ 11-2.30, 5-11; 11-11 Fri-Sat; 12-3, 7-10.30 Sun
☎ (01983) 298024
www.tjoy.co.uk

🍎 Westons

Offering one of the best choices of cask ales on the Isle of Wight, this well renovated and extended old country inn was the islands first beer exhibition house. Island drinkers owe much to the Travellers Joy, it is deservedly favoured by local CAMRA members who voted it Pub of the Year on no less than five occasions. Always at least eight beers on offer and a good range of home-cooked food. 🛏🛇⊛◑▲♣🖻P⊬

Kent

Red Lion
Ashford Road, ME13 0NX (on A251)
▶ 12-3, 6-11; 12-11 Fri-Sat; 12-10.30 Sun
☎ (01233) 740320

🍎 Johnsons

The pub dates from 1546 and its naturally cool cellar was once a morgue! Live bands perform on Friday evening. Beer festivals are held over Easter and August bank holidays. Camping available in pub grounds by prior arrangement. 🛏⊛◑▲♣🖻P

Yew Tree
CT15 7JH
▶ 12-3, 6-11 Tue-Fri (closed Mon); 12-11 Sat; 12-7 Sun
☎ (01304) 831619

🍎 Biddenden

Country pub and restaurant offering a wide choice of micro and small brewery ales, with particular emphasis on Kentish brews. Mild is usually available. Discounts are available to CAMRA members at certain times. Q⊛◑🖻P⊬

Three Chimneys
Hare Plain Road, TN27 8LW TQ826388 (On A262, 1 mile W of village)
▶ 11.30-3, 6-11; 12-3, 7-10.30 Sun
☎ (01580) 291472

🍎 Biddenden

Superb unspoilt country pub built in 1640. It has two bars and a separate dining room: the public bar is one of the finest in Kent. Excellent food from an imaginative menu. 🛏Q🛇⊛◑❶🖻P⊬

BRENCHLEY

Halfway House
Horsmonden Road, TN12 7AX
🍺 12-3, 6-11; 12-3, 7-10.30 Sun
☎ (01892) 722526

🍎 Chiddingstone

Attractive, recently refurbished pub providing a range of seating areas on different levels. Real ale is served from the cask and a good range of food is available. ♨Q✿✉🎐 🖃📷P✦✁

CANTERBURY

Simple Simon's
3-9 Church Lane, CT1 2AG
🍺 11-11; 12-10.30 Sun
☎ (01227) 762355

🍎 Biddenden

Stone-floored, heavily timbered Kentish Hall House built between 1350 and 1450. Regular live music. ♨✿🎐≈ (Canterbury West) 📷

CAPEL

Dovecote Inn
Alders Road, TN12 6FU OS643441
🍺 12-3, 6-11; 12-3, 7-10.30 Sun
☎ (01892) 835966

🍎 Chiddingstone

Set in a row of cottages in a hamlet half a mile west of the A228 between Colts Hill and Tudeley and featuring bare-bricked walls and beamed ceilings. The food is good value and the curry night on Thursday is popular. An attractive garden is complete with dovecote and climbing frame. ♨Q✿🎐Å📷P

COOLING

Horseshoe & Castle
The Street, ME3 8DJ
🍺 11.30-3, 7-11; 12-4, 7-10.30 Sun

☎ (01634) 221691
www.horseshoeandcastle.co.uk

🍎 Addlestones

Recently reprieved from the threat of Cliffe airport, the pub nestles in the middle of a peaceful village, close to an RSPB bird and nature reserve. Seafood is a speciality on an interesting menu (no food served Sun-Mon eve). The local graveyard boasts tombstones that were described in Charles Dickens' Great Expectations and the nearby ruined castle was once owned by Sir John Oldcastle on whom Shakespeare's Falstaff was modelled. ♨Q✿✉🎐 📷P

DOVER

Blake's
52 Castle Street, CT16 1PJ
🍺 11-3, 6-11; 6-10.30 Sun (summer only)
☎ (01304) 202194
www.blakesofdover.com

🍎 Thatchers

Located in a mid-19th-century terrace 100 metres from the Market Square, this popular cellar bar has a fine selection of malt whiskies and a ground-floor restaurant renowned for its seafood. Q✿✉🎐≈ (Dover Priory) 📷

EDENBRIDGE

Wheatsheaf Inn
Marsh Green, TN8 5QL
🍺 11-11; 12-10.30 Sun
☎ (01732) 864091
www.thewheatsheaf.net

🍎 Biddenden

A friendly country pub in the centre of the village on the B2028. Up to eight real ales including a mild are always available. Home-cooked food with vegetarian options is served daily. ♨Q❦✿🎐🖃❄♣📷P

FOLKESTONE

Chambers
Radnor Chambers, Cheriton Place, CT20 2BB
🍺 12-11; 12-10.30 Sun
☎ (01303) 223333

🍎 Biddenden

Busy pub with spacious cellar bar divided into two areas with secluded seating corners. No food served Friday evening.
◑➔ (Folkestone Central) 🏠

FORDCOMBE

Chafford Arms
Spring Hill, TN3 0SA
🍺 11.45-3, 6.30-11; 11-11 Sat; 12-4, 7-10.30 Sun
☎ (01892) 740267

🍎 Chafford (draught & bottled)

Attractive Victorian building close to the village green and with a pleasant garden. Popular with diners; fish is a speciality eve meals Tue-Sat). ♨❀◑♣🏠P

GILLINGHAM

Will Adams
73 Saxton Street, ME7 5EG
🍺 7-11; 12-3, 7-11 Sat; 12-4, 8-10.30 Sun
☎ (01634) 575902

🍎 Moles, Westons

Small, friendly one-bar back-street local close to Gillingham Football Club. ❀➔ Gillingham) 🏠

GRAVESEND

Crown & Thistle
44 The Terrace, DA12 2BJ
🍺 11-11; 12-10.30 Sun
☎ (01474) 326049
www.crownandthistle.org.uk

🍎 Varies

A warm and convivial atmosphere fills

this small Georgian gem off the inner ring road near the River Thames. Indian, Chinese or Thai meals can be ordered at the bar (check times) to be consumed on or off the premises. Occasional live music but no TV, fruit machines or children. Local CAMRA Pub of the Year 2003
❀◑➔ (Gravesend) 🏠⌿

HACKLINGE

Coach & Horses
Sandwich Road, CT14 0AT
🍺 11-11; 12-10.30 Sun
☎ (01304) 617063

🍎 Westons

Restaurant and pub on the busy Deal to Sandwich road. Despite considerable refurbishment and modernisation it retains a rural atmosphere. Games played include bar billiards. Large car park. ❀◑♿♣🏠P⌿

LUDDESDOWN

Cock Inn
Henley Street, DA13 0XB
🍺 12-11; 12-10.30 Sun
☎ (01474) 814208

🍎 Varies

Popular two-bar country free house that welcomes hikers. May be approached by a footpath over fields from Sole Street station (OS664672). The modern, spacious conservatory leads to a garden with a pétanque area. No lunches served Sunday. ♨Q❀◑⊞▲♣🏠P

LYNSTED

Black Lion
ME9 0RJ
🍺 11-3, 6-11; 12-3, 7-10.30 Sun
☎ (01795) 521229

🍎 Pawley Farm

Next to the church in a small, pretty village a few miles south of Teynham. It boasts good food and a large garden but is still a drinkers' pub. The real ales all come from a small local producer. ⚲Q☸◑🏠P

PLAXTOL

Golding Hop
Sheet Hill, TN15 0PT OS600547
⏸ 11-3, 6 (5.30 Fri)-11; 11-11 Sat;
   12-3.30 (4 summer), 7-10.30 Sun
☎ (01732) 882150

🍎 Varies

This 15th-century pub usually serves a range of draught ciders including one made on the premises. Bar food is available except Monday and Tuesday evenings. Eggs from the resident chickens, ducks and geese are often on sale. ⚲☸◑♣🏠P

ROCHESTER

Man of Kent
6-8 John Street, ME1 1YN
⏸ 12-11; 12-10.30 Sun
☎ (01634) 818771

🍎 Varies

Small back-street pub with rare tiled exterior. It has a single L-shaped bar with two Kentish ciders usually available, one on handpump and the other on top pressure. Small producers from Kent provide real ales to supplement Belgian and German beers on draught. ⚲☸≠ (Rochester) ♣🏠

SNARGATE

Red Lion
TN29 9UK (on B2080, N of A259/B2070 at Brenzett)
⏸ 12-3, 7-11; 12-3, 7-10.30 Sun
☎ (01797) 344648

🍎 Varies

Totally unspoilt classic free house dating from 1540 is on CAMRA's National Inventory for Outstanding Pub Interiors. It has side rooms and alcoves to explore. The pub hosts several beer festivals each year, the main one in June. Dogs are welcome. ⚲Q☸♣🏠P

STANSTED

Black Horse
Tumblefield Road, TN15 7PR
⏸ 11-11; 12-10.30 Sun
☎ (01732) 822355

🍎 Biddenden

A somewhat austere Victorian building in a secluded downland village near Brands Hatch. It welcomes walkers and other visitors while still being a focus for the local community. The pub hosts a weekend in July when all the real ales, ciders and wines come from local producers. Thai cuisine is served Tuesday to Saturday evenings and the Sunday lunches are recommended, as is the accommodation. A large natural garden includes a children's play area. ⚲☸🛏🚲🐕◑Å🏠P✁

TONBRIDGE

Cask & Glass
64 Priory Street, TN9 2AW
⏸ 12-3, 5-9.30; 11-10 Sat; 12-9.30 Sun
☎ (01732) 359784

🍎 Varies (draught & bottled)

Friendly local off-licence with at least one draught cider always available as well as an excellent bottled selection. ≠ (Tonbridge) 🏠

TUNBRIDGE WELLS

Bitter End
107 Camden Road, TN1 2QY
⏸ 12-3 (not Mon), 5-10 (9 Mon);
   11-10 Sat; 7-9 Sun
☎ (01892) 522918

🍎 Varies (draught & bottled)

Specialist beer off-licence also stocking ciders and perries from Double Vision, Biddenden and Westons. JT (Tunbridge Wells)

North Pole
434 Red Hill, ME18 5BJ
OS696548
▮▶ 11-11; 12-10.30 Sun
☎ (01622) 812392

🍏 Westons

Good value food provided in both smoking and no-smoking areas. Five cask ales are offered alongside one guest ale. ✿⬤ ⬤P½

Anchor
High Street, CT3 1BJ
▮▶ 11-11; 12-10.30 Sun
☎ (01227) 720229

🍏 Biddenden

Traditional Kentish village pub in main street, set back from the road, with car parking to the front. Patrons can choose between a friendly public bar and a quieter saloon bar. ✿⇆⬤ ⬤P

Swan
1 Swan Street, TN30 7PH
▮▶ 11-11; 12-10.30 Sun
☎ (01797) 270913

🍏 Double Vision

A 17th-century two-bar drovers' pub at the village centre. Good food is served in large portions. Regular live music and summer and winter beer festivals are hosted. This local CAMRA Pub of the Year 2003 also has a large car park and small garden and patio. 🏚✿⬤ ⬤Å♣ ⬤P

Lancashire

Spinners Arms
23 Church Street, PR7 4EX
▮▶ 12-2 (not Mon), 5-11; 12-11 Wed-Sat; 12-10.30 Sun
☎ (01257) 481170

🍏 Saxon

Situated on the main road that runs through Lower Adlington, the Spinners is a cosy local dating from 1838. It has a sizeable bar area with alcoves plus a no-smoking dining area. At the front of the pub is an attractive outdoor drinking area. The guest beers are mostly sourced from northern and Scottish micros. There is another Spinners in the upper part of the village so be sure to visit the right one! 🏚✿◗⇌ (Adlington) ⬤P½

Eagle & Child
Malt Kiln Lane, L40 3SG
▮▶ 12-3, 5.30-11; 12-10.30 Sun
☎ (01257) 462297

🍏 Saxon

Outstanding 16th-century local, boasting antique furniture and stone-flagged floors. Renowned for its food, a popular feature is the monthly themed menu evening (1st Mon of the month – booking advisable). An annual beer festival is held over the first May bank holiday in a marquee behind the pub. Tables around the bowling green offer wonderful views of the surrounding countryside, while the front of the pub overlooks the village green. 🏚Q✿◗⬤ ⬤P½

Black Horse
72 Redearth Road, BB3 3DE
▮▶ 12-11; 12-10.30 Sun

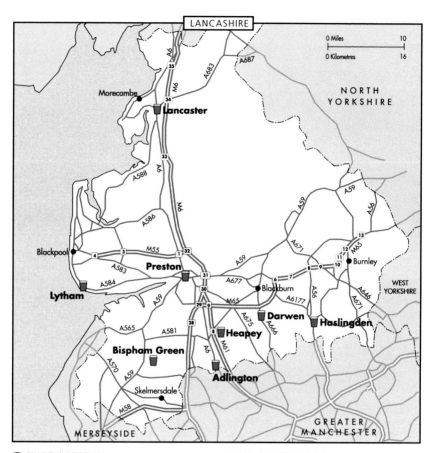

☎ (01254) 873040

🍎 Varies

This very lively community local stocks quality ales and cider. Its annual rare beer festivals showcase over 30 ales and draws visitors from far and wide. Smaller months end mini festivals also take place. Meal deals on Sunday afternoons and at beer festivals are a speciality. Picnic tables adorn the enclosed yard to the rear.
❀◖⅋≋ (Darwen) ♣🏠

⏸ 12-11; 12-10.30 Sun
☎ (01706) 214021

🍎 Saxon

This fine community pub is the home of the Porter Brewing Company. The pub is open-plan with a separate games area. In the large lounge area a picture window overlooks the countryside to the north and the valley below to the Worth. The window in the bar area overlooks the hills across the valley to the west. ⛰♣🏠

HASLINGDEN

Griffin
86 Hudrake, BB4 5AF

HEAPEY

Top Lock
Copthurst Lane, PR6 8LS

▮♦ 12-11; 12-10.30 Sun
☎ (01257) 263376

🍎 Saxon

An annual beer festival is held each October at the picturesque Top Lock, which sits beside the Leeds-Liverpool canal at the series of locks called Johnson's Hillock. This fine country pub comprises a single bar downstairs and an upstairs dining area. Popular with walkers and narrow boat owners, there are eight handpumps serving at least five guest beers including a dark mild and a stout. An authentic Indian menu is served alongside more traditional pub fayre. ⊛🌒❀💼P

LANCASTER

Bobbin
8 Chapel Street, LA1 1NZ
▮♦ 11-11; 12-10.30 Sun
☎ (01524) 32606

🍎 Westons

A substantial late 19th-century street corner pub. Varnished floor, conspicuous curtains and 'cotton industry' theme. The clientele is mainly goth and metal. Music staged Thursday and a quiz Tuesday. Lunchtime meals served 11-3 (4 Sat) and 12-4.30 Sunday. 🌒❀⇌ (Lancaster) 💼

Yorkshire House
2 Parliament Street, LA1 1PB
▮♦ 7-11; 2-11 Sat; 2-10.30 Sun
☎ (01524) 64679
www.yorkshirehouse.enta.net

🍎 Westons

🍷 Westons

On the fringe of the town centre. It features bare floorboards and walls with film posters and pictures of old rock stars. A large room upstairs is used for live music Friday and Saturday and a jazz club Thursday. 💼

University of Lancaster Graduate College Bar
Alexandra Park, LA1 0PF
▮♦ 7 (6 Thu-Fri)-11; 7-11 Sat; 7-10.30 Sun
☎ (01524) 592824
www.gradbar.co.uk

🍎 Saxon

A modern student bar, more like a pub than most, with a much better beer range – eight pumps, not all in use all the time. In a confusing cluster of buildings south west of the main campus. ⊛💼P

LYTHAM

Taps
Henry Street, FY8 5LE
▮♦ 11-11; 12-10.30 Sun
☎ (01253) 736226
www.thetaps.com

🍎 Westons

This snug multiple award-winning ale house is just off the main square and decorated in Hogshead style, with bare floorboards and brick. It is regularly turfed wall-to-wall for major golf tournaments. Look out for the portraits of regulars and local characters adorning the walls! Home-cooked food is available as well as a good selection of ales, with the house beers brewed by Titanic. Service is always fast and friendly even when busy. Runner up for CAMRA National Pub of the Year 2004. 🍺Q⊛🌒⇌💼

PRESTON

New Britannia
6 Heatley Street, PR1 2XB
▮♦ 11-3, 6-11; 11-11 Sat; 7-10.30 Sun
☎ (01772) 253424

🍎 Saxon

This CAMRA multi award-winning single bar, town centre pub attracts real ale enthusiasts from near and far. It enjoys an excellent reputation for the high quality and range of its beers served. Note the splendid Britannia windows. The tasty home made food represents good value (meals served Mon-Fri only). Small patio to rear of pub. Current holder of local CAMRA Pub of the Year. ⚘◖⇌ (Preston) ▥

Leicestershire

BARKBY

Malt Shovel
27 Main Street, LE7 3QG
⫼ 11-3, 5.30 (5 Fri)-11; 10.30-11 Sat; 12-10.30 Sun
☎ (0116) 269 2558

🍏 Westons

Thriving village local with several guest beers and a small restaurant. Pétanque is played in the summer. ≜Q⚘◖♣▥P⚡

CROFT

Heathcote Arms
Hill Street, LE9 3EG
⫼ 11.30-11; 12-10.30 Sun
☎ (01455) 282439

🍏 Varies

Everards Brewery owned community local set on a bank overlooking the village. Though there have been alterations in recent years, the Heathcote still retains a number of distinct areas and long alley skittles. Q⛵⚘◖⊟♣▥P

KEGWORTH

Red Lion
24 High Street, DE74 2DA
⫼ 11-11; 12-10.30 Sun
☎ (01509) 672466
www.tynemill.co.uk

🍏 Westons

Excellent multi-roomed village local that

includes Polish and Ukrainian vodkas among its offerings. Skittles and pétanque are played. There is a no-smoking family room inside and children's play area in the large garden. ≜Q⛵⚘✿⇌◖⊟♣▥P⚡

LEICESTER

Black Horse
1 Foxon Street
LE3 5LT
⫼ 3-11; 12-11 Fri-Sat; 12-4, 7-10.30 Sun
☎ (0116) 257 0030

🍏 Westons

Traditional two-bar pub – a rare survivor in an area full of style bars. Everards beers and guests are available. Acoustic music is played on Tuesday evening. The Black Horse also boasts Leicester's longest-running quiz night (Sun). Q⊟▥

Criterion
44 Millstone Lane, LE1 5JN
⫼ 12-11; 12-10.30 Sun
☎ (0116) 262 5418

🍏 Varies

🍶 Varies

Home-baked pizza and tapas are specialities at this two-bar city local. There is also a range of guest beers and bar billiards. Live music is staged Saturday lunchtime. ◖⊟⇌ (Leicester) ♣▥

Out of the Vaults
24 King Street
LE1 6RL
⫼ 12-11; 12-10.30 Sun
☎ 07976 222378 / 07974 932186 (No landline)
www.outofthevaults.com

🍏 Varies

🍶 Varies

Award-winning city centre ale house run by a manager and regulars from the

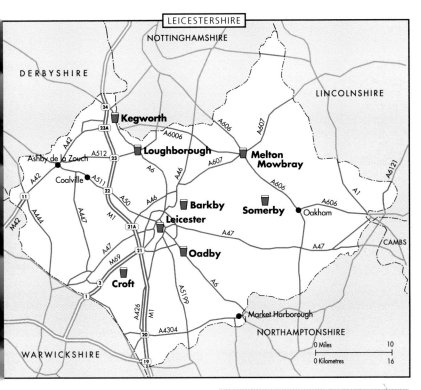

now-closed Vaults pub. Up to 12 real ales are served with regular beer festivals. The ciders are kept chilled and changed regularly. ◖▸⇌ (Leicester) 🏠🍺

Swan & Rushes
19 Infirmary Square, LE1 5JN
▸ 12-11; 12-10.30 Sun
☎ (0116) 233 9167
www.swanandrushes.co.uk

🍎 Varies

🍷 Varies

Corner local close to Leicester football and rugby grounds, it can be crowded on match days. A wide range of real ales and continental beers plus up to three guest ciders or perries are available. Regular beer festivals are held. ⊛◖⊡⇌ (Leicester) ♣🏠✂

LOUGHBOROUGH

Tap & Mallet
36 Nottingham Road, LE11 1EU
▸ 12-2.30, 5-11; 11.30-11 Sat; 12-10.30 Sun
☎ (01509) 210028

🍎 Varies

🍷 Varies

Genuine free house, handy to the rail station. Several guest beers have been brought in from mainly micro-brewers. The walled garden features a children's play area and pets corner. ♨Q⊛⇌ (Loughborough) ♣🏠

Swan in the Rushes
21 The Rushes, LE11 5BE
▸ 11-11; 12-10.30 Sun

☎ (01509) 217014
www.tynemill.co.uk

🍏 Varies (draught & bottled)

Two-bar Tynemill pub, popular with real-ale drinkers from all walks of life. It holds regular music sessions and twice-yearly beer festivals feature real cider.
🏨Q☎☼🚲⏻🖲🚻➼ (Loughborough) 🏠P⌖

MELTON MOWBRAY

Mash Tub
58 Nottingham Road, LE13 1NW
🍺 11-11; 12-10.30 Sun
☎ (01664) 410051
www.themashtub.co.uk

🍏 Westons

Locals' pub close to the livestock market (home to Melton Beer Festival). Younger crowds frequent it at weekends. ➼ (Melton Mowbray) ♣🏠

OADBY

Cow & Plough
Stoughton Farm Park, Gartree Road, LE2 2FB
🍺 12-3 (not Mon), 5-11 (10 Mon); 12-11 Sat; 12-4, 7-10 Sun
☎ (0116) 2720852
www.steamin-billy.co.uk

🍏 Westons (draught), Sheppy's (bottled)

Winner of several awards, this popular ale house serves its own Steamin' Billy beers and several guest ales. Memorabilia from old pubs and breweries adorns the place. There is now an excellent restaurant in an adjacent building (no meals Sun & Mon eve). Q☎☼⏻🖲🚻♣🏠P⌖

SOMERBY

Stilton Cheese
High Street, LE14 2QB
🍺 12-3, 6-11; 12-3, 7-10.30 Sun

☎ (01664) 454394

🍏 Varies

Two-room village pub popular for its food. It has a pleasant courtyard at the rear and guest beers and ciders are served. The pub may have a local cider in future. 🏨Q☎☼⏻🏠P⌖

Lincolnshire

LINCOLN

Golden Eagle
21 High Street, LN5 8BD
🍺 11-11; 12-10.30 Sun
☎ (01522) 521058

🍏 Westons

Former coaching inn at the south end of the High Street which has a cosy lounge at the front and a lively public bar at the back. It is home to sports teams and popular on Lincoln City FC match days. The large garden, unusual for a city pub, is popular in summer. Q☼🖲➼ (Lincoln) ♣🏠P

Portland
50 Portland Street, LN5 7JX
🍺 11-11; 12-10.30 Sun
☎ (01522) 560564

🍏 Westons

Brick-built 1950s pub just off the High Street, south of the city centre. There is a plain, lively public bar with games – and a quieter lounge. Up to eight real ales are also available. With the ground only a five-minute walk away, it is often busy when Lincoln City FC are at home. ☼🖲➼ (Lincoln) ♣🏠P⌖

Tap & Spile
21 Hungate, LN1 1ES
🍺 11.30-11; 12-10.30 Sun
☎ (01522) 534015

🍏 Westons

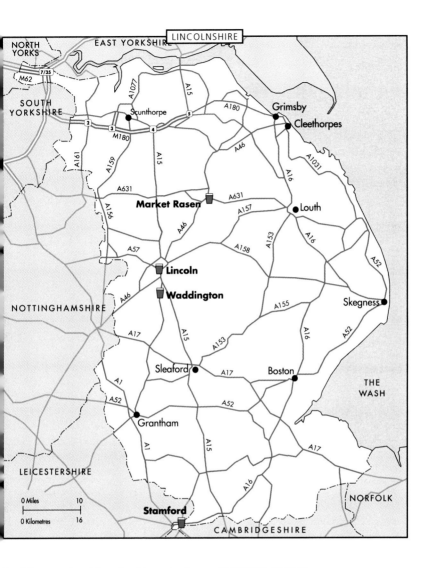

LINCOLNSHIRE

Small but comfortable pub with a mixed clientele, just off the upper High Street. A no-smoking area is part of the bar. Live music is staged occasionally. Up to eight real ales are available. ≋ (Lincoln) 🏠⚲

Victoria
6 Union Road, LN1 3BJ
🍴 11-11; 12-10.30 Sun

☎ (01522) 536048

🍎 Biddenden

Up to eight real ales available in this small town pub that nestles behind the West Gate of Lincoln Castle. Food is served 12-2.30 daily; Sunday roast lunches are also available in the upstairs room (booking advised). Q⚲🕻🖵🏠⚲

Green Man
29 Scotgate, PE9 2YQ
⏮ 11-11; 12-10.30 Sun
☎ (01780) 753598

🍺 Saxon

🍏 Saxon (summer only)

Stone-built former coaching inn features guest real ales from micro-breweries plus European bottled beer. Two beer festivals are held each year in the secluded patio. Two ciders are always available, plus perry in summer. ♨️🕸🅒▲⇌ (Stamford) ♣📷🚭

Clickem Inn
Binbrook Road, LN8 6BS
⏮ 12-3 (not Mon), 7-11; 11.30-11 Sat; 12-3, 7-10.30 Sun
☎ (01472) 398253

🍺 Westons

Isolated country pub on the Grimsby to Binbrook road. Entrance via the games area leads to the bar section and annexe restaurant. There are two small side rooms in which to enjoy quiet conversation. Four-times local CAMRA Country Pub of the Year. Q🕸🅒♣📷P

Brandy Wharf Cider Centre
DN21 4RU (off A15) TF 015 969
⏮ 12-3, 7-11; 12-11 Sat; 12-10.30 Sun
☎ (01652) 678364

🍺 Varies (draught & bottled)

🍏 Varies

Riverside cider tavern – no real ale. Up to 15 draught ciders are among the 60 usually available. Bar meals available most times – ring first if travelling any distance (especially on busy bank holidays). Children

are welcome in all rooms and also have their own play area in the large grounds. This is a smoke-free pub. Q🕸🅒🅓🚻🛏P🚭

Greater London (North)

Wenlock Arms
26 Wenlock Road, N1 7TA
⏮ 12-11; 12-10.30 Sun
☎ (020) 7608 3406
www.wenlock-arms.co.uk

🍺 Varies

🍺 Varies

Famous ale house, usually stocking eight ales, one of which will be a mild and one from the local Pitfield micro-brewery. The draught cider or perry changes constantly. During their October beer festival the range of draught cider and perry rises to three or four. ♨️⇌ (Old Street)⊖♣

Oakdale Arms
283 Hermitage Road, N4 1NP
⏮ 12-11; 12-10.30 Sun
☎ (020) 8800 2013
www.individualpubs.co.uk/oakdale

🍺 Varies

Large two-bar inter-war pub in the back streets between Manor House and Seven

Sisters tube stations. Up to eight real ales from Milton and other East Anglian micros. During three annual beer festivals five ciders and a perry will be stocked. The draught cider range may also be increased for October cider month promotions. Toasties and jacket potatoes served at mealtimes. 🦽◁🄴♣🏠P🄵

Greater London (North west)

NW1: EUSTON

Head of Steam
1 Eversholt Street, NW1 1DN
▥ 11-11; 12-10.30 Sun
☎ (020) 7383 3359
www.theheadofsteam.com

🍎 Westons

💧 Westons (autumn)

Railway-themed free house on the first floor overlooking the bus station in front of Euston Station. Up to 10 real ales are stocked, seven of them guests, and frequent themed beer festivals hosted. Perry is stocked in the autumn and served on gravity. ◁▶⇌⊖ (Euston) 🏠✄

NW3: HAMPSTEAD

Duke of Hamilton
23 New End, NW3 1JD
▥ 12-11; 12-10.30 Sun
☎ (020) 7794 0258

🍎 Biddenden (draught & bottled)

💧 Varies (autumn)

Good-value local in one of London's most distinctive villages. Fuller's London Pride and ESB are supplemented with a guest beer. Biddenden bottled ciders are also stocked and, during the autumn, the draught cider may vary and be joined by

a perry. 🦽◁⇌ (Hampstead) 🏠

NW5: DARTMOUTH PARK

Dartmouth Arms
35 York Rise, NW5 1SP
▥ 11-11; 10-11 Sat; 10-10.30 Sun
☎ (020) 7485 3267
www.dartmoutharms.co.uk

🍎 Newtons (draught), Varies (bottled)

💧 Varies (bottled)

Two-bar local with a mixed clientele. Real ale consists of Adnams Bitter plus two guests, usually one from a micro such as Cottage or Archers and one from a regional. The pub makes a feature of its good food and wine plus an extensive list of bottled cider and perry. 🅼◁▶⇌ (Gospel Oak) ⊖ (Tufnell Park) ♣🏠

Greater London (South East)

ADDISCOMBE

Claret Free House
5a Bingham Corner, Lower Addiscombe Road, CR0 7AA
▥ 11.30-11; 12-10.30 Sun
☎ (020) 8656 7452
john@claretfreehouse.co.uk
www.claretfreehouse.co.uk

🍎 Biddenden

Family-owned free house with one small bar, greatly improved after the installation of new air filters. An ever-changing range of guest beers make this an ale lover's paradise. Note that the cider has to be fetched from the cellar. Two TV sets mean it is busy during major sporting events, at other times it is quieter with board games in progress. Local CAMRA's Pub of the Year is handy for buses (289, 312, 494) and trams. ⊖ (Tramlink) ♣🏠

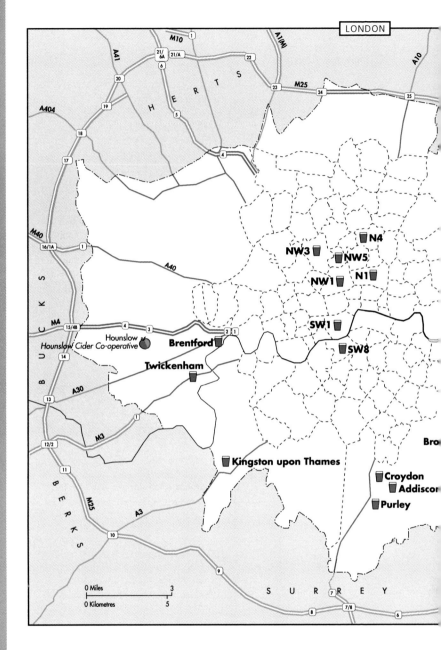

LONDON

N4

NW3

NW5

NW1 N1

SW1

SW8

Hounslow
Hounslow Cider Co-operative

Brentford

Twickenham

Kingston upon Thames

Bro

Croydon
Addiscor

Purley

HERTS

BUCKS

BERKS

SURREY

M10

A1(M)

A41

A404

M40

M4

A40

A30

M3

M25

A3

A10

A404

0 Miles   3
0 Kilometres   5

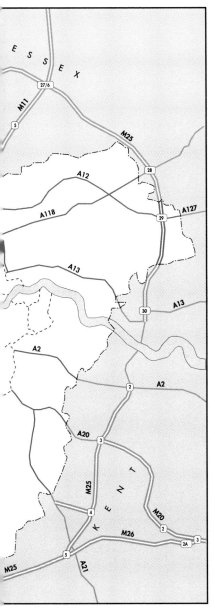

BROMLEY

Bitter End
139 Masons Hill
BR2 9HY
⏵5-9 Mon; 12-3, 5-10
Tue-Fri; 11-10
Sat; 12-2, 7-9 Sun
☎ (020) 8466 6083
nigel@thebitterend.biz
www.thebitterend.biz

🍎 Varies (draught & bottled)

A beer festival in a shop, this gem
of an off licence sells a number of
draught ciders and real ales, in poly
containers or bring your own. Good
bottled selection of ciders, ales and
foreign beers. Caters for functions.
Well worth the visit as it is a short
walk from Bromley South Station.
≋ (Bromley South) 🍶

CROYDON

Beer Circus
282 High Street CR0 1NG
⏵ 12-11; 6-10.30 Sun
☎ (07910) 095945
thebeercircus@yahoo.co.uk
www.thebeercircus.co.uk

🍎 Varies

A foreign beer bar selling a selection
of ciders (normally two or three) from
the Wholesaler Jon Hallams list. This
bar has an extensive range of foreign
beers in bottles and a number on
draught. Also has a few real ales
available including a regular of Dark
Star's Hophead. Well worth visiting
for an excellent selection to drink in a
good atmosphere. Hosts occasional
beer festivals. **Q**≋ (East & South
Croydon) ⊖ (George Street) 🍶

PURLEY

Foxley Hatch
8-9 Russell Hill Parade, Russell Hill Road, CR8 2LE
⏸ 10-11; 10-10.30 Sun
☎ (020) 8763 9307

🍎 Westons

The Wetherspoons formula operating in former 1990s shop premises; small compared to their current ambitions. Plenty of glass, dark wood, partitioning and ornate front windows belie its former retail use. A big addition to Purley's beer drinking scene from its opening, it offers up to three guest beers plus all the usual 'Spoon's promotions and festivals. Q◑&⇌ (Purley) 🏠✁

Greater London (South West)

SW1V: PIMLICO

Chimes
26 Churton Street, SW1V 2LP
⏸ 12-3, 5.30-11 Mon-Sun
☎ (020) 7821 7456
www.chimes-of-pimlico.co.uk

🍎 Varies

Small bar area specialising in traditional ciders, perry and fruit wines. The restaurant serves traditional English food, all prepared on the premises, it also sells a range of country wines. The pub has a bright 'country style' environment with wooden floors and church pews with a relaxed, friendly service. There is a function room for private parties. Cider and cask perry are only sold by the half pint, though it can be bought by the two pint flagon. Q✿◑&⊖ (Victoria / Pimlico) ✁⊟

Priory Arms
83 Landsdowne Way, Stockwell, SW8 2PP

⏸ 11-11; 12-10.30 Sun
☎ (020) 7622 1884
www.priory-arms.com

🍎 Thatchers

Multi-winner of local CAMRA's Pub of the Year. Five real ales and an excellent German and Belgian bottled beer selection complement the real cider. This is a popular, friendly, genuine free house in a surprising inner city suburb. Stockwell tube station is just five minutes' walk away. Bus 77 or 77a Wandsworth Road. ✿◑⊖ (Stockwell) 🏠

KINGSTON UPON THAMES

Kings Tun
153 Clarence Street
KT1 1QT
⏸ 10-11; 12-10.30 Sun
☎ (020) 8547 3827

🍎 Westons

Large Wetherspoons pub in a former music hall with the usual facilities. Trade moves from shoppers at lunchtime to a younger crowd in the evening. ◑&⇌ (Kingston) 🏠✁

Greater London (West)

BRENTFORD

Magpie & Crown
128 High Street
TW8 8EW
⏸ 11-11; 12-10.30 Sun
☎ (020) 8560 5658

🍎 Varies

🍺 Varies

For nearly 10 years this wonderful pub has been serving the finest selection of real ales, ciders and perries. It has been in the Good Beer Guide for many years and has twice been local CAMRA Pub of the Year. It is sought out by visitors from all over the country due to its proximity to Brentford Football ground. The bar recently moved from one cider or perry at a time to three, including one dedicated cider handpump. ✿⊨≈ (Brentford) ♣🏠

TWICKENHAM

Fox
39 Church Street
TW1 3NR
⫶ 11-11; 12-10.30 Sun
☎ (020) 8892 1535

🍏 Thatchers

A nice little back-street pub just off the main shopping street in Twickenham. It has five real ale handpumps and recently took on real cider. Home-cooked food is served at lunchtimes and evenings. Experienced and knowledgeable bar staff and landlord provide a first-rate service. ⚏✿⊂⊃≈ (Twickenham) 🏠

Greater Manchester

ALTRINCHAM

Old Market Tavern
Old Market Place, WA14 4DN
⫶ 12-3 (Tue only), 5-11; 12-11 Wed-Sat; 12-10.30 Sun
☎ (0161) 927 7062

🍏 Varies

Large black and white coaching inn on the main A56 road, only five minutes walk from the bus, rail and tram stations. Opened in the early 1990s, this pub has a bare-boarded beer house style. A recent refurbishment has made it brighter. It stocks the largest selection of cask ales in the area. ⚏≈ (Altrincham) 🏠⊬

BURY

Trackside
East Lancs Railway Bolton Street Station, Bolton Street
BL9 0EY
⫶ 12-11; 11-11 Sat; 12-10.30 Sun
☎ (0161) 764 6461

🍏 Varies

Free house with nine handpumps and draught cider from the cellar. Simple wooden tables and chairs give a traditional railway buffet bar feel. The vast array of pump clips on poles attached to the ceiling give testimony to the past choice of beers that have been available. Can be very busy at weekends when the ELR holds special events. Good choice of foreign bottled beers. Q✿⊂⊃&≈ (Bolton Street) ⊖ (Bury Metrolink) 🏠

CHEETHAM

Queen's Arms
6 Honey Street
M8 8RG
⫶ 12-11; 12-10.30 Sun
☎ (0161) 834 4239
www.queensarmsmanchester.co.uk

🍏 Biddenden

Located just outside Manchester's Northern Quarter, this well established two-room free house, with its impressive tiled Old Empress Brewery façade, justly rewards the uphill walk from the city centre. A large garden to the rear has a children's play area overlooking the industrialised Irk Valley, whilst inside up to six guests are usually available from micro-breweries together with a wide selection of bottled and draught continental beers. The pub is 'biker friendly' and a quiz is held on Tuesdays. ⚏✿⊂⊃≈ (Manchester Victoria) ⊖ (Victoria) ♣🏠

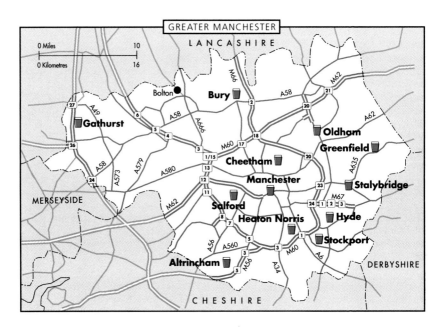

GATHURST

Navigation
162 Gathurst Lane, WN6 8HZ
⫯ 12-11; 12-10.30 Sun
☎ (01257) 252856

🍎 Westons

Extended canalside pub next to Bridge 46 on the Leeds-Liverpool Canal, popular with boaters, walkers and cyclists. Named after the Douglas Navigation Company, who kept the adjacent River Douglas navigable during the 19th-century. The point of transfer for barges from the river to canal is still visible alongside the nearby locks. Food is available daily in the pub and adjoining restaurant (lunchtime meals are seasonal, Apr-Sep). 🛏🌳🐕🍽⇌ (Gathurst) ♣🏠P✂

GREENFIELD

Railway
11 Shaw Hill, Bank Road, OL3 7JZ
⫯ 12-11; 12-10.30 Sun
☎ (01457) 872307

🍎 Westons

Unspoilt pub where the central bar and games area draw a good mix of old and young. The tap room boasts a log fire and old Saddleworth photos. In a picturesque area, it provides a good base for various outdoor pursuits and there are beautiful views across Chew Valley. The venue for live Cajun, R&B, jazz and pop on Thursday, Friday (unplugged night) and Sunday. It hosts top class entertainment each month. Lunches are served at weekends. 🛏🌳🐕🍽🍴❄▲⇌ (Greenfield) ♣🏠P

HEATON NORRIS

Navigation
1 Manchester Road, SK4 1TY
⫯ 12-11; 12-10.30 Sun
☎ (0161) 480 6626

🍎 Varies

🍂 Varies

Beartown Brewery and the licensee have

transformed what was previously a moribund pub into a multi award-winning thriving local. With a long, comfortable lounge and a smaller vault, both served by a central bar sporting half a dozen handpumps, the Navigation is well worth the short walk up Lancashire Hill from Stockport. The cider and perry is brought up from the cellar. Check the noticeboard for which ciders and perries are available. ⊛🚽♣🏠P

HYDE

Cheshire Ring
72-74 Manchester Road, SK14 2BJ
⏷ 2 (1 Sat)-11; 1-10.30 Sun
☎ (0161) 366 1840

🍎 Westons

🍂 Varies

Friendly local with wide range of Beartown beers with guests plus draught and bottled foreign lagers. ⊱⊛◖⇌ (Hyde Central) ⊖♣🏠P✕

MANCHESTER

Bar Fringe
8 Swan Street, M4 5JN
⏷ 12-11; 12-10.30 Sun
☎ (0161) 835 3815

🍎 Thatchers

An excellent example of a Belgian 'Brown Bar'. The 'Fringe Twins' offer a friendly yet robust and occasionally boisterous experience in this characterful pub with its ever-changing wall posters, framed cartoons and bare floorboards. Stocking an extensive selection of continental draught and bottled beers alongside its four handpumps with their local micro-brewery offerings, the pub is very much an alternative to the other nearby free houses in the Northern Quarter. A secluded patio can be found to the rear. ⊛◖⇌ (Victoria) ⊖ (Shudehill) 🏠

Beer House
6 Angel Street, M4 4BR
⏷ 12-11; Closed Sun
☎ (07733) 431153

🍎 Rich's

🍂 Varies

Famous free house being returned to its former glory by enthusiastic licensees. The bar dominates a single bare floorboarded room, dispensing up to six quality guest beers, putting the pub firmly back on the Northern Quarter drinking circuit. Real cider and perry plus an interesting range of bottled beers complete the picture. Function room available upstairs. ⇌ (Victoria) ⊖ (Shudehill) 🏠

Knott
374 Deansgate, M3 4LY
⏷ 12-11 (12 Thu; 1am Fri-Sat); 12-11 Sun
☎ (0161) 839 9229

🍎 Varies

Built into a railway arch in historic Castlefield, the Knott has established itself as an enthusiastically run pub for good beer lovers of all backgrounds. Its unusual layout, furniture and outside balcony (best tried in summer) all add to the atmosphere. As well as Marble beers and guests from local micros, draught and bottled beers from Belgium and Germany feature. The unique open kitchen serves up a menu as varied as the selection on the juke box. 🐾🌓⇌ (Deansgate) ⊖ (G-Mex) 🍴

Marble Arch
73 Rochdale Road, M4 4HY
⮕ 11.30-11; 12-11 Sat; 12-10.30 Sun
☎ (0161) 832 5914
www.marblebeers.co.uk

🍎 Varies

💧 Varies

A street corner entrance takes you into a narrow sloping lounge with its interesting tiled walls, old stone bottles, barrel-vaulted ceiling and mosaic floor. The doorway in the bottom corner leads through to a no-smoking room and the Marble Brewery. In addition to Marble's own organic vegan beers, guest beers from far and wide are always on tap plus a changing guest cider or perry. Excellent quality meals are available throughout the day to 8pm (6pm on Sun). 🌓⇌ (Victoria) ⊖ (Shudehill) 🍴⅄

OLDHAM

Ashton Arms
28-30 Clegg Street, OL1 1PL
⮕ 12-11; 12-10.30 Sun
☎ (0161) 630 9709

🍎 Westons

A friendly welcome awaits in this mid terraced, split level traditional pub. Situated in the town centre conservation area, opposite the old town hall, this free house provides up to six real ales plus a permanent cider and various continental beers are also stocked to accompany the good value food. A seat by the 200-year-old stone fireplace makes a change from the trendy outlets nearby. An array of guest beers, many from independent breweries make this pub well worth a visit. Meals finish at 6pm. ⚒Q🌓⇌ (Mumps) ♣🍴

SALFORD

Crescent
18-21 Crescent, M5 4PF
⮕ 11.30-11; 12-10.30 Sun
☎ (0161) 736 5600
www.beerfestival.com/crescent

🍎 Thatchers

Thriving terraced free house near Salford University, attracting an eclectic mix of locals, students and real ale fans. One central bar serves three drinking areas plus a side vault. Guest ales from micro-breweries are complemented by Thatchers cider and a range of draught and bottled foreign beers. Additional beers are served from the cellar at the regular festivals. Wednesday's curry night is the highlight of the excellent value food (serving times vary). A pub which really does have something for everyone. ⚒🐾🌓⇌ (Salford Crescent) 🍴P🚻

STALYBRIDGE

Stalybridge Station Buffet Bar
Platform 1, Stalybridge Station, Rassbottom Street, SK15 1RF
⮕ 11-11; 12-10.30 Sun
☎ (0161) 303 0007
www.buffetbar.co.uk

🍎 Varies

A national institution amongst discerning drinkers, the Buffet Bar continues its quest to bring new beers to entice the palettes of the good burghers of Stalybridge. Far enough away from the brash concentration of 'young persons venues' in the town, the Buffet Bar remains popular with its cosy and intimate feel and late Victorian charm. Four different rooms each have their attractions and the wholesome, simple food well complements the quality beer. Folk club on Saturday evenings. ⚒Q🌓⊟⇌ (Stalybridge) 🍴P

STOCKPORT

Crown
154 Heaton Lane, SK4 1AR
12-2.30 (Thu only), 6-11;
12-11 Fri-Sat; 6-10.30 Sun
(0161) 429 0549

Varies

Not only is the Crown a relatively rare outlet for real cider in this part of the world, but it even has something for the real ale drinker – 14 handpumps offer an ever-changing range with an emphasis on local micros and a mild. Also has regular music events. (Stockport)

Railway
1 Avenue Street
Great Portwood Street
SK1 2BZ
12-11; 12-10.30 Sun
(0161) 429 6062

Varies

Varies

The jewel in the crown of the Porter Brewing estate. All Porter beers are showcased here plus three guest ales at weekends. A large selection of foreign bottles is also on offer. No lunchtime meals served on Sunday. The Railway has won many CAMRA awards but is soon to be lost (within the next couple of years) to redevelopment.

Merseyside

BIRKENHEAD

Dispensary
20 Chester Street, L41 5DQ
11.30-11; 12-10.30 Sun
(0151) 649 8259

Addlestones

Superbly refurbished Cains tied house,

the ceiling over the bar has been removed to display a central glass apex. A comprehensive range of Cains ales are served from a central bar. Serves weekday lunches. Close to Birkenhead Town Hall, the law courts and the Mersey Ferries. (Hamilton Square)

Hotel California
2 New Chester Road
Tranmere, CH41 9AY
noon-2am; noon-12.30am
(0151) 650 1393

Varies

Multi-roomed, large Victorian pub, once a watering hole for the nearby Cammel Lairds shipyard, it has now been themed as a rock music venue. Features ornate mosaic flooring in the back bar and lots of carved wood. Serves up to five real ales from a central bar, one handpump regularly featuring local micro-brewery beers. Many people come from far and wide to listen to live music several nights a week. It can be noisy but always has a vibrant atmosphere and attracts a wide age range. Serves snacks every lunchtime and puts on a carvery on Sunday. (Green Lane) P

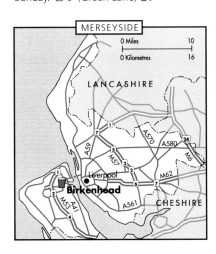

Norfolk

Old Red Lion
The Green, NR11 7AA
⫸ 11-11; 12-11 Sat; 12-10.30 Sun
☎ (01263) 761451

🍏 Westons (summer only)

Overlooking the village green, this 17th-century oak beamed pub also sells beer from Winter's Brewery. 🛏️❀☞✈🏠P✕

BARFORD

Cock Inn
Watton Road, NR9 4AS
⫸ 12-3, 6-11; 12-4, 7-10.30 (12-10.30 summer) Sun
☎ (01603) 757646

🍏 Banham

Former coaching inn with two bars. It is also home to Blue Moon and Spectrum breweries. 🛏️❀◖♣🏠P

GREAT YARMOUTH

Red Herring
24-25 Havelock Road, NR30 3HQ
⫸ 11-11; 12-6 Sun
☎ (01493) 853384

🍏 Westons

Atmospheric single-bar corner local near the old fishing quarter. ♣🏠

KING'S LYNN

Live & Let Live
18 Windsor Road, PE30 5PL
⫸ 12-11; 12-10.30 Sun
☎ (01553) 764990

🍏 Westons

Traditional community pub just off London Road with two bars, a cosy lounge and a larger public bar with TV and a pool table. Four real ales are available on handpump. The cider is kept in the cellar — ask at the bar. 🍺♣🏠🌳

Ouse Amateur Sailing Club
Ferry Lane (off King Street), PE30 1HN
⫸ 12-5, 7-11; 12-11 Fri-Sat; 12.30-5, 8.30-10.30 Sun
☎ (01553) 772239

🍏 Varies

Popular cosy local club which was awarded CAMRA National Club of the Year in 1998 and was a runner-up in 2001. The cider on offer varies and is sometimes from local producers. Seven beers are also available. Lunch is served from Monday to Saturday. Entry is subject to club rules; CAMRA members should ask to be signed in. ❀◖🏠

NORTH ELMHAM

Railway
40 Station Road, NR20 5HH
⫸ 11-11; 12-10.30 Sun
☎ (01362) 668300

🍏 Norfolk (summer only)

Comfortable village local which is set back from the road, with armchairs around an open fire. Camping allowed in the garden. 🛏️❀◖▲♣🏠P✕

NORWICH

Black Horse
50 Earlham Road, NR2 3DE
⫸ 11-11; 10.30-11 Sat; 12-10.30 Sun
☎ (01603) 624682
www.blackhorsenorwich.com

🍏 Norfolk

Large, friendly pub with restaurant facilities and occasional live music. Food served all day with breakfast from 8.30am. Accommodation is provided in the annexe. 🛏️☞◖♿🏠P✕

Coach & Horses
82 Thorpe Road, NR1 1BA
11-11; 12-11 Sat; 12-10.30 Sun
☎ (01603) 477077

Banham

Brewery Tap for Chalk Hill Brewery. A glorious mix of customers – office workers, rugby players, itinerant musicians et al – mingle happily in this no-frills pub with excellent food. Banham cider is always available. The pub is the nearest to the railway station and therefore popular with football supporters. ✺◑⇄ (Norwich Thorpe) 🍴P

Fat Cat
49 West End Street, NR2 4NA
12-11; 12-10.30 Sun
☎ (01603) 624364
www.fatcatpub.co.uk

Banham

A Mecca for all good real ale fans, the Fat Cat was National Pub of the Year in 1998 and 2004 making it the first pub to win this award twice. A bewildering array of real ales, foreign beers and Banham cider caters for all tastes. Rolls and snacks are available. No music but there is a TV tucked away in a quiet corner of the extension for those important sporting occasions. Miss this pub at your peril. Q✺🍴

Ribs of Beef
24 Wensum Street, NR3 1HY
11-11; 12-10.30 Sun
☎ (01603) 619517

www.ribsofbeef.co.uk

Norfolk

Family-run free house that supports local producers. It is set on the river bank so drinkers can moor their boats and enjoy pints while sitting on the jetty. ⌘✺◑♣🍴⚔

Rosary Tavern
95 Rosary Road, NR1 4BX
11.30-11; 12-10.30 Sun
☎ (01603) 666287
www.rosarytavern.cwc.net

Norfolk (draught & bottled)

One-roomed bar near the railway station with a separate function room and large garden for summer relaxation. Bar billiards is among the traditional games available. It is a locals' pub that extends a friendly welcome to everyone crossing the portals. ✺◑⇄ (Norwich Thorpe) ♣🍴P

Take 5
17 Tombland, NR3 1HF
11-11; 12-10.30 Sun (may vary, phone to confirm)
☎ (01603) 766785

Addlestones, Crones

Popular café bar opposite the cathedral in former Louis Marchesi (founder of the Round Table) public house. Wholesome home-cooked food, a good range of real ales and two ciders on draught are available. An upstairs gallery houses occasional exhibitions. ◑🍴

Trafford Arms
61 Grove Road, NR1 3RL
11-11; 12-10.30 Sun
☎ (01603) 628466
www.traffordarms.co.uk

Norfolk (bottled)

A busy and welcoming local on the edge of the city centre, which was awarded local CAMRAPub of the Year 2005.

Annual Valentine beer festival, monthly
Sunday quizzes and occasional music
nights are hosted. There is an
entertaining landlord, especially when he
is engaged in conversation about
Norwich City FC. 🐾🍺🍴

SETCHEY

Beers of Europe
Garage Lane, PE33 0BE
⮕ 9-6; 10-4 Sun
☎ (01553) 812000
www.beersofeurope.co.uk

🍏 Varies (bottled)

🍎 Varies (bottled)

Based in a large warehouse near King's
Lynn, signposted off the A10 in the village
of Setchey, is probably Britain's largest
beer shop. As well as an enormous range
of beers from all over the world, it also
stocks a good selection of ciders from a
number of British producers. Some French
ciders are also available. **P**

THORNHAM

Lifeboat Inn
Ship Lane, PE36 6LT
⮕ 11-11; 12-10.30 Sun
☎ (01485) 512236
www.lifeboatinn.co.uk

🍏 Westons

Pub and hotel on the edge of the
saltmarshes. The traditional bar is made
cosy and welcoming with a fire and lots
of dark wood. A light and airy
conservatory leads onto the gardens for
drinking in good weather.
🏨Q🛏🐾🍴🚭♿♣🅿🍴

WARHAM ALL SAINTS

Three Horseshoes
Bridge Street, NR23 1NL
⮕ 11.30-2.30, 6-11; 12-2.30, 6-10.30 Sun

☎ (01328) 710547

🍏 Whin Hill (Summer only)

Traditional pub with cider and beers from
the barrel, which also serves excellent
food. 🏨Q🛏🐾🍴🚭♿♣🅿🍴

WATTON

Breckland Wines
80 High Street, IP25 6AK
⮕ 9-9 Mon-Sun
☎ (01953) 881592

🍏 Varies (bottled)

🍎 Varies (bottled)

Well-stocked traditional off-licence
offering a good selection of bottled cider,
including possibly the best range of
bottled Norfolk ciders.

WELLS-NEXT-THE-SEA

Whin Hill Cider
The Stables, Stearmans Yard, NR23 1BW
⮕ 11-5.30 (Wed-Sun, Jul & Aug); 11-5.30
Sat & Sun (Easter-June, Sept & Oct)
☎ (01328) 711033
www.whinhillcider.co.uk

🍏 Whin Hill (draught & bottled)

🍎 Whin Hill

Cider maker with free tasting, off-sales and
a courtyard garden for on-sales. The cider
and apple juice is made from its own
orchards. Iceni beers are also available here.
The shop is open Easter to October – phone
for information at other times. 🐾♿🍴

WEYBOURNE

Ship
The Street, NR25 7SZ
⮕ 12-3, 6 (7 winter)-11; 11-11 Sat;
12-3, 7-10.30 Sun (phone to confirm)
☎ (01263) 588721
www.norwichinns.com

 Banham (summer only)

Handy for the North Norfolk Railway, the Coastliner bus and the Muckleburgh Military Collection, this pub serves a selection of guest real ale, locally sourced food and Banham cider. Original Steward & Patteson brewery windows are a feature along with wooden floors in the bar and a real fire. ⚏⚙◑⊟▲⇌ (North Norfolk Railway) ♣🏠P

WINTERTON-ON-SEA

Fisherman's Return
The Lane, NR29 4BN
 11.30-2.30, 6-11; 11-11 Sat;
    12-10.30 Sun
☎ (01493) 393305

 Westons

Cider is served in the surrounds of a 300-year-old Norfolk knapped-flint building. Long-standing landlord and landlady have a stirring collection of long-since-closed locals adorning the walls. This local is a survivor of the Watneys slaughter of the 1960s and 1970s — and rightly so! ⚏⚑⚙⊗◑⊟▲♣🏠P⚘

Northamptonshire

DENFORD

Cock
High Street, NN14 4EC (off A45/A14)
 12-3 (not Mon), 5.30-11; 6.30-11 Sat;
    12-3, 7-10.30 Sun
☎ (01832) 732565
www.cock-inn.co.uk

 Westons

Charming 16th-century Nene Valley pub situated on probably the smallest village green in England. The Cock has an L-shaped bar with a low beamed ceiling, bare floorboards and a roaring fire. The landlord serves up to three guests, often direct from the cellar. Northants skittles feature with the pub having its own team. The landlady is a qualified chef and serves good home-cooked food and excellent authentic curries in the no-smoking restaurant. Very friendly staff and good beer make this the CAMRA Country Pub of the Season and Year 2004. Well worth visiting. ⚏Q⚙◑⊟♣🏠

KETTERING

Piper
Windmill Avenue, NN15 6PS
 11-3 (4 Sat), 5 (6 Sat)-11;
    12-10.30 Sun
☎ (01536) 513870

 Westons

Excellent 1950s, two-room pub, a previous local CAMRA Pub of the Year. The landlord supplies a changing guest beer range, six in all with a good choice of fruit wines. The bar/games room is lively and popular with the young, while the lounge is quieter with a no-smoking policy. A beer festival is held in August. On Sunday evening there is a quiz. Good value pub meals are served every night. Handy for Wicksteed Park close by. ⚙◑⊟♣🏠P⚘

NORTHAMPTON

Malt Shovel Tavern
121 Bridge Street, NN10 1QF
 11.30-3, 5-11; 12-3, 7-10.30 Sun
☎ (01604) 234212
www.maltshoveltavern.com

 Varies

This award-winning free house is full of brewery memorabilia from Phipps and NBC who brewed nearby. Apart from the nine beers regularly available, including a mild, there are bottled and draught Belgian beers, English country wines and up to 50 single malts, make this a discerning drinkers' paradise. Home-cooked food is sold and top live blues bands perform on Wednesday evening. There are regular beer festivals, based on counties. Local CAMRA Pub of the Year 2003 and Regional Pub of the Year 2004. Q🕭🏠🌝⛃⇌🍺

Racehorse
15 Abington Square, NN1 4AE
⏸ 12-11; 12-10.30 Sun
☎ (01604) 631997

🍎 Varies

Lively town centre pub with a mixed clientele and excellent beer range. The pub is divided into two and has a large back room for live bands and other functions. The large rear garden is a fun place to be in the summer, especially when barbecues are held. Children not allowed in the pub but are welcome in the garden. A great place to escape the shops. 🌝🍺P

Romany
Trinity Avenue, NN2 6JN
⏸ 11.30-11; 12-10.30 Sun
☎ (01604) 714647

🍎 Westons

🌢 Westons

This former local CAMRA Pub of the Year is a 1930s two-room community pub situated one and a half miles from the town centre (bus No 8 or 25). An excellent choice of ales is available, sourced from all over the country. The landlord organises many events and stages live bands in the lounge. The public bar has Northants skittles, pool and darts and is always lively. Card-carrying CAMRA members receive a 10% discount on ales on Tuesday and Wednesday evenings. 🌝🍽🍀 🍺P

White Swan
22 Main Street, PE8 5EB
⏸ 12-2.30, 5.30-11; 12-11 Sat;
12-10.30 Sun

☎ (01780) 470381

🍎 Varies

In the centre of the village, the pub consists of one long room with a wooden partition separating the bar and drinking area from the dining area. Five real ales include a guest and a house beer. 🕭Q🌝🍽🍴🍺P

Northumberland

Dipton Mill Inn
Dipton Mill Road, NE46 1YA
⏸ 12-2.30, 6-11; 12-3 Sun
☎ (01434) 606577

🍎 Westons (draught & bottled)

Brewery tap for Hexhamshire Brewery in idyllic setting two miles from Hexham. This former local CAMRA Pub of the Year is noted for its fine home-cooked meals. Ask for the cider – it is brought direct from cellar. 🕭Q🌝🍽🍴🍀🍺P🍷

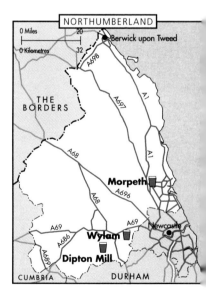

ap & Spile
3 Manchester Street, NE61 1BH
◗ 12-2.30, 4.30-11.30; 12-11 Fri-Sat;
12-10.30 Sun
☐ (01670) 513894

◖ Westons

mall, two-roomed traditional pub behind
he bus station. A selection of real ale is
vailable and the cider is brought up
irect from the cellar. Lunchtime meals are
erved 12-2. Q◖ (Wed-Sat) ⌸◉⦸

oathouse
tation Road, NE41 8HR
◗ 11-11; 12-10.30 Sun
☎ (01661) 853431

◖ Varies

uperb multi-roomed pub adjacent to the
ailway station, offering fine food and up
o nine ales (meals served 12-3 Sat-Sun). It
as quite a following for the cider, and acts
s the brewery tap for the nearby Wylam
rewery. It was local CAMRA Pub of the
ear 2004. ⌂Q⊛◖⌸⇌ (Wylam) ♣◉P

Nottinghamshire

ictoria Hotel
overcote Lane, NG9 1JG SK533362
◗ 11-11; 12-10.30 Sun
☎ (0115) 925 4049

◖ Varies

◖ Occasional

Many-roomed, superbly restored
raditional pub and a Mecca for real ale
rinkers. The pub offers quality food and
p to 13 beers at any time. It features a
overed outdoor area and holds a
summer beer festival. ⌂Q⊛◖⌸⟿⇌
(Beeston) ♣◉P

Bold Forester
Botany Avenue, NG18 5NF SK528606
◗ 11-11; 12-10.30 Sun
☎ (01623) 623970

◖ Westons

This large pub offers a range of six or
more real ales. Lunchtime and early
evening meals are served in the no-
smoking restaurant. There are live bands
on Sunday evening and the occasional
beer festival. ⊛◖⟿◉P⦸

Fox & Crown
4-6 Appleton Gate, NG24 1JY
◗ 11-11; 12-10.30 Sun
☎ (01636) 605820
www.tynemill.co.uk

◖ Westons

◖ Westons

In the centre of Newark, this pub
comprises four distinct drinking areas and
a no-smoking section. Six or more real
ales, foreign bottled beers and malt
whiskies are stocked as well as cider and
perry. Good-value home-cooked food is
served all day. ◖⇌ (Northgate) ◉

Bunkers Hill Inn
36-38 Hockley, NG1 1FP SK577402
◗ 12-11; noon-1am Fri-Sat;
12-10.30 Sun
☎ (0115) 910 0114
www.pubpeople.com

◖ Westons, Varies

Single-roomed pub with high ceiling,
recently tastefully refurbished with mixed

seating styles. Ideally situated next door to the Nottingham Ice Arena, it can get busy at times. It has a varied clientele and occasional live bands in upstairs rooms. Six real ales and a comprehensive menu are available. ❀◑≉ (Nottingham) ⊖ (tram – Lace Market) ♿🍽

Langtry's
4 South Sherwood Street, NG1 4DY SK572402
▮▸ 11-11; 12-10.30 Sun
☎ (0115) 947 2124

🍎 Westons

Busy Hogshead pub just north of the Market Square. At least eight real ales as well as food and cider are always available. Convenient stop-off for those visiting Nottingham by tram. ◑⊖ (Tram – Royal Centre) 🍽

Moot Hall Inn
27 Carlton Road, NG3 2GD SK583402
▮▸ 11-11; 12-10.30 Sun
☎ (0115) 954 0170

🍎 Westons

Two-storey warm and friendly local, originally a chapel, whose features have been retained upstairs. A family-run business with up to 10 real ale pumps, this real ale Mecca is worth seeking out. Lunchtime meals served 11-2. Disabled access available in downstairs areas. ◑♿🍽

Newshouse
123 Canal Street, NG1 7HB SK576395
▮▸ 11-11; 12-10.30 Sun
☎ (0115) 950 2419

🍎 Varies

Traditional modernised, two-room Tynemill pub, one room having a large TV screen and a bar billiards table. The walls are adorned with memorabilia from BBC Radio Nottingham and the Nottingham Evening Post. The pub's name harks back to a time when the

national news was read to customers. Look for brewery names etched into the ceramic wall tiles. Continental beers, both draught and bottled, are available. Lunchtime meals served 12-2 weekdays only. ❀◑⊞≉ (Nottingham) ⊖ (Tram – Lace Market) ♣🍽

Vat & Fiddle
12-14 Queensbridge Road, NG2 1NB SK573391
▮▸ 11-11; 12-10.30 Sun
☎ (0115) 985 0611

🍎 Westons (draught & bottled)

The Castle Rock Brewery tap. Part of the Tynemill chain, this friendly pub is handy for Nottingham station and the terminus of the NET tram line. Ten real ales offered, always including a mild and at least three beers from Castle Rock. No evening meals are served Sunday. Food is currently limited to hot and cold rolls and chilli, however there are plans to extend into the brewery next door, which would enable proper meals to be served. German and Belgian beers and 70 malt whiskies are available. Q❀◑♿≉ (Nottingham) ⊖ (Station Street) 🍽

Lion Inn
44 Mosley Street, New Basford, NG7 7FQ SK556419
▮▸ 12-11; 12-10.30 Sun
☎ (0115) 970 3506
www.pubpeople.com/houseinfo/lion.htm

🍎 Varies

The Lion is adjacent to Shipstone Street tram stop. The pub has a central bar that sells guest ciders and 10 real ales. Food is served throughout the day. An outside drinking area is open in the summer. Live bands play regularly. ♨❀◑♿⊖ (Shipstone Street) 🍽P

NOTTINGHAM: WEST

Red Lion
21 Alfreton Road, Canning Circus, NG7 3JE SK563403
⏸ 11-11; 12-10.30 Sun
☎ (0115) 952 0309

🍎 Westons

A few yards up the Alfreton Road from Canning Circus, this back-street local serves a range of five or more real ales. Weston's cider is always available. An outside drinking terrace is reached via a flight of steps. Good-value food is served at lunchtimes. ✤◑🍴

RADCLIFFE-ON-TRENT

Black Lion
Main Road, NG12 2FD SK647393
⏸ 12-11; 11-11 Sat; 12-10.30 Sun
☎ (0115) 933 2138

🍎 Westons

Spacious, comfortable pub in the centre of the village. Six real ales including guest ales are available as well as cider. Food, with the emphasis on home-cooked dishes, is served all day. There is a large screen TV in the public bar. ▲✤◑⊟&⇌ (Radcliffe-on-Trent) ♣🏠P

SELSTON

Horse & Jockey
Church Lane, NG16 6FB SK464539
⏸ 12-2.30, 5-11; 12-3, 7.30-10.30 Sun
☎ (01773) 781012

🍎 Westons

Family-run village local dating back to 1664 that is reputedly haunted. This former local CAMRA Pub of the Year features low, beamed ceilings and flagstone floors in all rooms. Good food is served (no meals Sat-Sun). The pub is one mile north of Selston; best approached from the B6018. ▲Q☗✤◑&♣🏠P

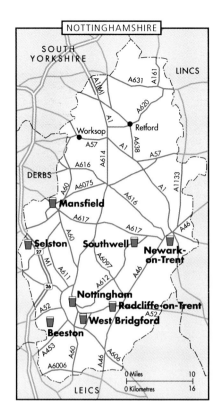

NOTTINGHAMSHIRE

SOUTH YORKSHIRE

LINCS

A631

A1(M)

A620

Worksop · Retford

A57

A638

A57

A616

A614

DERBS

A6075

A1133

A616

🍺 **Mansfield**

A617

A46

🍺 **Selston** **Southwell** 🍺 **Newark-on-Trent**

A6097

M1

A611

A612

A46

26

🍺 **Nottingham** 🍺 **Radcliffe-on-Trent**

A52

A52

🍺 **West Bridgford**

🍺 **Beeston**

A453

A60

A606

A6006

0 Miles 10
0 Kilometres 16

LEICS

SOUTHWELL

Old Coach House
69 Easthorpe, NG25 0HY
⏸ 5 (4 Fri)-11; 12-11 Sat; 12-10.30 Sun
☎ (01636) 813289

🍎 Varies (summer only)

On the A612, near to Southwell's Minster and racecourse. Six real ales are available on a rotating basis. In summer the patio area is popular and cider is available. ▲✤⊟♣🏠

WEST BRIDGFORD

Stratford Haven
2 Stratford Road, NG2 6BA
⏸ 10.30-11 (12 Fri & Sat); 12-10.30 Sun
☎ (0115) 982 5981

🍏 Westons

Part of the Tynemill (Castle Rock beers) pub chain, this friendly pub is tucked away next to the Co-op supermarket. The good food range makes a point of not doing chips. Up to 10 real ales, including a mild, are available. The pub is quiet except on monthly brewery nights. Park at the adjacent pay-and-display car park. Q❄️◑🍴P⌇⚮

Oxfordshire

ALBRIGHTON

Tite Inn
Mill End, OX7 3NY
⫤ 12-2.30, 6.30-11; closed Mon; 12-3, 7-10.30 Sun
☎ (01608) 676475
www.titeinn.com

🍏 Thatchers

Family-run Cotswold stone free house with attractive gardens and fine views of the countryside. Two comfortable furnished connecting bars and restaurant are supplemented by the garden room in summer. Excellent freshly prepared food, together with five well-kept ales and a cider are a focus for village activities. The pub is closed Mondays except on bank holidays. Local CAMRA Pub of the Year 2005. ⚶Q❄️◑♿▲⇌ (Charlbury) ♣🍴P

CHARLBURY

Rose & Crown
Market Street, OX7 3PL
⫤ 12-11; 11-11 Sat; 12-10.30 Sun
☎ (01608) 810103

🍏 Moles

Popular town centre free house which has a simply furnished, split level bar with separate no-smoking area. It also has a patio courtyard on Oxfordshire Way. Walkers are welcome to bring their own

food. The pub – which has twice been local CAMRA Pub of the Year – is one for the discerning drinker who enjoys an excellent pint. ❄️▲⇌ (Charlbury) 🍴⚮

GREAT TEW

Falkland Arms
19-21 The Green, OX7 4DB
⫤ 11.30-2.30, 6-11; 11.30-11 (summer) Sat; 12-3, 7-10.30 Sun (12-10.30 summer)
☎ (01608) 683653

🍏 Inch's

Set in a quiet thatched village with lovely views over the valley, this pub has oak-panelled walls, flagstone floors and a beamed ceiling. It is a Wadworth House with four Wadworth beers and two or three varying guest beers. ⚶Q❄️🛏️◑ 🍴⚮

SWINBROOK

Swan Inn
OX18 4DY
⫤ 11.30-3, 6.30-11; 12-3, 7-10.30 Sun
☎ (01993) 822165

🍏 Westons

Unspoilt 16th-century country inn in an idyllic setting by the River Windrush. The comfortable tap room has a flagstone floor, old settles, corner cupboard and log-burning stove. The cosy dining room has an open fire, unusual alcove seats and an excellent reputation for its food. The large garden with seating completes this pub. ⚶Q❄️◑♣🍴P

Shropshire

ALBRIGHTON

Harp
40 High Street, WV7 3JF
⫤ 12-11; 12-10.30 Sun
☎ (01902) 374381

🍎 Biddenden, Westons

A two-roomed pub by the village green. Cider and perry are included in the two annual beer festivals. The pub is a venue for live jazz. 🏮🕮⌂▲⇌ (Albrighton) ♣🏠

ALL STRETTON

Yew Tree
Shrewsbury Road
SY6 6HG
🍺 12-3 (3.30 Sat), 7-11; 12-3.30, 7-10.30 Sun
☎ (01694) 722228

🍎 Westons

Comfortable free house on B4370 north of Church Stretton, the hills of the Long Mynd rising directly behind the pub. There are two bars; a small public bar and a larger lounge and dining room. No evening meals are served Monday in winter. 🏮Q🕮◖⌂♣🏠P

BISHOP'S CASTLE

Three Tuns
Salop Street SY9 5BW
🍺 12-11; 12-10.30 Sun
☎ (01588) 638797

🍎 Westons

🍏 Westons

A three-roomed pub in this attractive small town on the Welsh border. In the early 1970s it was one of Britain's last four home-brew pubs but the Tower Brewery in the yard behind is now a separately owned business. Live music features on some Friday evenings (pub open until 12.30am on live music nights). No evening meals served Sunday. 🏮Q🕮◖⌂♣🏠

BRIDGNORTH

Hare & Hounds
8 Bernards Hill, WV15 5AX

🍺 7-11; 12-3, 7-11 Fri-Sat; 12-3, 7-10.30 Sun
☎ (01746) 763043

🍎 Thatchers

A locals' pub tucked away off the main road (A442) in Low Town. There are two bars – a public at the front and a small lounge at the back. The beer garden offers pleasant views to the west across the Severn Valley to High Town (Bridgnorth centre). 🏮🕮⌂▲⇌ (Bridgnorth SVR) ♣🏠

Railwayman's Arms
Severn Valley Railway Station
Hollybush Road
WV16 5DT
🍺 11.30-4, 6-11; 11-11 Sat; 12-10.30 Sun
☎ (01746) 764361
www.svr.co.uk

🍎 Thatchers

An excellent watering hole for railway buffs (particularly steam), based in the Northern Terminus of the railway. There is much railway memorabilia to gaze at in the bar and a platform that forms the outside drinking area. Drinkers do not pay parking charges. 🏮🕮▲⇌ (Bridgnorth SVR) 🏠P

BURWARTON

Boyne Arms
WV16 6QH
🍺 10-3, 6-11; 10-11 Sat; 12-10.30 Sun
☎ (01746) 787214

🍎 Westons

The pub is in the centre of this small village on the scenic and hilly Bridgnorth-Ludlow road (B4364), below the Brown Clee Hill. It is an 18th-century coaching inn with two bars and a dining room. No meals are served Sunday evening. 🏮🕮⌂◖⌂▲♣🏠P

SHROPSHIRE

CLEOBURY MORTIMER

Stables Tavern
1 Talbot Square
DY14 8BQ
🍺 11-11; 12-10.30 Sun
☎ (01299) 270382

🍎 Thatchers

In the alleyway next to the Talbot Hotel, this is a multi-roomed pub on various levels. There is a good range of food on offer. The Talbot Square public car park serves as the pub car park. 🛏🍺♿⚓♣📷

CLUN

White Horse Inn
The Square
SY7 8JA
🍺 11-11; 12-10.30 Sun
☎ (01588) 640305
www.whi-clun.co.uk

🍎 Westons

In the old market square of this timeless village in A. E. Houseman country, the pub is a comfortable 18th-century inn with a low-beamed L-shaped bar. A good selection of real ale can always be found. 🛏🐕🛏🍺♣📷

CORFTON

Sun
SY7 9DF
(on B4368 from Craven Arms)
🍺 12-2.30, 6-11; 12-3, 7-10.30 Sun
☎ (01584) 861239

🍎 Varies

🍐 Varies (occasional)

Early 17th-century inn in scenic Corvedale with Wenlock Edge behind. There is a front public bar and a lounge, with an extensive dining room. The pub is the home and brewery tap of the Corvedale Brewery. 🛏🐕🍺🍺♿⚓♣📷

ELLERDINE HEATH

Royal Oak
TF6 6RL
🍺 12-11; 11-11 Sat; 12-10.30 Sun
☎ (01939) 250300

🍎 Thatchers

This pub is known locally as the Tiddly. The landlord, a cider enthusiast, hosts an annual cider festival on the last Saturday in July. The cider is brought from the cellar. 🛏🍺🍺♿⚓♣📷P

HEATHTON

Old Gate
WV5 7EB
🍺 12-2.30, 6.30-11 Tues-Sat; 12-3, 7-10.30 Sun
☎ (01746) 710431
www.oldgateinn.co.uk

🍎 Addlestones

Tucked away in the lanes of east Shropshire, close to the Staffordshire border and Halfpenny Green Airport. This is a comfortable inn with two bars – the old stable snug being several stairs down from the other bar. There is an attractive garden with swings. No smoking in either bar until 9.30pm. No meals served Sunday evening. 🛏🐕🍺⚓📷P

LLANFAIR WATERDINE

Waterdine
LD7 1TU
🍺 12-3, 7-11 Tues-Sat; 12-3 Sun
☎ (01547) 528214
www.waterdine.com

🍎 Westons

🍐 Westons (occasional)

Situated in a quiet hamlet in a remote corner of south-west Shropshire, overlooking the River Teme at the back. The pub is a former Welsh long house

(built 1540) with two separate dining areas. No meals served Sunday evenings. Although the emphasis is on food, the drinker will not be disappointed.
🏛Q🕸🍺🍴◑ 🅰🏠P✂🗄

Bull Hotel
Corve Street, SY8 1AD
🍺 11-11; 12-10.30 Sun
☎ (01584) 873611

🍏 Westons

Former coaching inn in the centre of town, opposite the historic Feathers Hotel. Parking is in the courtyard through the arch. Inside, the serving area is in a central position with a drinking space beyond and a cosy drinking area down steps to the front. 🏛🍴◑⇌ (Ludlow) 🏠P

Charlton Arms
Ludford Bridge, SY8 1PJ
🍺 11-11; 12-10.30 Sun
☎ (01584) 872813

🍏 Aspells, Gwatkin (draught), Mahorall (bottled)

🍏 Gwatkin

On the south side of the town over Ludford Bridge from the south gate, the pub looks down over the River Teme – a great place for an outside drink. Good-value traditional food is available. The pub has just undergone an extensive refit. 🏛🍴◑🚹🅰⇌ (Ludlow) ♣🏠P🗄

Marches Little Beer Shop
2 Old Street, SY8 1NP
🍺 11-2 (closed Tue & Thu); 11-5 Fri-Sat; 12-4 Sun (summer only)
☎ (01584) 878999

🍏 Varies (draught & bottled)

🍶 Varies (draught & bottled)

Exceptionally well-stocked off-licence in this attractive medieval and Georgian town. The proprietors own a small craft brewery in rural Herefordshire and the beer (Golden Ales & Bitters) is sold on draught and in bottle from the shop.

Nelson Inn
Rocks Green, SY8 2DS (Just over A49 bypass on A4117 Kidderminster road)
🍺 12-3, 5-11; 11-11 Fri-Sat; 12-10.30 Sun
☎ (01584) 872908

🍏 Mahorall, Thatchers

A 300-year-old pub of character to the east of Ludlow. There are two bars, the lounge walls being decorated with musical instruments. Mahorall cider is produced on the southern slopes of the nearby Titterstone Clee Hill. 🏛Q🕸◑🍴⇌ (Ludlow) ♣

All Nations
20 Coalport Road, TF7 5DP
🍺 12-2.30, 5-11; 12-11 Fri-Sat; 12-10.30 Sun
☎ (01952) 585747

🍏 Westons

Welcoming one-room pub opposite Blists Hill Museum. This was one of the four remaining brew pubs in England in 1970, brewing having started in 1832. Although there was a two-year break before 2002, there are now up to two ales being brewed at the back of the pub. Rolls and pork pies available. 🏛🕸♣🏠P🗄

Crown Inn
Market Street, TF2 6EA
🍺 12.30-3, 5-11; 12-11 Thu-Sat; 12.30-10.30 Sun
☎ (01952) 610888
www.crown.oakengates.com

🍏 Varies

Friendly pub opposite the Station Hotel, noted for its variety of guest ciders and tremendous beer offering. The owner is keen on entertainment and the pub is well-known for its music. Perry is always available at the two beer festivals. A public car park can be found at the back. No lunchtime meals weekends or in August. ♒❀◑🍺👦♿ (Oakengates) ♣🍺½

Station Hotel
42 Market Street, TF2 6DU
🍺 11-11; 12-3.30, 7-10.30 Sun
☎ (01952) 612949
www.station-hotel.net

🍏 Addlestones, Varies

A thriving pub in the main street opposite the Crown Inn, with an excellent selection of beer and cider. Two beer festivals are held (May and August). There are three rooms, one of which is a lounge. Baps and sandwiches are available. The lounge is smoke free on weekdays. ❀🍺👦♿ (Oakengates) ♣🍺½

RATLINGHOPE

Horseshoe Inn
The Bridges, SY5 0ST OS 394965
🍺 11-11; 12-10.30 Sun
☎ (01588) 650260

🍏 Westons

A 400-year-old inn with literary connections. Picturesquely located just off the back road from Shrewsbury to Bishop's Castle, it is in a dip with the River Eastonny in front and the Long Mynd rising behind. ♒Q❀◑♣🍺P½

SHREWSBURY

Coach & Horses
Swan Hill, SY1 1NF
🍺 11-11; 12-10.30 Sun
☎ (01743) 365661

🍏 Addlestones

Comfortable hostelry on a corner site, just off the town centre, dating at least from the 18th-century. There is a wood panelled front bar with a side snug, a lounge bar behind and a dining room beyond that. Look out for the superb floral displays in summer. ◑🍺👦♿ (Shrewsbury) 🍺

Dolphin
48 St Michael's Street, SY1 2EZ
🍺 5-11; 12-2.30, 5-11 Fri-Sat; 12-3, 7-10.30 Sun
☎ (01743) 350419

🍏 Westons

Two-roomed pub on the road due north from the railway station, near the historic flax mill (first iron-framed building in the world). The room on the right is the bar, that on the left is the restaurant – the landlord is a French-trained chef. The Dolphin Brewery is based in the pub. ♒◑👦 (Shrewsbury) 🍺

UPPER AFFCOT

Travellers Rest Inn
SY6 6RL
🍺 11-11; 12-10.30 Sun
☎ (01694) 781275
www.travellersrestinn.co.uk

🍏 Westons

Large, comfortable roadside inn on A49 between Church Stretton and Craven Arms, with an extensive car park on one side. There is always a good selection of real ale. Q❀❀🍺◑♿♣🍺P½

WELLINGTON

Cock Hotel
148 Holyhead Road, TF1 2DL
🍺 4-11; 12-11 Thu-Sat; 12-4, 7-10.30 Sun
☎ (01952) 244954
www.cockhotel.net

🍏 Westons

A lively and popular house in an 18th-century coaching inn on the B5061 (old A5). There are three rooms, a spacious front lounge and two smoke-free rooms, one of which is wood panelled. The pub is close to the football ground. Q❀✉⇌ (Wellington) ♣🏠P⚤🛇

WOOTTON

Cider House
WV15 6EB
🍺 11.30-2.30, 7-10.30; 12-2, 7-10.15 Sun
☎ (01746) 780285

🍎 Thatchers (draught & bottled), Westons (bottled)

Originally owned by Bulmers, this cider house sells only cider and spirits. It is situated down the lanes off the A458 Bridgnorth-Stourbridge road, close to the Staffordshire border. There is a comfortable snug and a larger bar, as well as two outside serving hatches and outside drinking areas. Parking is extensive. ⛺❀🍴🛇♣P

YORTON

Railway Inn
SY4 3EP OS504239
🍺 12-3.30, 6.30-11; 12-3.30, 7-10.30 Sun
☎ (01939) 220240

🍎 Thatchers

A small, friendly country pub at the bottom of the hill to Clive and only 200 yards from the station – a request stop on the Shrewsbury-Crewe line. It has been run by the same family for almost 70 years. The cider is fetched from the cellar. Food is restricted to sandwiches. ⛺Q❀◖♣🏠P

Somerset

ASHCOTT

Ring O'Bells
High Street, TA7 9PZ
🍺 12-2.30, 7-11; 12-2.30, 7-10.30 Sun
☎ (01458) 210232
www.ringobells.com

🍎 Wilkins

Cosy pub near the church and village hall. The main bar is on three levels but there is level access to most facilities via the modern function room and skittle alley. There is a large garden at the rear. The same menu is available in the bars and the no-smoking restaurant and the home-made food has gained several awards. Families are welcome at this local CAMRA Pub of the Year 1998. Q⛄❀◖🍴♣🏠P⚤

AXBRIDGE

Lamb
The Square, BS26 2AP
🍺 11-2.30, 6.30-11; 12-10.30 Sun
☎ (01934) 732253

🍎 Thatchers

Lovely pub in the square at the heart of the village. There is a separate dining room (children allowed). Q❀✉◖♣⚤

BARTON ST DAVID

Barton Inn
TA11 6BZ (Turn off at W end of Keinton Mandeville)
🍺 12.30-2, 4-11; 12-11 Sat; 12-10.30 Sun
☎ (01458) 850451

🍎 Varies (draught & bottled)

Lovely village pub with a large and changing cider range thanks to the landlady who is always seeking new and unusual ciders. Usually up to 12 different ciders available! Curries are a speciality. ⛺⛄❀◖🍴♣P⚤🛇

BATHFORD

Broadlands Fruit Farm
Box Road, BA1 7LR
⏸ 9-5 Tue-Sat; 10-4 Sun
☎ (01225) 859780

🍏 Broadlands (draught), Varies (bottled)

🍎 Broadlands

Farm shop on the outskirts of Bath that produces its own cider. Also on sale are various bottled ciders from other producers, usually Thatchers. It also sells a range of wine including Lyme Bay. As well as all this, it stocks pickles, fruit, eggs, cheese and garden supplies. P

BISHOPS LYDEARD

Blue Ball
TA4 3HE
⏸ 12-2.30, 7-11; 12.30-3, 7-10.30 Sun
☎ (01984) 618242

🍏 Thatchers

Unusual multi-level pub with emphasis on fine food. Dogs and walkers stay away, though! Q🕭🏵◑⛨🍽P

BRIDGWATER

Bristol & Exeter Inn
135 St Johns Street, TA6 5JA
⏸ 8.30am-11; 8am-11 Sat; 8.30am-10.30 Sun
☎ (01278) 423722

🍏 Thatchers (draught & bottled)

A cider house – it sells more cider than beer! Otherwise, it is a typical one-roomed back-street boozer, on the road from the station to the town centre. Named after the forerunner of the Great Western Railway. Q⇌ (Bridgwater) ♣

BURTLE

Ye Olde Burtle Inn
Catcott Road, TA7 8NG
(Follow signs to Burtle from A39)
⏸ 11-11; 12-10.30 Sun
(closed 4-6pm in winter)
☎ (01278) 722269
www.burtleinn.fsnet.co.uk

🍏 Burtles (draught), Thatchers (bottled)

In the heart of the levels, offering cycle hire and a range of menus from tapas to carvery. Originally a cider house, although now much larger, the inn has retained many original features such as open log-burning fires, beamed ceilings, tiled floors and cob walling. 🏚Q🕭🏵◑⛨🅰♣🍽P

CANNINGTON

King's Head
12-14 High Street, TA5 2HE
(On village main street)
⏸ 11.30-3, 6.30-11; 12-4, 7-10.30 Sun
☎ (01278) 652293

🍏 Rich's

Three-room pub with good home-cooked food. It was the 1999 winner of Les Routiers Pub of the Year. Carvery is open Tuesday to Friday. Q🕭🏵⛨◑🍴♣🍽P✄

Malt Shovel Inn
Blackmore Lane
TA5 2NE
(Off A39 E of Cannington)
⏸ 11.30-3, 6.30 (7 winter)-11; 12-3, 6.30-10.30 (12-5 winter) Sun
☎ (01278) 653432
www.cannington.org.uk

🍏 Rich's

A 300-year-old free house with good-value home-cooked food. It is near the coast and Quantock Hills and understandably popular with walkers and cyclists. High chairs are available for children. 🏚Q🕭🏵◑♣🍽P

King William Inn
Lippets Way TA7 8HU
⏸ 12-2.30, 6 (5 Fri)-11; 12-2.30,
   7-10.30 Sun
☎ (01278) 722374

🍎 Taunton

Small, cosy bar and large restaurant in
village-centre pub. Catcott is signposted
from the A39.
Q☕❄◑⊞♣📷P

Bell & Crown
Coombe Street TA20 1JP
(take Coombe St Nicholas Road from
Chard centre)
⏸ 12-2.30 (Tue-Fri), 7-11; 12-3,
   7-11 Sat; 12-3, 7-10.30 Sun
☎ (01460) 62470

🍎 Westons

Converted from cottages, this traditional
pub retains its original gas lighting
around the bar. ❄◑♣📷P

White Hart
The Bays
BS27 3QN
⏸ 12-2.30 (not winter Mon-Wed),
   6-11; 12 (11 summer)-11 Sat;
   12-10.30 Sun (hours may vary)
☎ (01934) 741261

🍎 Thatchers

Friendly, welcoming back-street local
near Cheddar Gorge. The large,
single but cosy bar with a stone
fireplace displays local memorabilia of
White Hart charabanc trips of the
1930s. The small snug doubles as a
smoke-free family room. Regular
music and quiz nights are staged.
❄◑♣📷P✄

Poachers Pocket
BA4 4PY
⏸ 12-3, 6-11; 12-3, 7-10.30 Sun
☎ (01479) 880220
www.poachers-pocket.co.uk

🍎 Wilkins

A part 14th-century village pub with an
emphasis on food. Bare flagstone floors,
plain wooden furniture and a fire
produce a welcoming atmosphere. The
bar area and adjacent function room and
skittle alley are popular with locals. The
pub offers a good choice of three regular
real ales plus a guest beer and real cider.
In recent years it has hosted annual beer
and cider festivals and also supports local
arts and folk music events. 🏚❄◑♣📷P

Queens Arms
DT9 4LR (3 miles S of Sparkford)
⏸ 12-2.30, 7-11; 12-3 Sun
☎ (01963) 220317

🍎 Thatchers

Situated in ideal walking country with
accommodation available. Real ales from
all over the UK are on offer, along with a
guest cider in summer. 🏚Q❄🛏◑⊞📷P

George
Long Street, BA5 3QH
⏸ 12-2.30, 7-10.30 Mon-Tue; 12-2.30,
   6-11 Wed-Fri; 11.45-3, 7-11 Sat;
   12-3, 7-10.30 Sun
☎ (01749) 342306

🍎 Thatchers

A 17th-century former coaching inn. An
early landlord, James George, introduced
his own coinage in 1666 depicting
George and the Dragon. The pub has
been sympathetically refurbished since

2000 by the present landlord whose use of many personal photographs and mementoes give the feel of being welcomed into a family home. The large main bar has a smaller, adjacent no-smoking area. There is a separate restaurant and dining room as well as a skittle alley in an outbuilding in the back garden. Very limited parking is available in front of the pub. ⚒️🌸🚪◀️🍺♣️🏠P✂️

CROWCOMBE

Carew Arms
TA4 0AD (Just off A358 at the foot of the Quantock Hills)
🍺 11-4, 6-11 (11-11 summer Sat); 12-4, 6-10.30 Sun
☎ (01984) 618631

🍎 Lanes, Thatchers

Charming old thatched pub in village centre, listed on CAMRA's National Inventory of Outstanding Pub Interiors. Quaint public bar features stone-flagged floors and ancient settles; other rooms, each with different character, include a converted skittle alley. It also has eight letting rooms. Q🛏️🌸◀️🍺🏠P

DINNINGTON

Dinnington Docks (Rose & Crown)
Lower Street, TA17 8SX OS404132 (Off Crewkerne Road, 3 miles E of Ilminster)
🍺 12-2, 7-11; 12-11 Sat; 12-4, 7-10.30 Sun
☎ (01460) 52397

🍎 Burrow Hill

Old pub once called the Rose & Crown, popular with friendly locals and known for its themed food nights.
⚒️Q🛏️🌸◀️♣️🏠P

DOULTING

Abbey Barn
BA4 4QD

🍺 12-2.30, 6-11; 12-2.30, 7-10.30 Sun
☎ (01749) 880321

🍎 Thatchers

A friendly, well-run pub that serves excellent food but still retains all the character of a village local. Real fires heat both the separate lounge and public bars. A skittle alley, which is also used for private functions, leads off from the public bar. An extensive and growing collection of clocks decorates the lounge. The name is probably linked to the nearby medieval tithe barn, which would once have belonged to Glastonbury Abbey. ⚒️🌸🚪◀️🍺♣️🏠

DOWLISH WAKE

New Inn
TA19 0NZ
🍺 11-3, 6-11; 12-3, 7-11 Sun
☎ (01460) 52413

🍎 Perry's

Old world country pub with oak beams, handily situated for a visit to nearby Perry Brothers Cider Mill and Museum. It is a food orientated pub. ⚒️Q🛏️🌸◀️♣️🏠P✂️

FAULKLAND

Tucker's Grave
BA3 5AX
🍺 11-3, 6-11; 12-3, 7-10.30 Sun
☎ (01373) 834230

🍎 Thatchers

This is a real treasure of a local that has not changed much since it was built in the mid 17th-century. All beers and ciders are served direct from the cask in an alcove rather than a bar. The clientele is drawn from all walks of life and from miles around. Tucker hanged himself in 1747 and is buried at the crossroads. The pub was immortalised in song by the Stranglers. ⚒️Q🌸♣️🏠P

FITZHEAD

Fitzhead Inn
TA4 3JP
(Take B3227 off Wiveliscombe Road).
⏻ 7-11; 12-3, 7-10.30 Sun
☎ (01823) 400667

🍏 Thatchers

Charming village inn with courtyard and separate restaurant. 📶Q❀🎋🚭🏠

GLASTONBURY

Rifleman's Arms
Chilkwell Street, BA6 8DD
⏻ 12-11; 12-10.30 Sun
☎ (01458) 831023

🍏 Wilkins

A traditional town centre pub with three open fires; home-made meals all under £5. 📶👶❀🎋🚭🍴♣🏠P

HUISH EPISCOPI

Rose & Crown (Eli's)
Wincanton Road, TA10 9QT (On Langport-Wincanton Road, A372).
⏻ 11.30-2.30, 5.30-11; 11.30-11 Fri-Sat; 12-10.30 Sun
☎ (01458) 250494

🍏 Burrow Hill

17th-century thatched pub with several cosy rooms, universally known as Eli's. It is unusual in serving cider from wooden barrels in flagged tap room. Cider brandy is also available. Q👶❀🎋🚭🍴♣🏠P

KINGSBURY EPISCOPI

Wyndham Arms
TA12 6AT
⏻ 12-3, 6.30-11; 12-3, 7-10.30 Sun
☎ (01935) 823239
www.wyndhamarms.com

🍏 Burrow Hill

Pleasant, old hamstone inn in the village centre. With exposed beams, flagstone floors and two open fires, it has remained unchanged for many years. Used by locals as well as walkers and cyclists, home-cooked local dishes are a speciality. In the upstairs room a Blues and Roots club meets occasionally, featuring well-known artists. It is served by buses 630/2/3 (not Sun or eves).
📶Q❀🎋🚭🍴♣🏠P

LOWER ODCOMBE

Masons Arms
BA22 8ZX (Off the old Yeovil-Montacute Road)
⏻ 12.30-3 (not Mon-Tue), 7-11; 12-11 Sat; 12-3, 7.30-10.30 Sun
☎ (01935) 862591

🍏 Taunton

Country classic in charming old hamstone and thatch village. ❀🚭🍴▲♣🏠P

LUXBOROUGH

Royal Oak of Luxborough
TA23 0SH
⏻ 12-2.30, 6-10.30 (11 Thu-Sat); 12-3, 6-10.30 Sun
☎ (01984) 640319

🍏 Rich's, Thatchers

A 14th-century pub with bar with four real ales and three restaurants. A separate hotel entrance leads to 12 letting rooms. It is south of picturesque Dunster. 📶Q👶❀🚭🍴♣🏠P✄

MIDSOMER NORTON

White Hart
The Island, BA3 2HQ
⏻ 11-11; 12-10.30 Sun
☎ (01761) 418270

🍏 Varies

This pub is a gem of Victorian design. Its multi-room layout has not changed in years and is worth a visit for this alone. In addition to the Victoriana there is memorabilia from the past mining heritage of the area and also old pub pictures. The beers are served direct from the cask and there is usually a choice of two ciders. This is a popular local in the centre of town. Good bar snacks available. 🚶❀🍴🍺🦽♣📷

NETHER STOWEY

Cottage Inn
TA5 1HZ (on A39)
🍺 11-11; 12-10.30 Sun
☎ (01278) 732355

🍎 Thatchers

A converted cider barn with three separate rooms. Unusually, there is an air pistol shooting range!
🚶Q🌳❀🍴🍺🦽♣📷P

NORTH PETHERTON

Globe Inn
High Street, TA6 6NQ
🍺 11-11; 12-11 Sat; 12-10.30 Sun
☎ (01278) 662999

🍎 Taunton, Thatchers (draught & bottled)

A warm welcome awaits visitors to this recently refurbished traditional pub, situated among some of the oldest buildings in town. Photographs of bygone days hang in the bar room. Outside is a patio and children's play area. Parties can be catered for in the skittle alley. Note that the High Street is not the main A38 but parallel and to the west of it. Q❀♣📷P

PITNEY

Halfway House
Pitney Hill, TA10 9AB (On Langport road, 3 miles W of Somerton)

🍺 11.30-3, 5.30-11; 12-3.30, 7-10.30 Sun
☎ (01458) 252513

🍎 Hecks, Wilkins

Unspoilt rural gem with all the trimmings, including a flagstone floor. A recent National Pub of the Year. Excellent food, ale and cider. 🚶Q🌳❀🍴▲♣📷P

PORLOCK

Ship Inn
High Street, TA24 8QD
🍺 11-11; 12-10.30 Sun
☎ (01643) 862507

🍎 Perry's

At the foot of Porlock's (in)famous hill. A 13th-century part-thatched house where trace horses once were stabled for the climb. It has a large bar and several rooms leading off it. There is a separate restaurant for diners and residents. Guest cider is offered in summer.
🚶Q🌳❀🍴🍺🦽♣📷P⌁

SOUTH PETHERTON

Brewer's Arms
18 St James Street, TA13 5BV
(Just off A303)
🍺 11.30-2.30, 6-11; 12-10.30 Sun
☎ (01460) 241887

🍎 Taunton

A 17th-century coaching inn with a separate restaurant in the centre of a beautiful hamstone village. A beer and cider festival is held in August. Free parking availale 100 yards from the pub.
🚶🌳❀🍴🍺▲♣📷

STOKE-SUB-HAMDON

Half Moon Inn
TA14 6RL
🍺 7-11; 11-11 Fri-Sat; 12-10.30 Sun
☎ (01935) 824890

🍺 Burrow Hill

Several interconnecting rooms (some steps) create separate dining and drinking areas. From the village centre, follow the signs to Stoke-sub-Hamden. Free public parking available 50 yards away.
🏚️🕸️🌙♣️🏠P

TAUNTON

Coal Orchard
Bridge Street, TA1 1UD
🍺 10-11; 12-10.30 Sun
☎ (01823) 447330

🍺 Sheppy's

Typical Wetherspoon outlet serving a wide variety of food and drinks.
Q🕸️🌙♿⇌ (Taunton) 🏠½

WANSTROW

Pub
Station Road, BA4 4SZ
🍺 6-11 Mon; 12-2.30 (3 Fri-Sat), 6-11 Tue-Thu; 12-3, 7-10.30 Sun
☎ (01749) 850455

🍺 Thatchers

This is a gem; a friendly village local where the lounge bar, with open fire and flagstone floors, leads to a small restaurant. The pub is a regular outlet for the nearby Blindman's Brewery and in addition serves up to six guest beers on handpump or gravity. Blindman's seasonal beers are also offered. It also serves two ciders. Games include skittles, bar billiards and ring the bull. A small but imaginative menu is offered and all food is home-made (No lunchtime meals Mon). 🏚️Q🕸️🌙♿♣️🏠P

WELLINGTON

Blue Ball Inn
Sampford Moor, TA21 9QL (1 mile S of A38 Wellington bypass)

🍺 12-2.30, 5-11 (closed Mon in winter); 12-11 Sat; 12-10.30 Sun
☎ (01823) 663112

🍺 Thatchers

Friendly local with excellent food and home to darts, skittles and pool teams.
🏚️🍂🕸️🌙♿♣️🏠P½

Green Dragon Inn
23 South Street, TA21 8NR
🍺 11-2, 5.30-11; 12-2, 7-10.30 Sun
☎ (01823) 662281

🍎 Vickery's

Two-roomed locals' pub with a quiet front bar where conversation reigns and a livelier back bar with pool and darts. There is also a skittle alley and table skittles. Q🕸️🚲🍴♿♣️🏠

WELLOW

Fox & Badger
Railway Lane, BA2 8QG
🍺 11.30-3.30; 11.30-11 Fri-Sat; 12-3, 6-10.30 Sun
☎ (01225) 832293
www.foxandbadger.co.uk

🍺 Thatchers

Cosy, two bar pub in the village centre that serves well-kept ales. The lounge and public bar both have flagstones. There is a skittle alley at the rear. Extensive and good-value menu of traditional and more unusual dishes. A separate (no-smoking) dining room is available. A quiz night is held once a month. Can be difficult to park.
🏚️🕸️🌙🍴♿♣️🏠

WELLS

City Arms
69 High Street, BA5 2AG
🍺 10-11; 12-10.30 Sun
☎ (01749) 673916
www.thecityarmsatwells.co.uk

🍎 Thatchers

The City Arms first became a public house in 1810, having been the city jail for the preceding 200 years. Set on three sides around a cobbled courtyard, it is a wonderful atmospheric building, retaining the small barred windows and low vaulted ceilings from its former existence. One of the few free houses left in Wells, the landlord prides himself on maintaining a choice of six real ales at all times. 🌳🕸🌓♣🏠

WEST HUNTSPILL

Crossways Inn
Withy Road, TA9 3RA (On the A38, south of Highbridge)
⬤ 12-3, 5.30-11; 12-4.30, 7.30-10.30 Sun
☎ (01278) 783756

🍎 Rich's

Large half-timbered pub on a crossroads. Five separate drinking and dining rooms.
🏨Q🌳🕸🚃🌓♿🛖🏠P

WILLITON

Foresters Arms Hotel
55 Long Street, TA4 4QY
⬤ 11-11; 12-10.30 Sun
☎ (01984) 632508

🍎 Rich's

Charming, friendly pub with good food and accommodation. Five minutes walk from West Somerset railway station on the road to the village centre.
🏨🕸🚃🌓🍺♿🚉 (West Somerset) ♣🏠P✂

WITHAM FRIARY

Seymour Arms
BA11 5HF
⬤ 11-2.30, 6-11; 12-3, 7-10.30 Sun
☎ (01749) 850749

🍎 Rich's

This is a rural gem that has been in the same family for over 60 years. It requires a bit of a trek to find but is well worth the visit. Flagstone floors and traditional bar billiards, real fires and no piped music. The real ale and cider are served straight from the cask. No food is served at all. This pub has not changed in the last 50 years. The pub also possesses a large beer garden. 🏨Q🌳🕸♣🏠P

WRANTAGE

Canal Inn
TA3 6DF (A378, 1.5 miles E of jct with A358)
⬤ 12-2, 5-11; 12-3, 7-10.30 Sun
☎ (01823) 480210

🍎 Burrow Hill

Large roadside pub divided up into cosy separate areas by partitions. It was closed until a local campaign forced its reopening in 2003. The pub serves five real ales plus Belgian beers. 🏨🌳🕸🌓🏠P

Staffordshire

ALSAGERS BANK

Gresley Arms
High Street, ST7 8BQ (On B5367)
⬤ 12-3, 6-11; 12-11 Sat; 12-10.30 Sun
☎ (01782) 720297

🍎 Biddenden, Thatchers

An old village pub with views over the Cheshire plain. A quiz night is held on Monday. 🌳🌓🍺♣🏠✂

BURNHILL GREEN

Dartmouth Arms
Snowdon Road, WV6 7HU OS787006
⬤ 12-3, 6-11 (closed Mon); 12-3, 6-10.30 Sun
☎ (01746) 783268

🍎 Westons

🍺 Westons

A small rural pub on the Staffordshire-Shropshire border, well-known for its excellent home-cooked food. ✿◐⊟📷P✂

BURTON-ON-TRENT

Coopers Tavern
43 Cross Street, DE14 1EG SK245232
🍺 12-3, 5-11; 12-3, 7-10.30 Sun
☎ (01283) 53232

🍎 Thatchers, Varies

A 19th-century Tynemill ale house. The tap area has barrel tables and bench seats and beer is served direct from the stillage. It hosts occasional folk music nights. ✿◐⇌ (Burton-on-Trent) ♣📷✂

Plough Inn
7 Ford Street, Stapenhill, DE15 9LE
🍺 12-3.30, 7-11; 12-3.30, 7-10.30 Sun
☎ (01283) 548160

🍎 Westons, Various

🍶 Westons

Local CAMRA Pub of the Year 2004. A traditional pub tucked away in a council estate in Stapenhill. The first pub in Burton to sell real cider. 3-4 real ales. Two beer festivals are held. ✿♣📷P

KIDSGROVE

Blue Bell
25 Hardingwood, ST7 1EG (off A50)
🍺 7-11 (closed Mon); 1-4, 7-11 Sat; 7-10.30 Sun
☎ (01782) 774052

🍎 Gwatkins, Varies

🍶 Varies

This canalside pub has won local CAMRA Pub of the Year many times. It has a good selection of real ales and foreign beers with ever-changing ciders and perries. ⌂Q✿⇌ (Kidsgrove) 📷P✂

MILWICH

Green Man
ST18 0EG (On B5027)
🍺 12-2 (not Mon), 5-11; 12-11 Sat; 12-10.30 Sun
☎ (01889) 505310
www.greenmanmilwich.com

🍎 Thatchers, Westons

A pub since 1775, this free house also offers guest beers from regionals and micro-breweries nationwide. The current licensee is in his 15th year. A list of his predecessors dating back to 1792 hangs in the bar. Serves lunches and evening meals (in 16 seater restaurant) Tuesday to Sunday. ⌂✿◐♣ 📷P✂

NEWCASTLE UNDER LYME

Old Brown Jug
43 Bridge Street, ST5 2RY
(off A52 / A34 ring road)
🍺 6-11 (1am Wed & Fri); 12-1am Sat; 12-10.30 Sun

☎ (01782) 711393

🍎 Westons

This popular drinking venue is slightly off the beaten track. The interior has been opened up over the years but still retains two separate drinking areas. Regular jazz nights are hosted on Wednesday and mixed music nights on Sunday. A late licence has been granted for music nights and weekends. The Jug also holds occasional food nights and mini beer festivals. ✿♣🏠P

NORTON CANES

Railway
63 Norton Green Lane, WS11 9PR
⫸ 12-2.30 (not Mon-Tue), 5-11;
12-11 Fri-Sat; 12-10.30 Sun
☎ (01543) 279579

🍎 Westons

A little off the beaten track, this hostelry is a bright, brassy community pub with a warm welcome. Local CAMRA Pub of the Year 2003-04, it offers Weston's Old Rosie cider together with a selection of six beers, two of which are changing guest ales. It also has a fully enclosed rear garden with a well-equipped children's play area. Lunchtime meals are available Wednesday to Saturday. ✿◑♣🏠P

STAFFORD

Spittal Brook
106 Lichfield Road, ST17 4LP
⫸ 12-3, 5-11; 12-11 Sat; 12-4,
7-10.30 Sun
☎ (01785) 245268

🍎 Varies

Originally a beer house, the Spittal Brook was renamed the Crown Inn to commemorate the coronation of Queen Victoria. It reverted to its former name in 1998. This thriving, traditional two-roomed pub, adjacent to the west coast main line, has been much improved in recent years. The premises are licenced for civil weddings and accommodation comprises three twin-bedded rooms. No food is served on Sunday evening. Entertainment includes a folk night each Tuesday and a quiz on Wednesday evening. 🚪✿🛏◑⊟⇌ (Stafford) ♣🏠P

Suffolk

BRENT ELEIGH

Cock
Lavenham Road, CO10 9PB (on A1141)
TL941478
⫸ 12-3, 6-11 (closed Mon); 12-3,
7-10.30 Sun
☎ (01787) 247371

🍎 Castlings Heath

A National Inventory pub with two small bars; a must to visit. It gives a true step back into history – how pubs used to be. Q✿🛏⊟♣🏠P

BURY ST EDMUNDS

Barwells Food
Abbeygate Street, IP33 1BR
⫸ 9-5 Mon-Sat; Closed Sun
☎ (01284) 754084
www.barwellsfood.com

🍎 Perry's (bottled)

A small fine-food shop that also operate mail-order supplies.

HAWKEDON

Queen's Head
Rede Road, IP29 4NN TL798530
⫸ 5-11; 12-11 Sat; 12-10.30 Sun
☎ (01284) 789218

🍎 Westons

🌢 Westons

Well worth hunting down, this village pub has good views across farmlands and features low, timbered ceilings, stone flag floors and a large open fire. Meals are served Friday to Sunday. 🏚️🕭🕪🍴🕭🏠P

IPSWICH

Dove Inn
76 St Helens Street, IP4 2LA
🍺 12-11; 11-11 Sat; Closed Sun
☎ (01473) 211270
www.dovestreetinn.co.uk

🍏 Varies

Character pub retaining three drinking areas with bare floorboards and bench seating in the main bar and more comfortable furnishings elsewhere. Excellent beer and cider festivals are held in the back yard. Up to three ciders are available including Westons Old Rosie and Cheddar Valley. Q🕭🕪🍴🏠P🕭

Fat Cat
288 Spring Road, IP4 5NL
🍺 12-11; 11-11 Sat; 12-10.30 Sun
☎ (01473) 726524
www.fatcatipswich.co.uk

🍏 Varies

This twice-winner of local CAMRA Pub of the Year is a traditional, simple pub with bare floorboards and lots of atmosphere. This is a sister pub to the Norwich Fat Cat – twice national winner of Pub of the Year. Evening meals are served 6-7.30 (Mon-Fri). Q🕭🚬 (Derby Road) 🍴🏠

LOWESTOFT

Triangle Tavern
29 St Peters Street, NR32 1QA
🍺 11-11; 12-10.30 Sun
☎ (01502) 582711

🍏 Varies

The Triangle Tavern is also the

Greenjack Brewery pub and a real ale house with wood floors, an open fire and friendly atmosphere. There are live music nights in the front bar on Thursday and Friday. No food is served but you can bring your own. Beer festivals are held in spring, summer and at Christmas. 🏚️🕭🕪🏠🚬
(Lowestoft) 🍴🏠P

Surrey

ABINGER

Kingfisher Farm Shop
RH5 6QX
(on A25) OS096474
🍺 9-6; 10-4 (5 summer) Sun
☎ (01306) 730703

🍏 Westons (bottled)

🥃 Westons (bottled)

A farm shop selling bottled ciders. P

CATERHAM

Clifton Arms
110 Chaldon Road, CR3 5PH OS328556
🍺 11-2.30, 4-11; 12-11 Sat;
   12-10.30 Sun
☎ (01883) 343525

🍏 Westons

🥃 Westons

This pub is host to an amazing collection of artefacts relating to both local history and militaria that has to be seen to be believed; photos, uniforms, flags, deactivated firearms, swords, musical instruments, enamel advertisements plus much more cover almost every inch of the walls! Games enthusiasts can choose between darts, pool and shove-ha'penny. Evening meals are served Tuesday to Saturday. 🕭🕪🍴🏠P

CHURT

Crossways

Churt Road, GU10 2JE (A287)
- 11-3, 5-11; 11-11 Fri-Sat; 12-4, 7-10.30 Sun
- ☎ (01428) 714323

🍎 Varies

Charming village pub with six real ales and four ciders always available, sometimes more. A beer festival is held in July with extra ciders. Q❀◖◀◗▲♣🏠P

COLDHARBOUR

Plough

Coldharbour Lane, RH5 6HD OS152441
- 11.30-11; 12-10.30 Sun
- ☎ (01306) 711793
- www.ploughinn.com

🍎 Biddenden

Home of the Leith Hill Brewery, the pub dates from the 17th-century when it was on one of the coaching routes from London to the south coast. Despite being tucked away in a sleepy village, first-rate meals are served in the restaurant and six en-suite rooms are available. In summer the large garden comes into its own.
🏨⋈❀⇥◗♣🏠P

CROWHURST

Brickmakers Arms

Tandridge Lane, RH8 9NS OS377480
- 11-3, 6-11; 12-10.30 Sun
- ☎ (01342) 892212 / 893042

🍎 Biddenden

Split-level, single-bar country free house with a log fire in each part. The building dates from the 15th-century. Walkers and dogs are welcome, with dog biscuits available on the bar. The food is home-cooked with a meat and fish specials board to supplement the normal menu (child portions available). An all-you-can-eat buffet is offered on Sundays.
🏨Q❀◗🏠P

FRIDAY STREET

Stephan Langton

RH5 6JR OS128456
- 11-3 (not Mon), 5-11; 11-11 Sat; 12-8 Sun
- ☎ (01306) 730775

🍎 Westons

This gastro-pub is named after a local man who became the Archbishop of Canterbury in 1206 and was involved in the writing of the Magna Carta. The bar has a welcoming open fire and dogs are allowed if on a lead. Situated in good walking country, by an old hammer pond, it gets especially busy in the summer and booking is often essential for meals. The menu changes daily and all food is freshly cooked, even the bread. (No lunch Mon, no evening meals Sun-Mon). There is a nearby walkers' car park if the limited parking area outside is full. Evening meals are served Tuesday to Saturday. 🏨❀◗🏠P⊬

MERSTHAM

Feathers

36 High Street
RH1 3EA OS290534
- 11-11; 12-10.30 Sun
- ☎ (01737) 645643

🍎 Addlestones

Imposing multi-balconied and half-timbered edifice on the A23, displaying much evidence of the arts-and-crafts movement. Although internal divisions have long gone, careful retention and modification of the original heavy wooden bar, plus differing styles of décor, help divide the pub into distinctive areas, including a rear no-smoking room. Also serves a wide selection of real ales.
❀◗&⇌ (Merstham) 🏠⊬P

MUGSWELL

Well House Inn
Chipstead Lane
CR5 3SQ OS258553
⏱ 12-11; 12-10.30 Sun
☎ (01737) 830640
www.wellhouseinn.com

🍎 Addlestones

A rural gem nestled in attractive countryside down a narrow lane, yet, surprisingly not far from the M25. The building dates from the 16th-century and in the garden is St Margaret's Well or Mag's Well, which is reputedly mentioned in the Domesday Book and gives the area its name. There are three bars; each with a log fire, and a conservatory has recently been added at the rear. Food is of a high standard (no meals Sun eve). Cider may not be available in winter.⚬Q❀◑ 🗏P✄

NEWDIGATE

Surrey Oaks
Parkgate Road
Parkgate, RH5 5DZ
OS205436
⏱ 11.30-2.30; 11-3, 6-11 Sat; 12-3, 7-10.30 Sun
☎ (01306) 631200
www.surreyoaks.co.uk

🍎 Moles

The Soaks probably has done more to support micro-breweries than any other pub in the area. Two guest beers are available and these are constantly changing. On average a new beer to the pub comes on sale every day. The pub has been voted local CAMRA Pub of the Year on various occasions. The building itself dates in part from the 16th-century, but only became a pub in 1850 having previously been a wheelwright's cottage. Home-cooked food is a feature and a number of daily specials are always available – particularly recommended are the chef's pies and the landlady's pâtés. (No meals Sun-Mon eve). Outside is a large garden with goats, an aviary and a children's play area. ⚬Q❀◑♣🗏P✄

PUTTENHAM

Good Intent
62 The Street, GU3 1AR
(off B3000)
⏱ 11-2.30, 6-11; 11-11 Sat; 12-10.30 Sun
☎ (01483) 810387

🍎 Addlestones, Mr Whitehead's

Nestling beneath the Hog's Back (A31) with the North Downs Way running past the front door, this is a gem of a pub in a picturesque village. It is popular for food, especially fish and chips on Wednesday. ⚬Q❀◑▲♣🗏P

SOUTH NUTFIELD

Station Hotel
South Station Approach, The Avenue, RH1 5RY OS305492
⏱ 11-11; 12-10.30 Sun
☎ (01737) 823223

🍎 Westons

🍏 Westons

A much-altered, large, late-Victorian establishment, built for Mellersh & Neale's brewery, to serve the community growing up around the Nutfield railway station. There is a pleasant garden to the side, which is always popular in the summer and features a children's play area. The landlord, a keen cider enthusiast, sells cider from an electric pump at a T-bar. Evening meals are served Tuesday, Thursday, Friday and Saturday. ❀◑⇌ (Nutfield) ♣🗏P

STAFFHURST WOOD

Royal Oak
Caterfield Lane, RH8 0RR OS407485
🍺 11-3, 5-11; 11-11 Thu-Sat;
12-10.30 Sun
☎ (01883) 722207

🍎 Biddenden

A rural pub with varied clientele. It is on a number of walkers' routes and both they and their dogs are welcome. Food is a strong presence, with as much as possible being bought from local farms and suppliers (no meals Sun eve). Goods views over the surrounding countryside can be had from the garden.
🏕Q🐕◑♣🐕P✄

TONGHAM

Hog's Back Brewery Shop
Manor Farm
The Street GU10 1DE
🍺 10-6 Mon-Tue; 10-8.30 Wed-Fri;
9-6 Sat; 10-4.30 Sun
☎ (01252) 783000
www.hogsback.co.uk

🍎 Varies (draught & bottled)

Off licence attached to award-winning brewery. A wide range of bottled ciders are stocked, alongside more than 300 bottled beers. Draught beer also available from the brewery. 🐕P

WOKING

Wetherspoon
51-59 Chertsey Road, GU21 5AJ
🍺 10-11; 12-10.30 Sun
☎ (01483) 722818

🍎 Westons

Large town-centre pub catering for everyone which can get busy at night. The theme is H.G. Wells' War of the Worlds – look for the backwards clock!
Q◑♿⇌🐕✄

WOOD STREET

Royal Oak
89 Oak Hill, GU3 3DA
🍺 11-3, 5-11; 11-3.30, 5-11 Sat;
12-2.30, 7-10.30 Sun
☎ (01483) 235137

🍎 Thatchers

A warm welcome awaits at this free house north-west of Guildford. Six real ales including a mild are always available. 🐕◑🐕P

East Sussex

BRIGHTON

Cobblers Thumb
10 New England Road, BN1 4GG
🍺 1-11; 12-11 Fri-Sat; 12-10.30 Sun
☎ (01273) 605636

🍎 Westons (draught & bottled)

This Victorian street corner pub proclaims that it is an Aussie themed English boozer – hence Aboriginal art everywhere, including an impressive mural in the small courtyard garden. Besides Weston's ciders, there is a good selection of real ales plus guests. No food available. Separate pool room (competitions Wednesday evening).
🐕⇌ (Brighton) ♣🐕

Evening Star
55-56 Surrey Street, BN1 3PB
🍺 12-11; 11.30-11 Sat; 12-10.30 Sun
☎ (01273) 328931
www.eveningstarbrighton.co.uk

🍎 Thatchers, Westons (bottled)

🍏 Varies (summer only)

This is a one-room bar brewpub close to Brighton station with friendly knowledgeable staff. It serves excellent baguettes 12-3 daily. It always has Thatchers Medium cider on handpump with one guest cider and occasionally one guest perry. Besides a selection of four Dark Star real ales, three guest ales are always available as well as both bottled and draught Belgian beers. ※◁⇌ (Brighton) ♣🏠

Lord Nelson Inn
36 Trafalgar Street, BN1 4ED
⮕ 11.30-11; 11-11 Sat; 12-10.30 Sun
☎ (01273) 695872
www.thelordnelsoninn.co.uk

🍎 Addlestones

Friendly mid-terraced, low-ceilinged Harvey's pub in the North Laine area of Brighton. There is an interesting picture gallery at the back, with a tree growing in the middle of it, the room being used for meetings as well as for drinking. Meals are available seven days a week and there is a pub quiz on Tuesday nights. 🏨Q◁⇌ (Brighton) ♣🏠

FIRLE

National Collection of Cider & Perry
Middle Farm BN8 6LJ (On A27)
⮕ 10-5 (Every day except Xmas Day, Boxing Day & New Years Day)
☎ (01323) 811411
www.middlefarm.com

🍎 Varies (draught & bottled)

This is probably the world's largest permanent collection of cider and perry. Part of a working farm and countryside centre, a flint farm building houses a vast array of cider and perry polycasks. You can try before you buy and there is also a wide selection of bottled ciders, meads, English country wines, fresh apple juice and draught Sussex ales.

PORTSLADE

Stanley Arms
47 Wolseley Road BN41 1SS

⮕ 2-11; 12-11 Sat; 12-10.30 Sun
☎ (01273) 430234
www.thestanley.com

🍎 Biddenden, Westons (bottled)

🍎 Varies (occasional)

Good old fashioned friendly back street free house with two bars and a small beer garden where barbecues are held in summer. Besides Biddenden cider there are three ever-changing real ales and a wide range of bottled Belgian beers. There is TV for the sports fans and the pub's own football and cricket teams. Always holds at least two annual beer festivals. 🏨🛏※◁⇌ (Fishersgate) ♣🏠🚭

West Sussex

HENLEY VILLAGE

Duke of Cumberland Arms
GU27 3HQ SU894258
⮕ 11-11; 12-10.30 Sun
☎ (01428) 652280

🍎 Rich's

Difficult to find but worth it – from the A286 turn off opposite the King's Arms and follow the road along. The pub sits in four acres of garden with trout ponds coming from a spring-fed pool. The small bar is little altered and partly lit by gas lamps. Four regular real ales and two guests are offered. Ciders vary occasionally. Meals are served Tuesday to Saturday. 🏨Q※◁♣🏠P

LAMBS GREEN

Lamb Inn
RH12 4RG (2 miles N of A264)
⮕ 11.30-3, 5.30-11; 12-4, 7-10.30 Sun
☎ (01293) 871366

🍎 Biddenden

Country pub selling good food and real

ale. The main bar features flagstone floors and wooden beams while the (smoke free) conservatory is more modern. ⏃⚘⛻⬤ ⬤P

MAPLEHURST

White Horse
Park Lane, RH13 6LL (2 miles S of Monks Gate, off A281)
⏃ 12-2.30, 6-11; 11.30-3, 6-11 Sat; 12-3, 7-10.30 Sun
☎ (01403) 891208

🍎 Varies

Wonderful country free house with a spacious garden, where the large bar has several areas rambling off it. A good range of food is served.
⏃Q⛱⚘⬤♣⬤P✂

SELHAM

Three Moles
Nr Midhurst, GU28 0PN OS935206
⏃ 12-2, 5-11; 11.30-11 Sat; 12-10.30 Sun
☎ (01798) 861303
www.thethreemoles.co.uk

🍎 Varies (draught, summer only), Westons (bottled)

The Three Moles served passengers at the adjacent Selham railway station until Dr Beeching came along, but is now a friendly free house with Skinner's Betty Stogs and three guest beers including a mild. No food served beyond crisps and pickled eggs – except for the barbecue at the beer festival in June! Draught cider is generally only available in summer. Caravans allowed. ⏃Q▲⬤P

SHOREHAM

Buckingham Arms
35-39 Brunswick Road, BN43 5WA
⏃ 11-11; 12-10.30 Sun
☎ (01273) 453660

🍎 Biddenden

Close to Shoreham station, this popular independent free house serves at least six real ales at any one time, has Biddenden dry cider most of the time and a good selection of real ciders at beer festivals in February and August. It has a large L-shaped bar with a mirror on one end wall, creating an impression of more space, and a patio garden at the rear. ⚘⬤⇌ (Shoreham) ⬤P

STAPLEFIELD

Jolly Tanners
Handcross Road, RH17 6EF
⏃ 11-3, 5.30-11; 11-11 Sat; 12-10.30 Sun
☎ (01444) 400335

🍎 Addlestones

A popular free house situated on the village green and a regular entry in CAMRA's Good Beer Guide. The food is home-cooked. ⏃⚘⬤ ⬤P

YAPTON

Maypole Inn
Maypole Lane, BN18 0DP OS978041
⏃ 11.30-11; 12-10.30 Sun
☎ (01243) 551417

🍎 Thatchers (bottled), Westons (draught & bottled)

🍏 Westons

This local CAMRA Pub of the Year 2004 sits down a secluded country lane and boasts three regular ales, including a mild, four guest ales from small breweries and extremely filling lunches. The public bar contains a pool table and jukebox, while the lounge has two log fires, a towering charity stack of 2p coins and lots of drinkers. Low-alcohol cider is available for drivers. Book ahead for the skittle alley. ⏃Q⚘⬤⬤♣⬤P

Tyne & Wear

GATESHEAD

Aletaster
706 Durham Road
Low Fell, NE9 6JA
⏻ 12-11; 11-11 Sat; 12-10.30 Sun
☎ (0191) 487 0770
www.looknorth-east.com/thealetaster/

 Westons

This former coaching inn offers the only real cider for some distance south of the River Tyne as well as 11 real ales, the widest range in the district. The pub also hosts weekly live music and a quiz as well as an annual beer festival. ⬛🍴♣🅿️P

JARROW

Robin Hood
Primrose Hill, Primrose, NE32 5UB
⏻ 11-11; 12-10.30 Sun
☎ (0191) 428 5454
www.jarrowbrewing.co.uk

🍎 Westons

Superb old coaching tavern dating from 1896, nestled on the banks of the River Don and home to Jarrow Brewery and Vincenzo's Restaurant. Six real ales are available, most of which are brewed on the premises, which is boosted to 12 at the bi-annual beer festivals. It was declared local CAMRA Pub of the Year 2004. No lunchtime meals Monday, no

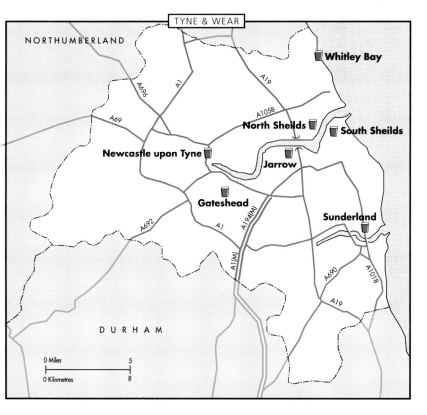

evening meals Sunday. Q✿◑&⊖
(Fellgate) ♣📷P✂

Bodega
125 Westgate Road, NE1 4AG
⫸ 11-11; 12-10.30 Sun
☎ (0191) 221 1552
www.sjf.co.uk

🍎 Westons

Large, single-roomed pub near the Tyne
Opera House. Interesting features include
two differently shaped original glass
ceiling domes. It is a multiple winner of
the local CAMRA Pub of the Year award.
Due to its proximity to the home of
Newcastle United FC, it can get very busy
on match days. ◑≋ (Newcastle Central)
⊖ (Central) 📷

Cumberland Arms
James Place Street, NE6 1LD
⫸ 4-11; 12.30-11 Sat-Sun
☎ (0191) 265 6151
www.thecumberlandarms.co.uk

🍎 Varies

A wonderfully vibrant, traditional pub
which stands alone overlooking the
Ouseburn valley at a short distance from
buses and Byker Metro station. It retains its
Victorian two-room layout either side of a
central entrance. Counter service in the
public bar (left) and a hatch service in the
'sitting room' (right). The pub has
developed a strong emphasis on real ale
and, more recently, cider, and is well
known for its traditional music which takes
place most Tuesdays-Fridays and Sunday
evenings. ▲Q✿◑🔄⊖ (Byker Metro) ♣📷P

Head of Steam
36 Lime Street, Byker, NE1 2PQ
⫸ 11-11; 12-10.30 Sun
☎ (0191) 230 4474

🍎 Westons

Large former bonding warehouse and
whisky bottling plant in the heart of the
historic Ouseburn Valley, now a top-class
music and arts venue. The large L-shaped
bar stocks a selection of real ales, some
quite diverse for the area. Also stocks
Belgian beers, both bottled and draught.
☲◑⊖ (Byker) 📷✂

Tap & Spile
184 Tynemouth Road, NE30 1EG
⫸ 12-11; 12-10.30 Sun
☎ (0191) 257 2523
www.tapandspile.org.uk

🍎 Westons

💧 Westons

This is a popular, award-winning pub
opposite the Magistrates Courts, which
sells a good selection of guest ales. It has
a strong cider following, hence
occasional guest ciders or perry. ✿🔄⊖
(North Shields) ♣📷

Maltings
9 Claypath Lane, NE33 4PG
⫸ 11-11; 12-10.30 Sun
☎ (0191) 455 7189

🍎 Westons

Opposite the town hall in the former co-op
dairy complex. Tastefully refurbished into a
ground floor micro-brewery producing
Jarrow Brewery ales and a traditional first
floor bar with full facilities for the disabled.
An oasis of real ale in a particularly desert
area of town. ◑&⊖ (South Shields) 📷P

Riverside
3 Mill Dam, NE33 1EQ
⫸ 11.30-11; 12-10.30 Sun
☎ (0191) 455 2328

🍎 Westons

Popular ale house at the top of the Mill Dam area and local CAMRA Pub of the Year 2003. Serves up to six real ales and sometimes a perry. The regular cider, Westons, is occasionally replaced by Biddendens. Beer festivals are held regularly. This is a sister pub to the Trimmers Arms. ⌘⊖ (South Shields) 🍺

Trimmers Arms
34 Commercial Road, Laygate, NE33 1RW
⊪ 11.30-11; 12-10.30 Sun
☎ (0191) 454 5550
www.trimmers-arms.co.uk

🍏 Westons

Newly built pub on the site of a former pub that never opened. The landlord is keen and serves a large choice of guest ales. The cider is usually Westons Old Rosie but others can feature when available. Beer festivals are held periodically. ⌘◑&⊖ (Chichester) ♣🍺P

SUNDERLAND

Fitzgeralds
10-12 Green Terrace, SR1 3PZ
⊪ 11-11; 12-10.30 Sun
☎ (0191) 567 0852
www.sjf.co.uk

🍏 Westons

The most popular city centre real ale pub, offering the best choice around and unofficial brewery tap for the nearby Darwin Brewery. It was declared local and Regional CAMRA Pub of the Year 2002. Up to nine guest ales compliment the changing cider or perry. No smoking allowed during mealtimes. ⌘◑⊟⇄ (Sunderland) ⊖ (University) 🍺✂

Smugglers
Marine Walk, Lower Promenade, Roker, SR6 0PL
⊪ 12-11; 12-10.30 Sun
☎ (0191) 514 3844
www.smugglerspub.com

🍏 Varies

'Real Ale, Real Cider, Real Music' is the slogan for this popular seafront muso's pub on Roker beach. Subdued lighting and nautical memorabilia enhance the drinking atmosphere. It is a cider stalwart pub. Although Westons is semi-permanent, others ciders are sourced as and when available. ⌘⊖ (Stadium of Light) 🍺P☐

WHITLEY BAY

Briar Dene
71 The Links, NE26 1UE
⊪ 11-11; 12-10.30 Sun
☎ (0191) 252 0926
www.sjf.co.uk

🍏 Westons

Large roadside ale house overlooking the links on the road to Blyth. A good selection of micro-breweries ales are sold and it is well known for its good food; busy during summer mealtimes.
🛏⌘◑⊟&🍺P✂

Fat Ox
278 Whitley Road, NE26 2TG
⊪ 12-11; 12-10.30 Sun
☎ (0191) 251 3852

🍏 Westons

A busy pub serving a selection of real ales in a popular seaside resort, it was once part of the Tap & Spile chain. The cider has been selling well for a long time now. 🏨⊖ (Whitley Bay) ♣🍺

Warwickshire

ASHORNE

Cottage Tavern
CV35 9DR OS303577
⊪ 12-3 (Wed-Fri), 5-11; 12-11 Sat; 12-4.30 Sun
☎ (01926) 651410

🍎 Westons

🍏 Westons

Friendly, popular village pub with a welcoming atmosphere. A cosy log fire warms the traditional drinking area at one end of the bar; at the other is a no-smoking dining area. When not in use for the great value food, the dining area hosts dominoes and crib matches. Guest beers change regularly, mostly selling out in two or three days, so you need to visit often or miss out on a really good beer from breweries both local and afar. ⚐⚑⚒⚓♣☗

RIDGE LANE

Church End Brewery Tap
109 Ridge Lane, CV10 0RD OS295947
🍺 6-11 Thu; 12-11 Fri-Sat; 12-10.30 Sun
☎ (01827) 713080

🍎 Varies

🍏 Varies

Converted from a working men's club, the brewery is visible from the bar of this popular tap. Four handpulled beers are served, some straight from the cask. The no-smoking pub has been awarded a silver certificate in the National Clean Air Award scheme. A large meadow-style garden offers alfresco drinking at all times. Hidden behind houses, look for the sandwich board opposite the unmarked drive. Lunches are served on Friday and Saturday only. Local CAMRA Pub of the Year 2004. Q⚒♣☗P⚘

ROWINGTON

Cock Horse
Old Warwick Road, CV35 7AA
🍺 12-11.30; 12-10.30 Sun
☎ (01926) 842183

🍎 Westons

Situated just south of Rowington, this

300-year-old traditional inn offers a good choice of ales and food. The pub has a single oak-beamed bar and an intimate restaurant. There is a regular beer festival on August bank holiday weekend, live music on Friday evenings, and a monthly folk club. Voted local CAMRA Most Improved Pub of the Year 2003, this is a popular local with a warm welcome for visitors. ⚐⚒⚓☗P

RUGBY

Alexander Arms
James Street, CV21 2SL
🍺 11.30-3, 5-11; 11-11 Fri-Sat; 12-10.30 Sun
☎ (01788) 578660
www.alexandraarms.co.uk

🍎 Addlestones

Awarded local CAMRA Pub of the Year in 2004 for the sixth time. The L-shaped lounge is a comfortable place where lively debate flourishes among the locals. The games room is a favourite with rock fans attracted by the well-stocked juke box. Skittles and bar billiards are also played. The garden serves as a venue for summer beer festivals with both open and covered seating. Guest beers include milds, stouts and porters from a wide range of breweries. There are plans to build a micro-brewery in the outhouses. Q⚒⚓♿⚖♣☗

Merchant's Inn
5-7 Little Church Street, CV21 3AW
🍺 12-11 (midnight Tue; 1am Fri-Sat); 12-10.30 Sun
☎ (01788) 571119
www.merchantsinn.co.uk

🍎 Varies

Local CAMRA 2003 Pub of the Year, this well-established ale and beer house has a warm, cosy atmosphere, wooden seating and comfortable sofas, flagstone floor and an abundance of brewery memorabilia. The pub stocks two regular beers, six guest ales and a superb selection of Belgian beers, cider, wines and malt whiskies. Home-cooked food is served every lunchtime. On Tuesday evenings the pub becomes a popular live music venue. Actively involved with the Brewery History Society, the pub hosts regular beer festivals. ⟨⟩&≈♣🏠P⅄

Regular quiz nights and occasional live music are hosted. ⚏Q⛄⊛◑⊟&♣🏠P⅄

West Midlands

BIRMINGHAM

Anchor Inn
Bradford Street, B5 6ET
⫢ 11-11; 12-10.30 Sun
☎ (0121) 622 4516
www.the-anchor-inn.fsnet.co.uk

🍏 Gwatkin (bottled), Thatchers (draught)

Traditional pub in the Irish quarter, built by Victorian architects James & Lister Lea. It has often won local CAMRA Pub of the Year. There are many real ales on offer and occasionally a different cider on draught in conjunction with themed ale festivals. Bottled Gwatkins has been a recent welcome addition. Q⊛◑⊟&≈ (Birmingham New Street) 🏠⅄

Wellington
37 Bennetts Hill, B2 5SN
⫢ 11-11; 12-10.30 Sun
☎ (0121) 200 3115

🍏 Varies

This pub opened in December 2004 and within six weeks was stocking cider in polybarrels behind the bar. Due to high demand, it now usually features three polybarrels at any one time. The landlord has a strong commitment to serving cider and perry and is hoping to diversify the producers range available. Q≈ (Birmingham New Street) 🏠

ULLENHALL

Winged Spur
Main Street, B95 5PA
⫢ 12-11; 12-10.30 Sun
☎ (01564) 792005

🍏 Varies (draught & bottled)

🍎 Westons

Unassuming, traditional pub in a quiet village. The name comes from the spur on the crest of the Knight family, who were associated with Ullenhall from 1554. The single open-plan room is split into different areas. Up to three guest beers are available. Voted the local CAMRA branch's Most Improved Pub 2004. Dogs are allowed in the pub if on a lead. No food is served on Sunday evening. ⚏⊛◑🏠P

WARINGS GREEN

Blue Bell Cider House
Warings Green Road, B94 6BP OS129742
⫢ 11-11; 12-10.30 Sun
☎ (01564) 702328

🍏 Varies

Friendly canal-side free house offering two or three real ales and five draught ciders, including a house special from Westons. Eight temporary moorings make it popular with boaters and walking, cycling and fishing parties are catered for. Both the large lounge and cosy bar have real fires during winter. Reasonably priced food includes a children's menu and vegetarian options.

BLACKHEATH

New Inn
90 Oldbury Road, B65 0PH
⫢ 11-11; 12-3, 7-10.30 Sun
☎ (0121) 559 1946

🍏 Westons

This recently refurbished edge-of-town local offers a friendly atmosphere in homely surroundings. Good food is available at an excellent price (no eve meals Sun). It is close to the railway station and well served by local buses. ⛊◗≒ (Rowley Regis) ♣🏠P

BRIERLEY HILL

George Gallagher
7 Church Street, DY5 3PT
⇥ 11-3 (4 Sat), 6-11; 12-4, 7-10.30 Sun
☎ (01384) 78692

🍎 Thatchers

Unspoilt local just off the Stourbridge end of Brierley Hill High Street. Formerly known as the Plough, it was recently renamed in honour of a late long-standing landlord. ⛊♣

HALESOWEN

Waggon & Horses
Stourbridge Road, B63 3TU
⇥ 12-11; 12-10.30 Sun
☎ (0121) 550 4989

🍎 Westons

Two-roomed pub serving a good range of guest ales in a thriving community atmosphere. Sandwiches and cobs available (no eve meals Sun). Note the 'Barbara Cartland' lounge with pink décor! ◗♿🏠

HARBORNE

White Horse
2 York Street, B17 0HG
⇥ 11-11; 12-10.30 Sun
☎ (0121) 427 6023

🍎 Westons

This traditional local pub is just off the High Street in the villagey suburb of Harborne, ten minutes by bus from the city centre. It offers many real ales and good value food and occasionally

features a different cider such as Thatchers Cheddar Valley. ⛊◗🏠

LOWER GORNAL

Fountain
8 Temple Street, DY3 2PE
⇥ 12-11; 12-10.30 Sun
☎ (01384) 242777

🍎 Varies

Close to Lower Gornal bus station, this excellent free house serves up to six guest beers from micros far and wide. Attracting locals and visitors, young and old, the pub has a great community feel. The vibrant bar is complemented by an elevated dining area. Wholesome, reasonably priced food is served 12-9 (not Sun eve). There is an outside area for summer drinking. Regular beer festivals are held. A range of draught and bottled Belgian beers and real cider make this local CAMRA 2002/03 Pub of the Year a must. ⛊◗♿♣🏠P⚲🍴

SEDGLEY

Bull's Head
27 Bilston Street, DY3 1JA
⇥ 12 (11 Thu-Fri)-11; 12-10.30 Sun
☎ (01902) 578905

🍎 Thatchers

A late 1990s refit of this former two-roomed local moved its bar six feet or so to the left, merging the basic front bar with the cosy back lounge. However, these two previously separate areas have retained their individual character. The enterprising licensee has extended the range of ales and brought back the traditional cider, making the Bull's Head a haven for the discerning drinker. Wednesday evening is games night. It is handy for the shops in the nearby bull ring. ⛺⛊🚪♿♣🏠P🍴

TIPTON

Rising Sun
116 Horseley Road, DY4 7NH
12-2.30, 5-11; 11-11 Fri-Sat; 12-3,
7-10.30 Sun
☎ (0121) 530 2308

🍎 Saxon

Refurbished internally in 2003, this
Victorian edifice boasts two distinct rooms.
The busy bar is decorated with pictures of
local sporting heroes. The more relaxing
lounge has two real fires. In summer the
back yard is occasionally open for outdoor
drinking. The pub, popular with locals and
visitors alike, keeps four guest beers and
two guest ciders as a rule (mainly from
smaller brewers) and is a 10 minute walk
from Great Bridge bus station. Buses from
Birmingham, West Bromwich and Dudley
stop here. Dudley Port railway station is
one mile away. 🏨🌳🍴🍺♣🏠

Waggon & Horses
131 Toll End Road, Ocker Hill, DY4 0ET
5-11; 12-11 Fri-Sat; 12-3.30,
7-10.30 Sun
☎ (0121) 502 6453

🍎 Thatchers

Two-roomed mock Tudor brew pub,
home of 'Toll End' beers. Open plan feel
in a pub possessing a spacious,
comfortable lounge and a basic bar with
darts and a sports screen. Outside
drinking available in a landscaped garden
and conservatory. 🏨🌳🍺♿⊖
(Wednesbury Parkway) ♣🏠

UPPER GORNAL

Crown
16 Holloway Street, DY3 2EA
11-3, 6-11; 11-11 Sat; 11-3,
7-10.30 Sun
☎ (07951) 781989

🍎 Thatchers

Traditional estate pub serving Banks'
beers plus guests. It has an open plan
public bar plus a lounge with a more
secluded feel. The patio area lends itself
to pleasant outside summer drinking.
🏨🌳🍺P

Jolly Crispin
25 Clarence Street, DY3 1UL
4-11; 12-11 Fri-Sat; 12-3, 7-10.30 Sun
☎ (01902) 672222
www.jollycrispin.co.uk

🍎 Thatchers, Westons

🍏 Westons

This wayside hostelry is rapidly becoming
a Mecca for ale drinkers, both local and
from further afield, drawn in by its
extensive range of draught beers and two
ciders/perries. Two steps below street
level is the tile-floored front bar (take care
on leaving!). The extended lounge at the
rear of the pub is very comfy and its walls
are hung with aircraft pictures, including
one showing a WWII duel between
Douglas Bader and Luftwaffe ace, Adolf
Galland. Q🍺♿🏠P

WALSALL

Rose & Crown
55 Old Birchills, WS2 8QH
12-11; 12-10.30 Sun
☎ (01922) 720533

🍎 Varies

A Grade II listed building built in 1901,
this traditional three-roomed local boasts
some fine tile work in the bar and corridor
and original woodwork behind the bar.
There is also an unusual clock above the
normally unused corner entrance. The
rooms consist of a long bar warmed by an
open fire on cold days, a smaller lounge
where children are welcome and a pool
room. The cider is from Thatchers but
rotates between four different varieties
🏨🍽🍺⇌ (Walsall) ♣🏠P

White Lion
150 Sandwell Street, WS1 3EQ
⮑ 12-11; 12-10.30 Sun
☎ (01922) 628542

🍎 Westons

Imposing Victorian backstreet local with a classic L-shaped bar and a comfortable lounge. The bar floor slopes a little with signs on the bar doors indicating 'deep end' and 'shallow end'. There is also a games room with two pool tables. Popular with people from all walks of life, it is handy for Highgate Brewery and Walsall Football Club. ⚗☕♣🏠P

WEST BROMWICH

Wheatsheaf
379 High Street, B70 9QN
⮑ 11-11; 12-10.30 Sun
☎ (0121) 553 4221

🍎 Thatchers

A beacon of Black Country brewed ale on the High Street, sporting the full range of Holden's brews at reasonable prices. The busy front bar contrasts with the quieter extended lounge. The pub is popular with local office workers and football fans on match days. The guest beer usually comes from Nottingham Brewery. No-nonsense, competitively-priced food is served every lunchtime, including Sunday; this includes the local delicacy, grey peas and bacon. A must to visit when in the area. ⚗◖☕⊖ (Dartmouth Street) ♣🏠🍴

WOLVERHAMPTON

Tap & Spile
35 Princess Street, WV1 1HD
⮑ 11-11; 12-10.30 Sun
☎ (01902) 713319

🍎 Westons

This ever-popular city centre pub consists of a narrow bar and two snugs. There is one large screen TV and another three TV's around the pub, which are used for

sporting and music events. Very popular with Wolves fans on match days, due to its central location, it also attracts weekend clubbers. It boasts a darts team and two dominoes teams which is rare for a city centre pub. Well placed for the local bus and metro station. OWT (Wolverhampton) ⊖ (St Georges) ♣🏠

Wiltshire

BRADFORD-ON-AVON

Rising Sun
231 Winsley Road, BA15 1QS
⮑ 12-11; 12-10.30 Sun
☎ (01225) 862354

🍎 Inch's

On the outskirts of Bradford at the top of the hill, this is a popular local. There are two bars, the lounge, which is small and quiet and has pictures of various cricket pavilions adorning the wall, and the saloon, which is larger and livelier and possesses a large screen TV. Live music hosted at the weekends. ⌂⚗♣🏠🍴

CORTON

Dove
BA12 0SZ
⮑ 12-3 (3.30 Sat), 6.30-11; 12-4, 7-10.30 Sun
☎ (01985) 850109
www.thedove.co.uk

🍎 Varies

A village pub in the Wylye Valley. The candlelit conservatory together with a separate restaurant is where children are served. Recent improvements give drinkers a larger bar area bar that has a polished wood floor and centrally placed fire. Usually four ales on handpump. Food is excellent with a varied lunchtime menu and a more sophisticated evening choice using local ingredients including game and fish. There is a large garden. Accommodation is available. Corton is situated on the Wiltshire Cycleway. ♨Q❀🐾◑❀⅄♣🍴P✂

Worcestershire

BOURNHEATH

Nailers Arms
62 Doctors Hill, B61 9JE
🍺 12-11; 12-10.30 Sun
☎ (01527) 873045
www.thenailersarms.com

🍎 Varies

Originally a 1780s nailmakers workshop-cum-brewery, this whitewashed three gabled building has a good, traditional quarry tiled bar with a real fire. The lounge/restaurant is accessible via a corridor or a separate entrance. The décor, with comfortable seating and sofas, creates a distinctively modern Mediterranean feel. At least three guest ales and a real cider are usually available. No evening meals Sunday. ♨☎❀◑🍴🔌♣🍴P✂

BRETFORTON

Fleece
The Cross, WR11 7JE
🍺 12-3, 6-11; 11-11 Sat; 12-10.30 Sun
☎ (01386) 831173
www.thefleeceinn.co.uk

🍎 Varies

Famous old National Trust pub untouched by the passage of time until a fire in February 2004 gutted the upstairs living area. Fortunately the public area escaped almost unscathed – inglenooks, three open fires, antique furniture and its world-famous collection of 17th-century pewter all survived. The pub is one of the stars of CAMRA's National Inventory of Historic Pub Interiors. Families can enjoy the large garden with play area and orchard. There's a famous asparagus auction it its season.

An informal folk music gathering is held on Thursday in the Pewter Room. Fruit wines are available. ♨Q❀◑🔌🍴🍴

CHADDESLEY CORBETT

Fox Inn
Bromsgrove Road, DY10 4ON
🍺 11.30-2.30, 5-11; 11-11 Sat;
12-10.30 Sun
☎ (01562) 777247

🍎 Thatchers

Roadside pub to the south of this attractive village with a tidy L-shaped lounge and a pool room to the side. An air-conditioned no-smoking restaurant area serves a popular, good value carvery (Tue-Sun lunchtimes; Wed and Fri eves). A comprehensive range of main meals and snacks is available every day. Bottle conditioned beers are normally available. The guest beer is usually from an independent micro-brewery. ♨☎❀◑♣🍴P

Swan
High Street, DY10 4SD
🍺 11-3, 6-11; 11-11 Sat; 12-3, 7-10.30 Sun
☎ (01562) 777302
www.bathams.co.uk

🍎 Westons

Originally built in 1606 this comfortable village pub is set in a picturesque black and white timbered village with lots of good walks in the vicinity. The traditional bar (dogs welcome) enjoys a good atmosphere; large high ceilings, a snug to the rear and a restaurant to the side (No food Mon lunchtime or Sun-Wed eves). A jazz band plays every Thursday evening. ♨Q❀◑🔌♣🍴P✂

MONKWOOD GREEN

Fox
WR2 6NX OS803601
🍺 12-2.30 (not Mon-Thu), 5-11; 12-5, 7-11 Sat; 12-5, 7-10.30 Sun

☎ (01886) 889123

🍎 Barkers

🍺 Barkers

Friendly single-bar village local dating from Georgian times, affording good views of the Malvern Hills to the south. Guest beer usually comes from a local micro. A venue for many local events, including indoor air rifle shooting and a skittle alley is available. Music nights are held every last Friday of the month. Opening hours and food availability are flexible – phone ahead. Camping requires prior arrangement. ⚏Q☸🌙▲♣🏠P

OFFENHAM

Bridge Inn
Boat Lane,
WR11 8QZ
⮑ 11-11; 12-10.30 Sun
☎ (01386) 446565
www.bridge-inn.co.uk

🍎 Westons

Ancient riverside inn with its own moorings and a garden leading down to the Avon, known locally as the 'Boat' since the bridge was washed away in the 17th-century and replaced by a ferry. With extensive improvements in recent years, the Bridge features a vibrant public bar and excellent reputation for meals produced with locally grown fruit and vegetables. Regular mini beer festivals are held over the year. ⚏Q☸🌙🍴▲♣🏠P🍴

PENSAX

Bell
WR6 6AE
⮑ 12-2.30 (not Mon), 5-11;
12-10.30 Sun
☎ (01299) 896677

🍎 Westons

🍺 Westons

Winner of numerous awards including CAMRA's Regional Pub of the Year 2003, the bar serves at least four guest beers, usually from local independents. Children are welcome in the snug and no-smoking dining room. The food is prepared using local produce where possible. A beer festival is held on the last weekend of June and a monthly farmer's market (fourth Saturday). ⚏Q☸🌙☸🌙▲🏠P

East Yorkshire

BEVERLEY

Cornerhouse
2 Norwood, HU17 9ET
⮑ 12-2.30, 5-11; 11-11 Sat;
12-10.30 Sun
☎ (01482) 882652

🍎 Westons

Former Tetley pub, known as the Valiant Soldier, this historic listed building was gutted by the previous owners before its rebirth as the Cornerhouse in 1999. This well-respected pub/café bar serves quality food in colourful surroundings. Guest beers, real cider plus malt whiskies and cocktails add variety. Food is a speciality, mostly home made and served until 8pm. Tuesday is curry night and the pub opens early on weekends for English breakfast (10-1). ☸🌙🏠P

YORKSHIRE EAST RIDING

NORTH YORKSHIRE

Sledmere — A166

A614 — Bridlington

A165

A164

A614

A1079

A1079

A163

A1079

Beverley

Kingston upon Hull

M62 — 38

A1033

37

Goole

LINCS

0 Miles 10
0 Kilometres 16

Sun Inn
1 Flemingate
HU17 0NP
◉ 12-11; 12-10.30 Sun
☎ (01482) 881547

🍎 Westons

Medieval timber-framed building opposite the east front of the Minster and reputed to be Beverley's oldest pub. The Sun's Spartan interior with flagstone floors, brick walls and wooden seating dates from a 1994 refurbishment. OT (Beverley) ♣ 🐶✄

KINGSTON UPON HULL

Gardeners Arms
35 Cottingham Road, HU5 2PP
◉ 11-11; 12-10.30 Sun
☎ (01482) 342396

🍎 Westons, Varies

Local CAMRA Pub of the Year 2004 and finalist in the previous five years. The original front bar has seen many alterations but retains the matchwood ceiling that blends with the current ale house style. The large rear extension is comfortably furnished, housing numerous pool tables. Good value food is served 12-2.30 and 5-7 (12-6 at weekends). The six guest beers in the front bar include Cropton's seasonal brews. It hosts three weekly quizzes and is situated on a main bus route. 🐶◑ 🍺♿🐶P✄

Green Bricks
Humber Dock Street, HU1 1TB
◉ 11-11; 12-10.30 Sun
☎ (01482) 329502

🍎 Westons

Former Humber Dock tavern, extended in the 1990s. It is a large one-room pub with views of the marina. Good value food is served until 9pm daily. 🐶◑♿🐶✄

Minerva Hotel
Nelson Street, HU1 1XE
◉ 11-11; 12-10.30 Sun
☎ (01482) 326909

🍎 Westons

Overlooking the Humber Estuary and Victoria Pier, this well known pub, built in 1835, is a great place to watch the ships go by. Superb photos and memorabilia are a reminder of the area's maritime past. 🏔🐶◑♣🐶

Three John Scott's
Lowgate
HU1 1XW
◉ 10-11; 12-10.30 Sun
☎ (01482) 381910

🍎 Westons

Converted from the Edwardian Post Office opposite Hull Crown Court and St Mary's Church in the old town area, this large, open plan Wetherspoon's features modern décor. It was named after three past incumbents of the church. It draws a mixed clientele at lunchtime and circuit drinkers at weekends. A large rear courtyard has plentiful seating. Up to five guest beers are on tap plus cider. Food offers include a steak club (Tue) and curry club (Thu). 🐶◑♿🐶

Wellington Inn
55 Russell Street
HU2 9AB
◉ 12-11; 12-10.30 Sun
☎ (01482) 329486

🍎 Westons

🍷 Westons

Situated on the north eastern edge of the town centre. This former Mansfield pub became a free house in 2004 and is extremely popular, offering a range of real ales and foreign beers. 🐶🐶P✄

Whalebone
165 Wincolmlee, HU2 0PA
⏴ 12-11; 12-10.30 Sun
☎ (01482) 327980

🍎 Westons

Built in 1796 on the site of the old Lockwood's Brewery, the pub is situated at the former harbour in an old industrial area – look for the illuminated M&R Ales sign. The comfortable saloon bar is adorned with photos of bygone Hull and its sporting heritage. A new brewery, housed in the adjacent building, started brewing in 2003. Two real ciders and a selection of Gale's country wines are available, plus hot bar snacks. Dogs are allowed. ♨♣🏠

Ye Olde Black Boy
150 High Street, HU1 1PS
⏴ 12-11; 12-10 Sun
☎ (01482) 326516
www.yeoldeblackboy.co.uk

🍎 Westons

Old town pub on the medieval cobbled High Street, a five minute walk (across the River Hull footbridge) from 'The Deep' visitor attraction. It retains much of its old layout as a Victorian wine merchants; note the leaded display window and the carved head above the fireplace in the front room snug. An upstairs room houses a pool table. Up to five guest ales are stocked plus Lindisfarne fruit wines. Thursday is piano night at this local CAMRA Pub of the Year 2003. ♨Q♣🏠

SLEDMERE

Triton Inn
Main Street, YO25 3XQ
⏴ 12-3, 5-11; 12-11 Sat; 12-10.30 Sun
☎ (01377) 236644
www.thetritoninnsledmere.co.uk

🍎 Westons

This 18th-century coaching inn features a real fire, oak panelling and settles. The main bar is used to display horseshoes from classic winning throughbreds. Lunchtime and evening meals are served Friday-Monday only. ♨Q✿🚲◑♣🏠P✄

North Yorkshire

CROSS HILLS

Old White Bear
6 Keighley Road
BD20 7RN
⏴ 11.30-11; 12-10.30 Sun
☎ (01535) 632115

🍎 Westons

🍐 Westons

This brew pub has recently started alternating Westons cider and perry. Its separate dining room serves good value food and has a window into Naylors Brewery, situated in the former stables. ♨✿◑♣🏠P✄

HARROGATE

Tap & Spile
Tower Street
HG1 1HS
⏴ 11-11; 12-10.30 Sun
☎ (01423) 526785

🍎 Westons

Popular ale house which has three distinct drinking areas, one being smoke free. A mixture of exposed brick walls and wood panelling creates a warm and cosy atmosphere in this traditional pub. Regular live music sessions are also held: folk music on Tuesday, rock music on Thursday. Lunchtime meals are served Monday to Saturday. OLT (Harrogate) ♣🏠P✄◻

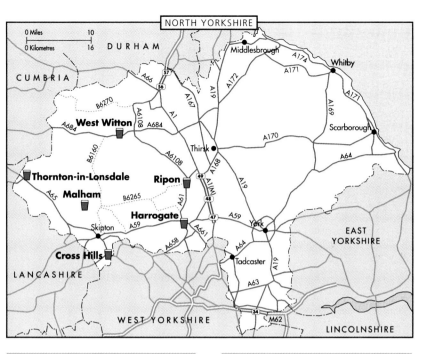

MALHAM

Lister Arms
Gordale Scar Road
BD23 4DB
▸ 12-3, 7-11; 12-11 Fri-Sat;
12-10.30 Sun
☎ (01729) 830330
www.listerarms.co.uk

🍏 Westons (summer only)

Opposite the village green, this 17th-century coaching inn takes its name from Thomas Lister, the first Lord of Ribblesdale. The tiled entrance opens to a main bar with a large inglenook and many other original features. A cider is available in the summer. There is also an extensive bottled foreign beer list. Food and accommodation are of the best quality. Internet access is available by the bar, as well as table football.
▥❀➪◑♣♠🏠P

RIPON

One-Eyed Rat
51 Allhallowgate, HG4 1LQ
▸ 12-3.30 (not Mon-Wed), 6-11 (5.30-11 Fri); 12-11 Sat; 12-3, 7-10.30 Sun
☎ (01765) 607704
www.oneeyedrat.co.uk

🍏 Biddenden, Thatchers

This is a popular base-boarded traditional pub consisting of one long, narrow room warmed by open fires. It is decorated in Edwardian style and centrally situated in a terrace close to the heart of this small historic city. ▥Q❀♣🏠

THORNTON-IN-LONSDALE

Marton Arms
LA6 3PB
▸ 11-3, 5.30-11 (11-11 summer); 11-11 Sat; 12-10.30 Sun

☎ (01524) 241281
www.martonarms.co.uk

🍎 Westons

This pub relies almost entirely on tourists and trippers for its clientele. It has 16 handpumps and a large selection of malt whiskies available. A traditional flagged passage leads to a bar dominated by light wood in which bar billiards are played. ❀🍴🍺♣🏠P✂

WEST WITTON

Fox & Hounds
Main Street, DL8 4LP
🍺 12-4, 7-11; 12-4, 7-10.30 Sun
☎ (01969) 623650
www.foxwitton.com

🍎 Pipkin (summer only), Westons

Character stone-built traditional pub situated in beautiful Wensleydale and run by a friendly and knowledgeable landlord. A chimney breast separates the cosy drinking area into a bar and a games area. 🏨❀🍴🍺♣🏠P

South Yorkshire

ROTHERHAM

Blue Coat
Feoffes, Moorgate Street, S60 2DJ
🍺 10-11; 12-10.30 Sun
☎ (01709) 539500

🍎 Westons

Situated behind the Town Hall, this pub is popular with the business community at lunchtimes. Q🍺❀🍴🍺♿≈ (Rotherham Central) 🏠P✂

George & Dragon
85 Main Street, Wentworth, S62 7TN
🍺 10-11; 10-10.30 Sun
☎ (01226) 742440

🍎 Addlestones

A friendly and popular pub set back off the main road in the village. 🏨Q❀🍴♿🏠P

Hare & Hounds
52 Wellgate, S60 2LR
🍺 11-11; 12-10.30 Sun
☎ (01709) 830993

🍎 Westons

A small cosy locals' pub just on the edge of the town centre. Very friendly and busy. Parking available on the street or in the multi-storey next door. 🍺♿🏠

Sportsman
55 Broad Street, Parkgate, S62 6DU
🍺 8-11 Mon & Thu; 7-11 Tue-Wed/Fri-Sat; 12-4, 8-10.30 Sun
☎ (01709) 522501

🍎 Addlestones

On the main road out of Rotherham towards Rawmarsh. A very welcoming, traditional pub which prefers to sell the real stuff (cider and beer). 🍺♿🏠P

SHEFFIELD

Cask & Cutler
1 Henry Street, S3 7EQ
🍺 12-2 (not Mon), 5.30-11; 12-11 Fri-Sat; 12-3, 7-10.30 Sun
☎ (0114) 249 2295

🍎 Westons

Enterprising free house with a range of

up to nine cask ales including a mild and a stout or porter. Occasional brews available from the pubs own Port Mahon Brewery in the grounds. A good range of Belgian bottled beers are also available. A popular beer festival is held in November. QOU (Tram, Shalesmoor) 🍴⅄🗍

Devonshire Cat
49 Wellington Street, S1 4HG
⏸ 11.30-11; 12-10.30 Sun
☎ (0114) 279 6700

🍎 Saxon

Spacious city centre café-bar style pub with modern wood-and-glass design. The wide range of varying real ales includes house bitter from Kelham Island. Set amid student accommodation but also popular with office workers lunchtimes and early evenings. ◑♿⊖ (West Street) 🍴⅄

Fat Cat
23 Alma Street, S3 8SA
⏸ 12-3, 5.30-11; 12-11 Fri-Sat; 12-3, 7-10.30 Sun
☎ (0114) 249 4801
www.thefatcat.co.uk

🍎 Varies

Sheffield's original real ale free house, and the first with a no-smoking room. It is close to Kelham Island Industrial Museum but most noted for its home-cooked food, especially the wide choice of vegetarian options (eve meals 6-7.30 Mon-Fri). 10 real ales are usually on tap, always including three or four from the adjacent Kelham Island Brewery, with the rest mainly from small independents. ♨Q♿◑ (Mon-Fri) ⊖ (Shalesmoor) 🍴⅄

Gardeners Rest
105 Neepsend Lane, S3 8AT
⏸ 12-11; 12-10.30 Sun
☎ (0114) 272 4978

🍎 Westons

🍎 Westons

Traditional two-roomed pub with conservatory extension and beer garden overlooking the River Don. The beer range usually includes beers from Timothy Taylor and Wentworth with up to five guests. It has one of Sheffield's few bar billiards tables as well as hosting a quiz night on Sunday and regular live music. Q♿♿⊖ (Infirmary Rd) ♣🍴⅄🗍

Kelham Island Tavern
62 Russell Street, S3 8RW
⏸ 12-11; 12-3, 7-10.30 Sun
☎ (0114) 272 2482

🍎 Saxon, Westons

Modernised L-shaped bar with new smoke-free extension. It was CAMRA's Yorkshire Regional Pub of the Year 2004 with 8-10 real ales always including a mild and a stout or porter. Live music sessions are held Sunday evening. Lunchtime meals are served 12-3 (not Mon). Q♿◑♿⊖ (Shalesmoor) 🍴⅄🗍

West Yorkshire

BAILDON

Junction
1 Baildon Road, BD17 6AB
⏸ 12-11; 12-10.30 Sun
☎ (01274) 582009

🍎 Biddenden, Saxon

Recently refurbished and increasingly popular free house. The games room features darts, dominoes and pool. Several guest real ales and two ciders are always on offer. ⛳♿◑⇌ (Shipley) 🍴♣P⅄

BRADFORD

Fighting Cock
21-23 Preston Street, BD7 1JE
⏸ 11.30-11; 12-10.30 Sun
☎ (01274) 726907

 Varies (draught & bottled)

A drinkers' paradise in an industrial area, one mile from the town centre off Thornton Road.

Fox & Goose
9 Heptonstall Road
HX7 6AZ
 11.30-3, 7 (6 Fri)-11; 12-10.30 Sun
 (01422) 842649

 Varies (draught), Westons (bottled)

This popular real ale pub now has a changing cider available on a mini handpump and two Weston's bottled ciders, including the organic. On the opposite side of town from the railway station but accessible by the 590 / 592 Halifax-Todmorden bus services. Q♣🏠⚲☰

Boltmakers Arms
117 East Parade, BD21 5HX
 11-11; 12-10.30 Sun
 (01535) 661936

 Varies

This town centre local is small but split onto two levels. The clientele are locals and visitors to the nearby steam railway. The changing real cider is complemented by a wide range of Taylor's beers and a guest. (Keighley & KWVR) ♣🏠

Duck & Drake
43 Kirkgate, LS2 7DR
 11-11; 12-10.30 Sun
 (0113) 246 5806
www.duckanddrakeleeds.co.uk

 Westons

A proper old fashioned ale house, resplendent in its scruffiness; well

trodden bare boards, beery posters, blackboards and a fine beer range. Two rooms, neither of which could be called a lounge, around a central bar. A Leeds institution. (Leeds) 🏠

Scarbrough Hotel
Bishopgate Street, LS1 5DY
 11-11; 12-10.30 Sun
 (0113) 243 4590
tobydflint@yahoo.co.uk

 Westons

 Westons

Conveniently positioned opposite Leeds train station, the Scarbrough is easily spotted – look for the toffee and cream coloured tiling. Many times local CAMRA award-winner for its good beers, many of which are from Yorkshire. (Leeds) 🏠

Brewers Pride
Low Mill Road, off Healey Road, WF5 8NB
 12-3, 5.30-11; 12-11 Fri-Sat;
 12-10.30 Sun
 (01924) 273865

 Addlestones

Popular free house offering nine real ales. The pub is five minutes walk from the Calder & Hebble Canal and the bus 21 stops within 200 metres. Home-cooked food is available on Wednesday nights; lunchtime meals are served 12-2 Monday to Saturday. The local folk club meets on Thursday night, with live music on the first Sunday of the month. Q🏠

Fanny's Ale & Cider House
63 Saltaire Road, BD18 3JN
 11.30 (5 Mon)-11; 12-10.30 Sun
 (01274) 591419

 Biddenden

Real ale haven close to World Heritage site of Saltaire. It has been local CAMRA Pub of the Season several times. ⚑Q⇌ (Saltaire/Shipley) 🍺

Fernandes Brewery Tap
5 Avison Yard
Kirkgate WF1 1UA
🍺 5-11; 11-11 Fri-Sat; 12-10.30 Sun
☎ (01924) 369547
www.fernandes-brewery.gowyld.com

🍎 Varies

A real-ale drinkers' paradise, it also has a Belgian Genever bar and bottled Belgian beers. It has won many National and local awards and always provides a friendly welcome. Q⇌ (Kirkgate/Westgate) 🍺

Talbot & Falcon
North Gate, WF1 3AP
🍺 11-11; 12-10.30 Sun
☎ (01924) 201693

🍎 Westons

A listed building in the heart of the city, popular with shoppers. Refurbished in 2003, the pub features a changing range of guest ales and stocks an extensive selection of fine wines. ⇌◖🍺

Two Pointers
69 Church Street
LS26 8RE
🍺 3-11; 12-11 Fri-Sat; 12-10.30 Sun
☎ (0113) 282 3124
thetwopointers@aol.com

🍎 Varies

Situated in a modern village, just one stop on the train out of Leeds, the Two Pointers is a tidy, friendly local; well decorated with lots of different drinking areas. Q❀⇌ (Woodlesford) 🍺P

Cider Outlets
Wales

Glamorgan

GILFACH FARGOED

Capel Hotel
Park Place CF81 8LW
⏸ 12-3, 7-11; 12-11 Fri-Sat;
12-4, 8-10.30 Sun
☎ (01443) 830272

🍎 Varies

This award-winning, friendly pub is among the finest for miles. Many original features give a homely touch, and it woulad be easy to imagine the bar full of tired colliers as it once was. Today's customers enjoy up to three guest beers plus a guest cider. Local CAMRA Pub of the Year 2004, with an enthusiastic approach to real ale. The local station is a 'request' stop. Annual beer festival held in early May.
Q❀♫➥ (Gilfach Fargoed) ♣🏠✂

GROESFAEN

Dynevor Arms
Llantrisant Road, CF72 8NS OS061810
⏸ 11-11; 12-3, 7-10.30 Sun
☎ (02920) 890530

🍎 Addlestones

Popular roadside village pub, it is comfortable with disabled and family friendly facilities. Well decorated on the inside, while on the outside it is colourfully signposted and painted in traditional pub colours. Ever-changing guest beers are stocked. An area is set aside for darts, dominoes and cards and either live music or a quiz is held on Sunday evenings. A dining area enhances the open plan bar facilities and a varied menu offers good value meals (no food Sunday evening).
❀◑&♣🏠P

MONKNASH

Plough & Harrow
CF71 7QQ
⏸ 12-11; 12-10.30 Sun
☎ (01656) 890209

🍎 Westons

This two-room pub is located in what was a medieval grange, the public bar having once been a mortuary. Visitors to the lounge are advised the handpumps are in the bar as are the casks on gravity. With up to five guests ales in winter and seven in summer, coupled with cider and food from 12-2 and 6-9 this is well worth a visit. ▲❀◑⊟&▲♣🏠P

NEATH

Borough Arms
New Henry Street, SA11 1PH
⏸ 4-11; 12-11 Sat; 12-10.30 Sun
☎ (01639) 644902

🍎 Varies

Traditional back street pub which has been transformed by the new owner into a brew pub and real ale oasis in a town where the emphasis is on nitrokegs. The L-shaped bar has a constantly changing choice of up to four real ales including many from micro-breweries and always one beer from the Eaglesbush Brewery, established in September 2004 at the rear. Q☼❀➥♣🏠

ST HILARY

Bush
CF71 7AD
⏰ 11.30-11; 12-10.30 Sun
☎ (01446) 772745

🍎 Westons

A 400-year-old thatched pub near to the church in an attractive village. The small bar has larger rooms opening off either side including a restaurant to the right. A pleasant outside drinking area adds to the appeal. A display of hops adorns the fireplace adding to the cosy atmosphere on a cold day. No meals Sunday evening.
🏚Q❀◑⊟🍴P

TYLEGARW

Boars Head
Coedcae Lane, CF72 9EZ
⏰ 11-11; 12-10.30 Sun
☎ (01443) 225400

🍎 Varies

Built in 1875 to serve the local heavy industries, it is now amidst modern light industry and houses yet retains its 'country pub' atmosphere with its very small bar, pool room and rural lounge. It is very popular in the locality, serving up to seven real ales. The no-smoking restaurant has a reputation for value, with reservations necessary for Sunday lunch. No meals served Sunday or Tuesday evenings. 🏚❀◑⊟👤⇌ (Pontyclun) 🍴P

Gwent

CLYTHA

Clytha Arms
Old Raglan Road, NP7 8BW
⏰ 12-3 (not Mon), 6-11; 12-11 Sat; 12-4, 7-10.30 Sun
☎ (01873) 840206

www.clytha-arms.com

🍺 Varies

🍎 Varies

Several times a local CAMRA Pub of the Year, the Clytha Arms is gaining a national reputation for the quality of its beer, cider and food. A former dower house, it is set in beautiful, extensive grounds. Six real ales are served including guests from a wide variety of independent breweries. These are complemented by draught ciders and perry. Highlights of the pub year are the festivals of Welsh beer and cheese and the Welsh cider festival, but every day is special here. Q❀⇌◑⊟♣🍴P

LLANTHONY

Half Moon
NP7 7NN
⏰ 12-3, 7 (6 Sat)-11; 12-3, 7-10.30 Sun (seasonal hours vary, ring to check)
☎ (01873) 890611

🍎 Addlestones

Situated in an area of outstanding natural beauty in the heart of the Black Mountains, the pub is just a few metres beyond the medieval ruins of Llanthony Priory. It opens only at the weekends in winter, but keeps more regular hours after Easter when walkers, trekkers and visitors boost the sparse population of this remote valley. This is a rare local outlet for Bulmastiff beers. The bar billiards table, bought secondhand 19 years ago, still operates on two shilling coins. 🏚Q🛏❀⇌◑⊟👤♣🍴P⌇

PANTYGELLI

Boat Inn
Lone Lane, NP25 4AJ
OS535098
⏰ 11-11; 12-10.30 Sun
☎ (01600) 712615

🍎 Local Producer

Unspoilt gem of a pub in a picturesque setting on the bank of the River Wye. The car park is across the river in the village of Redbrook, England and the pub is approached along a footbridge next to the disused railway line. Inside, there's a bar with a flagstone floor and a small side room. A stream runs through the pub garden. Up to five ales are normally available. Live music is hosted here on Tuesday and Thursday. 🏡🌢🍺P

Bell
NP7 8UH
🍺 11-11 (not Mon); 12-10.30 Sun
☎ (01600) 750235
www.skenfrith.co.uk

🍎 Broome Farm

🍏 Broome Farm

Nestling on the banks of the River Monnow under the walls of the ancient Norman Skenfrith castle, this former 17th-century village coaching inn has been transformed into a high quality hotel and restaurant while retaining a separate bar for locals and visitors. Beer comes from independent breweries and the draught cider is made at a farm just over the border in England.
🏡Q🏢🌢🍺P✂

Cherry Tree Inn
Forge Road, NP16 6TH
🍺 12-11; 12-10.30 Sun
☎ (01291) 689292
www.thecherry.co.uk

🍎 Varies (draught & bottled)

A gravity-lover's delight, the fizz-free Cherry thrives in its enlarged 21st-century form after extensive redevelopment. The

original bar remains for the serious business of drinking and conversation, both encouraged by an expansive stillage with constantly changing choices from small breweries. With live music every Thursday and two beer festivals a year this pub shouldn't be missed.

Lion Inn
NP25 4PA
🍺 12-3, 6 (7 Mon, 6.30 Sat)-11 (hours vary in winter); 12-3 (closed eve) Sun
☎ (01600) 860322
www.lioninn.co.uk

🍎 Varies

Local CAMRA Pub of the Year once and runner-up twice in the last three years, the Lion is a consistently excellent pub. With an open plan interior, there is a small bar to the right and a slightly larger dining area to the left. An exhibition of foreign bottled beers was held last year, in addition to the regular summer beer festival. Up to four beers are always available, nearly always from micros. The food menu ranges from the simple to the exotic: Hungarian dishes are a speciality.
🏡🏢🌢🍺P

Mid Wales

Boar's Head
Ship Street, LD3 9AL
🍺 12-11; 12-1am Fri-Sat; 12-10.30 Sun
☎ (01874) 622856

🍎 Westons

The Breconshire Brewery tap is an extremely popular town centre pub. The wood-panelled front bar displays a collection of old photographs of Brecon and the larger, livelier back bar houses the busy pool table and a large screen TV for sporting events. Live music is hosted on Friday. The patio garden boasts views of the River Usk and over to the Beacons. Special events are held throughout the summer and during the jazz festival. ⚐✿◑⊟☕P

Bull's Head
86 The Street, LD3 7LS
⮑ 12-3 (closed Mon), 6.30-11; 12-3, 7-10.30 Sun
☎ (01874) 622044

🍎 Varies

Now owned by Evan-Evans of Llandeilo, the beers are all sourced from them or the Wolverhampton & Dudley brewery. A range of bottled beers is also stocked. This popular two-room pub has three drinking areas. An excellent menu featuring home-cooked food caters for all including vegetarians and vegans. Good value B&B accommodation is available. ⚐Q✿⚑◑⊟☕

Vine Tree Inn
NP8 1HG
OS215180
⮑ 12-3, 6-11 (extended in summer); 12-3, 6.30-10.30 Sun
☎ (01873) 810514

🍎 Local Producer

Riverside pub where the emphasis is on food. However, drinkers are very welcome in the cosy, copper-covered bar, complemented by stone walls and quarry tiled floors. Cider is produced locally, exclusively for the pub. The impressive food menu boasts locally sourced meat and vegetables and ever-changing specials which are always good. Booking is advisable as the pub can be very busy. The riverside beer garden is an added attraction. ⚐Q✿◑☕P

Hollybush Inn
HR3 5PS OS198403
⮑ 11-11; 11-10.30 Sun
☎ (01497) 847371

🍎 Thatchers, Westons

🍏 Westons

Warm and friendly four-roomed pub. The two main rooms are part of the original building, with a slightly more modern annexe at one end, and a newly-built dining room to the side. The exposed beams in the bar are bedecked with locally-grown hops. Superb home-cooked food includes dishes for vegetarians and vegans. Land beside the pub is taken up by a spacious camping and caravan park, next to the River Wye and complete with woodland walks and an adventure area. Views of the Black Mountains and the Begwyn Hills mark the horizon. ⚐Q✿◑Å☕P⌿

Radnor Arms
LD8 2SP
⮑ 12-3, 7 (5 Fri)-11; 11-11 Sat; 12-10.30 Sun
☎ (01544) 350232

🍎 Ralph's (summer only)

🍏 Ralph's (summer only)

Set in the Welsh Marches and close to the English border, this cosy pub also offers accommodation, making it an ideal base for anyone looking for an away-from-it-all break. There is good walking, trekking and cycling, Offa's Dyke is nearby and Hereford 25 miles away. Food is served every day, with a popular Sunday carvery (booking advisable), and a children's menu. The restaurant is no-smoking and a take-away service is available, including excellent fish and chips. ⚐Q☎✿⚑◑⊟♣☕P

RHAYADER

Cornhill
West Street, LD6 5AB
11 (12 winter)-11; 12-10.30 Sun
☎ (01597) 811015
www.cornhillinn.co.uk

🍏 Thatchers

Despite alterations this early 16th-century pub retains not just its original character – with low ceilings and an inglenook – but reputedly a female ghost. Guest beers are mainly from smaller breweries and traditional cask and bottled cider is stocked. Vegan and vegetarian choices are included in the excellent menu of freshly-prepared meals. Self-catering accommodation is available in a detached former smith. Children are welcome. No food is served January-March. ♨Q❀✿⏻♣🏠

TALYBONT ON USK

Star Inn
LD3 7YX OS114226
11-3, 6.30-11 (11-11 summer);
11-11 Sat; 12-3, 6.30-10.30 Sun
☎ (01874) 676635

🍏 Westons

A large and lively pub beside the Monmouthshire and Brecon Canal. A vast display of pump clips reflects the enormous number of ales served by this CAMRA award-winning pub over the years. Beers from the nearby Breconshire Brewery are often available. Quiz nights and live music evenings are popular during the week. The large garden at the back, overlooking the canal, is very busy in summer. ♨❀✿⏻⊟⚓♣🏠

North East Wales

HALKYN

Blue Bell Inn
Rhosesmor Road, CH8 8DL OS209703

12-2.30 Wed-Fri summer; 5-11;
12-11 Sat; 12-10.30 Sun
☎ (01352) 780309
www.bluebell.uk.eu.org

🍏 Varies

The real ale renaissance of the Blue Bell started in April 2003 and a blackboard displays the number of different cask beers sold since then. A house beer, Blue Bell Bitter, from Plassey is a regular, together with two changing guest beers usually from local micros and a real cider (a rarity in north east Wales). The pub is situated on top of Halkyn Mountain and is the focal point for guided walks organised by Walkabout Flintshire. Good value Sunday lunches are served and evening meals are available Thursday-Saturday. Lunchtime weekday opening is restricted to Wednesday-Friday during summer only. ♨❀⏻⚓♣🏠P

MOLD

Gold Cape
8 Wrexham Road, CH7 1ES
9-11; 12-10.30 Sun
☎ (01352) 705920

🍏 Westons (draught & bottled)

A recent addition to the Wetherspoon's estate, the pub is named after the gold

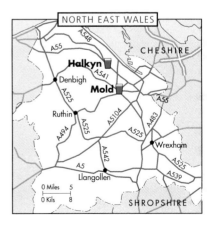

NORTH EAST WALES

cape found nearby by workmen in 1831. A replica stands in the foyer. The manager is a keen real ale fan and keeps a good selection. Standard pub food is available until one hour before closing time. Stories of local interest are told on wall plaques, such as the Mold riots of 1869, and the life of novelist Daniel Owen, Mold's most famous son. The pub was awarded Welsh Loo of the Year 2004! Q⌖❀◗🏠

North West Wales

LLANDUDNO

Palladium

7 Glodaeth Street,LL30 2DD OS781825
▮◗ 11-11; 12-10.30 Sun
☎ (01492) 863920

🍎 Westons

A huge Wetherspoons pub that was converted from a theatre. The boxes and upper seating can still be seen, although not used, and the walls are adorned with theatrical memorabilia including original programmes bearing the names of the performing stars of the day. Spacious areas on split levels including a family dining room. Lift available. There are seven real ales in addition to the cider. Q◗⧖⇌ (Llandudno) 🏠

Penrhyn Arms

Pendre Road, Penrhynside, LL30 3BY
OS814816
▮◗ 12-2 (Fri only), 5.30 (5 Wed-Fri)-11; 11-11 Sat; 12-10.30 Sun
☎ (01492) 541569
www.penrhynarms.com

🍎 Gwatkins, Ralphs

🍎 Gwatkins

Comfortable open-plan locals' pub at the heart of the community with a warm welcome always guaranteed. Spacious L-

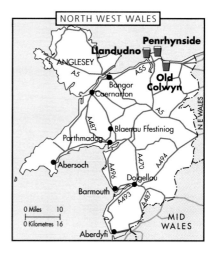

shaped bar, with pool at one end and darts at the other; plenty of comfy seating and a widescreen TV showing mainly sport. The pub has its own football team and the landlord is a keen fisherman. Framed pictures of noted drinkers such as Oliver Reed adorn the walls. There is always a real cider including one from Wales. 🏚❀♣🏠

OLD COLWYN

Plough

282 Abergele Road, LL29 9LN OS866783
▮◗ 12-3, 6-11 Mon-Wed; 12-11 Thu-Sat; 12-10.30 Sun
☎ (01492) 515387

🍎 Westons

The Plough is a popular community pub in the centre of the town. There is a spacious lounge area which surrounds the bar; a dining area on the left and a games room on the right, where pool and darts are played. Real cider is available and the guest beers are usually from independent breweries and include one on gravity. A popular quiz night is held on Thursdays. The landlord is a supporter of Colwyn Bay Football Club and holds regular fund-raising events for the team. Q❀◗🍴♣🏠

West Wales

CWMANNE

Cwmanne Tavern
SA48 8DR
🍺 5-11; 12-11 Sat; 12-10.30 Sun
☎ (01570) 423861
www.cwmanntavern.co.uk

🍎 Westons

Built in 1720 on a drovers route a quarter mile from Lampeter, all age groups are welcome here. The interior features three drinking areas with plenty of timber beams, posts and floors. The current owners have improved the quality of the beer considerably since acquiring the premises in 2004. There are two guest beers, a draught cider and a very good selection of bottled UK and European beers, most bottle conditioned. Live music Saturday night. Lunchtime meals are only served Saturday and Sunday, evening meals all week except Monday.
ΔQ❀⇆◖♣🐾P

Cross Inn
SA39 9HX
🍺 5-11 (closed Tue); 12-10.30 Sun
☎ (01559) 384838
www.crossinnwales.co.uk

🍎 Varies

This 16th-century drovers pub is now back in the 21st-century as far as real ale is concerned. Single bar with open fire, pool room and separate restaurant. Good quality food is served, all prepared and cooked on the premises. The specials menu offers a mouthwatering selection of meals prepared from locally sourced produce (lunchtime meals served weekends only). The well-organised annual Easter beer festival is very popular. The friendly licensees organise regular local events, which ensure this pub is a part of village life.
ΔQ❀◖⏢Å♣🐾P

Cider Outlets
Scotland
Central

CALLANDER

Waverley Hotel
88-94 Main Street
FK17 8BD
⬛▶ 11-midnight (1am Fri-Sat);
   11.30-midnight Sun
☎ (01877) 330245

🍎 Varies

Real ale is available in the Claymore bar, it normally carries a good range, particularly in the summer months when there can be up to eight beers stocked. The town is well placed for visiting tourists as it is close to the Trossachs and the Central Belt. Two beer festivals usually take place in September and December, each lasting a week. Good food is available, served all day. 🚲◑⚲🏠

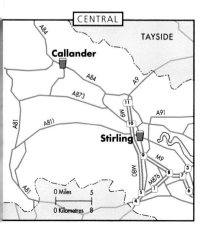

STIRLING

Settle Inn
91 St Mary's Wynd, FK8 1BU
⬛▶ 12-midnight (1am Fri-Sat); 12.30-
   midnight Sun
☎ (01786) 474609

🍎 Addlestones

Claimed to be the oldest pub in Stirling, dating from 1733, the Settle Inn is a peaceful but lively pub, popular with locals, students and visitors alike. The visitors' book bears witness to the friendliness of the welcome, the quality of the beer and the traditional cosy atmosphere. This is a pub with good community links, hosting a Halloween bash and a Burns Supper for regulars, as well as a Christmas party for pensioners. Sunday is quiz night, 'open mike' sessions feature on Tuesday and folk on Thursday evening. Look out for the two ghosts that have made the Settle Inn their home! 🏨🏠

Grampian

STONEHAVEN

Marine Hotel
9-10 Shorehead, AB39 2JY
⬛▶ 11-11 (midnight Thu; 1am Fri-Sat);
   11-midnight Sun
☎ (01569) 762155

🍎 Addlestones

This hotel's picturesque harbour-front location makes it a must, particularly in summer. Downstairs there is a

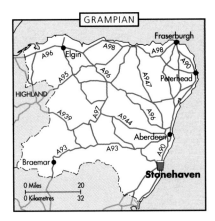

and wood. Situated on the rural Rosneath Peninsula, it offers superb views over Loch Long towards Blairmore and Strone. It has a safe anchorage with five moorings and a large garden. Local ales are regularly available. An hourly bus service runs from Helenburgh. 🏨🏡🍴🎴🎱P

Bon Accord
153 North Street, G3 7DA
▯▶ 11-midnight; 12.30-11 Sun
☎ (0141) 248 4427
www.thebonaccord.freeserve.co.uk

🍺 Varies (summer only)

Local CAMRA Pub of the Year, the Bon Accord continues to thrive under the current forward-thinking management team, assisted by a Cellarman who has worked in the pub for almost 25 years and the cheerful, well-informed bar staff. Beers from throughout the UK are served, many difficult to find locally. A range of foreign beers plus many malt whiskies are available. Entertainment includes an open stage (Tue), quiz (Wed) and live music (Sat). Food is served 11-7 (children are welcome). ◑◗♿⇌ (Charing Cross / Anderston) ♣🎱

Three Judges
141 Dumbarton Road, G11 6PR
▯▶ 11-11 (midnight Fri; 11.45 Sat); 10.30-11 Sun
☎ (0141) 337 3055

🍺 Varies (summer only)

Typical corner-tenement Glasgow pub that has won many CAMRA awards over the years. Recently sensitively refurbished, the decor has moved slightly upmarket, but a homely atmosphere still permeates. Beers, too numerous to mention, mostly from independent and small craft breweries, grace the L-shaped bar every year. Foreign beers are available, with cider often featured. Live jazz is performed on Sunday afternoon. ⇌ (Partick) ⊖ (Kelvinhall) 🎱

simple, wood-panelled bar serving five frequently-changing ales selected from both micro-breweries and the more enterprising regionals. The adjacent lounge is furnished with armchairs and settees, which together with a huge fire in winter make a comfortable contrast to the bustle of the small bar. Upstairs is the main eating area specialising in fresh, local produce, particularly seafood dishes. The house beer is Dunottar Ale brewed by Inveralmond. Children are allowed upstairs only. A former local CAMRA Pub of the Year. 🏨🏡🍴🎴◑◗🏕🗡🎱🍴

Strathclyde

Knockderry Hotel
204 Shore Road, G84 0NX
▯▶ 11.30-midnight; 12.30-11 Sun
☎ (01436) 842283
www.knockderryhotel.co.uk

🍺 Addlestones

Built circa 1851, this former Glasgow merchant's house boasts one of the best examples of works by architect William Leiper and designer Daniel Cottier. It is a stunning building with a recurring theme of the four seasons, in both stained glass

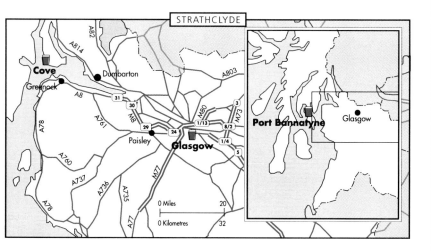

PORT BANNATYNE

Port Royal Hotel

37 Marine Road, PA20 0LW OS072672

▯ 12-1am (2am Sat); 12.30-1am Sun

☎ (01700) 505073

🍏 Westons

🍎 Westons

Famous for hosting Stella McCartney's wedding, the Isle of Bute also boasts this wonderful, award-winning, family-run re-creation of a Russian tavern. Bar-top casks serve local micros' ales on gravity. There is real cider and perry, bottled and draught foreign beers, a range of Russian vodkas, home-made soft drinks and frozen fruit yoghurts. The Russian-style food is prepared from fresh local ingredients and served all day. Popular with yachtsmen, locals and visitors, this hotel with splendid views over the harbour, enjoys a picturesque setting. Live Russian music is staged occasionally. Q🛏🌙◐🚭

Tayside

BLAIRGOWRIE

Ericht Alehouse

13 Wellmeadow, PH10 6ND

▯ 11-11 (11.45 Fri-Sat);
12.30-11 Sun

☎ (01250) 872469

🍎 Addlestones

Established in 1802, this traditional town centre pub has a friendly atmosphere. The pub has two seating areas split by a well-stocked bar. The lounge area boasts a log-burning open fire. Up to six beers are on tap from Scottish and English breweries – Inveralmond beers are a local favourite. Liefmans Frambozen is available on tap and a good selection of bottled beers. Although no food is available customers are welcome to take their own. Weekends can be busy with occasional live music. 🏛Q♿🌙📶🚭

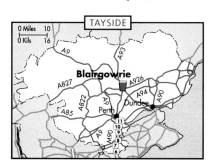

Cider Outlets
Isle of Man

Isle of Man

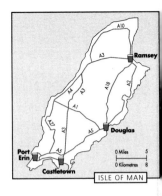
ISLE OF MAN

CASTLETOWN

Sidings
Victoria Road, IM9 1EF (by station)
⏸ 11.30-11 (midnight Fri-Sat);
12-10.30 Sun
☎ (01624) 823282

🍎 Westons

After many years' benign neglect under
brewery ownership, the refurbished
Duck's Nest became the Sidings with an
Isle of Man railway theme. An impressive
and ornate wooden bar counter displays
a large array of handpumps dispensing a
wide range of ales, both Manx and
imported. During fine weather the small,
secluded garden area is ideal for those
with children. It was awarded local
CAMRA Pub of the Year 2003. No food is
served Sunday. ◖≋ (IMR) 🍴

DOUGLAS

Rovers Return
11 Church Street, IM1 2AG
(behind Town Hall)
⏸ 12-11 (midnight Fri-Sat); 12-11 Sun
☎ (01624) 676459
www.bushys.com

🍎 Westons

Named after Blackburn Rovers Football
Club, this popular multi-roomed pub has
been extended into the former adjacent
tattoo parlour. The pub itself has
remained largely unaltered: the Rovers'
shrine remains, as do the meet and pool
rooms. The additional room has a real fire

and houses photos of many old Isle of
Man pubs. Note the unusual handpumps
fashioned from fire brigade brass branch
pipes. Archers beers are stocked
alongside the regulars. Generous portions
of reasonably priced food (Mon-Fri) make
this bustling pub even busier at
lunchtime. 🏔🏵◖≋ (IMR) ♣🍴

PORT ERIN

Bay Hotel
Shore Road, IM9 6HC (on lower promenade)
⏸ 12-midnight (including Sun)
☎ (01624) 832084

🍎 Westons

Large, established pub fronting the lower
promenade and beach. It has a traditional
feel with timber floors in an unspoilt
interior, encompassing bar, lounge and
separate vaults. A selection of imported
bottled beers and a varied menu is
available; the atmosphere is friendly and
welcoming. 🏔◖🏠♿≋ (IMR) 🍴✂

Ellan Vannin
West Quay, IM8 1JU
⏸ 12-11 (midnight Fri-Sat); 12-11 Sun
☎ (01624) 812131

🍎 Westons

This pub has recently undergone a
thorough refurbishment but retains its
welcoming open fire. A clutch of tall
tables with comfortable high chairs offer
an excellent perch for drinkers. Live music
is staged at weekends. 🏔◖🍴

Buy official CAMRA merchandise
and help campaign for real cider and perry

Pomona	Pomona T-shirts	Lapel
Fridge Magnet	£8.50 each Available in	Badge
£1.50	Green or White – Sizes M-XXL	£2.50

Quantity	Item	Size/Colour	Price	Total
		Postage		
		Total		

Card Number		Expiry Date	Issue Number
Name			Date
Signature		Membership Number	
Address			
Postcode		Telephone Number	

Postage is included in all prices for UK customers. Please add £2 per item in the European Union. Please add £4 per item Rest of the World. Please return this form with your card details or a cheque made payable to CAMRA to:

CAMRA, 230 Hatfield Road, St Albans, Herts AL1 4LW.

Orders can also be placed over the phone on 01727 867201, or via our website www.camra.org.uk/shop where you can see the full range of clothing and merchandise.

We deliver your order as soon as possible. We will normally send your order within 10 business days. This could extend to 15 days in peak periods.

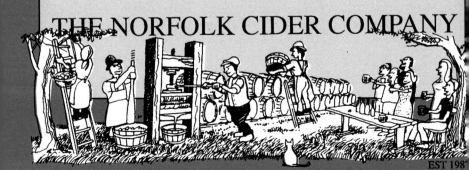

It takes all sorts to Campaign for Real Ale

CAMRA, the Campaign for Real Ale, is an independent not-for-profit, volunteer-led consumer group. We actively campaign for full pints and have campaigned successfully for more flexible licensing hours in England and Wales, as well as protecting the 'local' pub and lobbying government to champion pub-goers' rights.

CAMRA has 80,000 members from all ages and backgrounds, brought together by a common belief in the issues that CAMRA deals with and their love of good quality British beer. For just £18 a year, that's less than a pint a month, you can join CAMRA and enjoy the following benefits:

A monthly colour newspaper informing you about beer, cider and pub news and detailing events and beer festivals around the country.

Free or reduced entry to over 140 national, regional and local beer festivals.

Money off many of our publications including the *Good Beer Guide* and *CAMRA's Good Cider Guide*.

Access to a members-only section of our national website, **www.camra.org.uk**, which gives up-to-the-minute news stories and includes a special offer section with regular features saving money on beer and trips away.

The opportunity to campaign to save pubs and breweries under threat of closure, and to actively promote real cider and perry as well as real ale.

Log onto **www.camra.org.uk** for CAMRA membership information

Do you feel passionately about your cider and perry? Then why not join CAMRA

Just fill in the application form (or a photocopy of it) and the Direct Debit form on the next page to receive three months' membership FREE!

If you wish to join but do not want to pay by Direct Debit, please fill in the application form below and send a cheque, payable to CAMRA, to CAMRA, 230 Hatfield Road, St Albans, Hertfordshire, AL1 4LW.

Please tick appropriate box

☐ Single Membership (UK & EU) £18

☐ For under-26 Membership £10

☐ For 60 and over Membership £10

For partners' joint membership add £3 (for concessionary rates both members must be eligible for the membership rate).

Life membership information is available on request.

If you join by Direct Debit you will receive three months' membership extra, free!

Title _____ Surname _____

Forename(s) _____

Address _____

_____

_____ Postcode _____

Date of Birth _____ Email address _____

Signature _____

Partner's details if required

Title _____ Surname _____

Forename(s) _____

Date of Birth _____ Email address _____

Please tick here ☐ if you would like to receive occasional emails from CAMRA (at no point will your details be released to a third party).

Find out more about CAMRA at **www.camra.org.uk** Telephone 01727 867201

CAMPAIGN FOR REAL ALE

Instruction to your Bank or Building Society to pay by Direct Debit

DIRECT Debit

Please fill in the form and send to: Campaign for Real Ale Ltd. 230 Hatfield Road, St. Albans, Herts. AL1 4LW

Name and full postal address of your Bank or Building Society

To The Manager   Bank or Building Society

Address

Postcode

Name (s) of Account Holder (s)

Bank or Building Society account number

Branch Sort Code

Reference Number

Banks and Building Societies may not accept Direct Debit Instructions for some types of account

Originator's Identification Number

| 9 | 2 | 6 | 1 | 2 | 9 |

FOR CAMRA OFFICIAL USE ONLY
This is not part of the instruction to your Bank or Building Society

Membership Number

Name

Postcode

Instruction to your Bank or Building Society

Please pay CAMRA Direct Debits from the account detailed on this Instruction subject to the safeguards assured by the Direct Debit Guarantee. I understand that this instruction may remain with CAMRA and, if so, will be passed electronically to my Bank/Building Society

Signature(s)

Date

✂ detached and retained this section

This Guarantee should be detached and retained by the payer.

The Direct Debit Guarantee

- This Guarantee is offered by all Banks and Building Societies that take part in the Direct Debit Scheme. The efficiency and security of the Scheme is monitored and protected by your own Bank or Building Society.

- If the amounts to be paid or the payment dates change CAMRA will notify you 7 working days in advance of your account being debited or as otherwise agreed.

- If an error is made by CAMRA or your Bank or Building Society, you are guaranteed a full and immediate refund from your branch of the amount paid.

- You can cancel a Direct Debit at any time by writing to your Bank or Building Society. Please also send a copy of your letter to us.

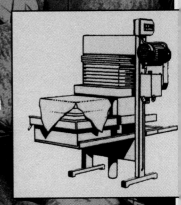

Books for Beer Lovers

CAMRA Books, the publishing arm of the Campaign for Real Ale, is the leading publisher of books on beer and pubs. Key titles include:

Good Beer Guide 2006

Editor: ROGER PROTZ

The Good Beer Guide is the only guide you will need to find the right pint, in the right place, every time. It's the original and the best independent guide to around 4,500 pubs throughout the UK; the Sun newspaper rated the 2004 edition in the top 20 books of all time! Now in its 34th year, this annual publication is a comprehensive and informative guide to the best real ale pubs in the UK, researched and written exclusively by CAMRA members and fully updated every year.

£13.99   ISBN 1 85249 211 2

300 Beers To Try Before You Die

ROGER PROTZ

300 beers from around the world, handpicked by award-winning journalist, author and broadcaster Roger Protz to try before you die! A comprehensive portfolio of top beers from the smallest microbreweries in the United States to family-run British breweries and the world's largest brands. This book is indispensable for both beer novices and aficionados.

£12.99   ISBN 1 85249 213 9

Big Book of Beer

ADRIAN TIERNEY-JONES

Everything you could ever want to know about the world's favourite drink; this beautifully illustrated book is an eye-opener to the world of beer articulated by well-known beer experts and those who brew it. A perfect gift for the 'real beer' connoisseur.

£14.99
ISBN 1 85249 212 0

Good Pub Food

SUSAN NOWAK & JILL ADAM

This fully revised sixth edition of Good Pub Food singles out over 600 real ale pubs in England, Wales, Scotland and Northern Ireland, which also specialise in fine cuisine. All are highlighted on easy to use maps and have a full description of their location, ales, menus, prices, vegetarian selections and facilities. Both Susan Nowak and Jill Adam have been involved in editing and compiling CAMRA guides for over 20 years. Published April 2006.

£13.99   ISBN 1 85249 214 7

Order these and other CAMRA books online at **www.camra.org.uk/books**
ask at your local bookstore, or contact:
CAMRA, 230 Hatfield Road, St Albans, AL1 4LW   Telephone 01727 867201

Map Index for Good Cider Guide

CAMRA's Cider Supplier List

his list is meant to be a guide to publicans (or anyone operating under a licence to sell alcohol) to assist them in choosing where to get Real Cider or Perry from. Below you will find a list of people, (Cider Specialists; Beer Agents/Cider Makers/Breweries; Wholesalers; and some Specialist Shops) willing to sell cider or perry to you.

Now all you have to do is spot who supplies your area and this will define the method of dispense, (polycasks, bag in a box system or bottle). Oh yes and the space on the bar! Enjoy.

This is only the second time a list like this has been drawn together, if anyone is missing or if you find any details are incorrect, please write to Gillian Williams C/O CAMRA HQ, so the list can be updated next time. Thanks.

Cider Specialists

Cider specialists have lists of ciders available which they can send to you and you place your order. Please note they get booked up at least two months in advance so approach early. The catchphrase seems to be the more you order the more viable the trip becomes:

Jon Hallam 01291 627242
Large & extensive lists which change seasonally of approximately 120 ciders & perries from some 50 makers; Delivery no fixed area or fixed delivery times. Some areas are multidrops, some pallet drops only, some quantity dependent, some not. Currently supplying from Sussex to Perthshire. Ring to discuss requirements.

Merrylegs AKA Jon Reekes,
07776 013787
Merrylegs has an impressive list of ciders & perries. Delivery North West England, Manchester, Devon. Ring to discuss logistics.

Beer Agents

Some Beer Agents carry and will deliver cider/perry at the same time as dropping off beer:

Waverley TBS
(formally Beer Seller) 01963 32255

Westons, Bulmers, Thatchers, Matthew Clark; Delivery whole of the UK

East-West Ales 01892 834040
Thatchers (inc. Moles Black Rat), Biddenden; Delivery all of England (including the North of England); Welsh Borders

Small Beer 01522 540431
Westons, Biddenden, Thatchers (inc. Moles Black Rat), Broadoak, Bulmers, Reedcutter; Delivery mainly East Midlands, & up as far North as Newcastle

Cider Makers

Some cider makers will deliver their own cider/perry usually within a defined area:

Biddenden Cider, Kent 01580 291726
Biddenden dry or medium both 8% or Bushells Cider 6%; Delivery South East, Kent, East Sussex, London. Supplied in 2 gallons/5 gallons/ or 9 gallon containers.

Broadoak Cider, Somerset 01275 333154
Moonshine, Kingstone Black & others in dry & medium in polycasks to the on trade. Off trade supplied in 3 or 2 litre bottles. Delivery West Country. Ring to discuss.

Westons Cider, Hereford 01531 660100
Old Rosie, Traditional Scrumpy, 1st Quality, GWR,

Bounds Brand Perry; Will deliver own products Nationwide. (Westons are moving from using polycasks to a bag in a box system which keeps the products fresh for up to three months).

Brewerys

Some Brewerys carry and will deliver cider/perry:

Crouch Vale 01245 322744
Eight to twelve products on their list which changes. Delivery Essex; South Suffolk, East & Central London.

RCH Brewery 01934 834447
Thatchers; Coombes, Rich's, Crossmans, Wilkins, Westcroft; Delivery South Devon, Somerset, Gloucestershire, West Midlands

Wylam Brewery 01661 853377
Perry's Cider Vintage & Leakham Dry (This is cider made by the Perry Family they do not make perry), supplied in polycasks; Delivery from the Scottish Borders to North Yorkshire.

Ringwood Brewery 01425 471177
Thatchers; Delivery Hampshire & 50 mile radius.

Wye Valley Brewery 01885 490505
Gwatkins cider & perry; Delivery the whole of Wales, most of England the further the distance from Hereford the longer lead in time needed. Ring to discuss viability of delivery.

Wolf Brewery 01953 457775
Kingfisher Farm Cider & Crones Cider; Delivery Norfolk only.

Church End Brewery 01827 713080
Carries a selection of cider/perry which can be delivered on the back of a beer order. Delivery Central England plus Somerset & parts of Yorkshire. Ring to discuss requirements.

St. Austell Brewery 01726 74444
Bulmers Medium; Delivery Cornwall & Devon.

Wholesalers

Wholesalers carry bottles to the trade:

Dartmouth Vintners 01803 832602
Heron Valley, Lyme Bay, & Ashridge (sparkling). Delivery Dartmouth & South Hams. area

Dayla 01296 420261
Thatchers, Westons, & Bulmers, bottles & polycasks. Delivery Thames Valley & Home Counties.

Infinity Wholefoods 01273 424060
Dunkertons & Westons. Delivery Sussex & The South, but can arrange delivery Nationally.

Rainbow Wholefoods 01603 630484
Organic only: Crones, & Dunkertons bottles only. Trade deliveriaes to East Anglia only. Also has a shop open to the public in Norwich City Centre.

Suma Wholefoods 01422 313840
Thatchers, Weston's & Dunkertons. Delivery Countrywide (including Glasgow).

Specialist Shops

Specialist shops are open to the public and do not usually operate mail order/ delivery. Bottles are generally either 500ml/750ml:

National Collection of Cider & Perry, East Sussex 01323 811324
Rod Marsh hosts the National Collection with 100 ciders & perries on draft and over 150 types of bottled ciders & perries. Sells wholesale or direct to the public. No delivery. Ring to discuss requirements.

Marches Little Beer Shoppe, Ludlow 01584 878999
Paul runs this wonderful outlet which deals directly with both the trade & the public. 30+ ciders & perries are stocked primarily from Herefordshire (with just about every Producers represented) but also stocks New Forest, Thatchers and others. Delivery Three

Counties (Gloucester/ Hereford/Worcester), Shropshire, & Mid-Wales.

Orchard Hive & Vine, Leominster 01568 611232
Geoff Morris runs this specialist Off Licence with about 60+ bottled varieties plus Westons, Malvern Magic & Gregg's Pit in manucubes (please ring regarding the manucubes well in advance). Delivery within a 30 mile radius free, otherwise £7.50 plus VAT (Nationwide mail order).

Real Ale Shop, Preston 01772 201591
Times Monday – Saturday 11am – 2pm & 5pm – 10pm; Sundays 12noon – 2pm & 6pm – 10pm. Dave or Adrian stock Thatchers,

Sheppys with other ciders, plus a selection of perries. All are in bottles and there is no delivery.

The Beer Shop, **Pitfield Street**, **London**, N1 020 7739 3701
Martin runs this shop with about 10 Bottled varieties of cider/perry also some draught products and polycasks can be arranged; ring to discuss requirements.

York Beer Shop, **York** 01904 647136
Jim & Eric stock five strong cider brands (Gwatkin, Burrow Hill, Sheppys, Dunkertons & Gospel Oak) & have several varieties of each Maker. They have sparking varieties & cider brandy etc. as well. Collection only.

Fine, distinguished ciders and perries made with unsprayed fruit from orchards in the Three Counties of Herefordshire, Worcestershire and Gloucestershire. Fermented by wild yeasts and matured in old oak barrels. Enjoy these unique ciders and perries in bottle and draught.

Tom Oliver on 01432 820569 email: oliverciderandperry@theolivers.org.uk. Ocle Pychard, Herefordshire HR1 3RE www.theolivers.org.uk

Producers Index for Good Cider Guide

Countryman Cider

TRADITIONAL CIDER MAKERS

Countryman Cider is locatde in the 15th Century stables of a former coachinh inn, on the Devon side of the lovely Tamar Valley on the Tavistock to Launceston Road. You are welcome to visit us all year round to see how our Traditional Farmhouse Ciders are made.

Coutryman Cider is available on Draught (Dry, Medium or a 3 year old Gold Label). Also, Somerset Royal Cider Brandy, Mead, Country Wines, Perry, Cider Vinegar, Sparkling Cider and Apple Juice.

- Demonstration Cider Apple Orchard
- Apple Mill and Cider Press
- Fermintation
- Bottling
- Sampling
- Off licence Shop

Opening hours: Mon-Sat 9.00am-6.30pm all year round.

HOW TO FIND US

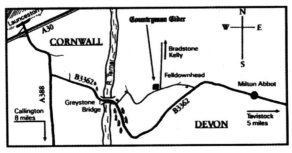

COUNTRYMAN CIDER
Felldownhead, Milton Abbot, Tavistock, Devon PL19 0QR
Tel: Milton Abbot (01822 870226)